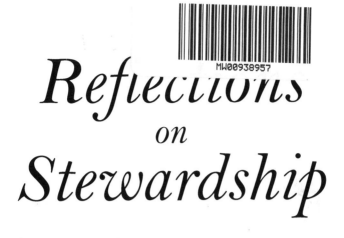

Reflections
on
Stewardship

**Articles written for *The Crossroads*
Gilbert Presbyterian Church
Gilbert, Arizona**

Eloise R. Annis

**Gilbert Presbyterian Church
235 E. Guadalupe Rd.
Gilbert, AZ 85234
www.azgpc.org**

Scripture quotations taken from The Holy Bible -
New International Version®. Copyright© 1995 Tyndale
House Publishers, Inc. Wheaton, Illinois and Zondervan
Publishing House Grand Rapids, Michigan.

Published by:
Gilbert Presbyterian Church
235 E. Guadalupe Rd.
Gilbert, AZ 85234
www.azgpc.org

ISBN: 9-781979-002813

Dedication

This book is dedicated to the memory of my husband, Roy Annis, and my parents, Omar and Mildred Robinson.

My husband will always be remembered for his kindness and generosity toward others. My parents are remembered for their industriousness, perserverness, and love for one another. I received my interest and ability for mathematics from my father and my appreciation for music from my mother.

Table of Contents

2008 - REJOICE WITH ME; I HAVE FOUND MY LOST SHEEP

2009 - I CAN DO EVERYTHING THROUGH HIM WHO GIVES ME STRENGTH

2010 - I WAS HUNGRY AND YOU GAVE ME SOMETHING TO EAT

2011 - LET THE LITTLE CHILDREN COME TO ME

2012 - I AM THE GOOD SHEPHERD

2013 - ON THIS ROCK I WILL BUILD MY CHURCH

2017 - THE LORD IS MY SHEPHERD

Foreword

*By The Reverend Doctor Theron (Terry) Palmer
Pastor, Gilbert Presbyterian Church*

Eloise Annis is the real-life embodiment of the familiar poster slogan, "Be patient! God isn't finished with me yet." Having spent a good portion of her life as a math teacher, writing a devotional column each month for the Gilbert Presbyterian Church newsletter was the farthest thing from her mind. Yet in her retirement, following the death of her husband, Roy, she found God calling her to explore many life-changing adventures, discovering gifts she never knew she had. She began taking piano lessons. She played in the church orchestra. She made regular trips to the gym. And she began to write about stewardship.

Contrary to many church planning calendars, "stewardship" knows no particular season. It is a year-round preoccupation. Eloise recognizes that basic truth of the Christian community. On the following pages, she reflects on God's call to respond with joyful generosity to the gracious gift of Jesus Christ in all seasons of life.

As you read through this compilation, I pray that the same Spirit who inspired Eloise will touch your heart and make you aware that all we have is a gift from God. And then I would encourage you to reflect on how God might be calling you to use all those gifts you have been given as a grateful response to God's love.

And when you think of Eloise, remember that God isn't finished with YOU yet, either!

By Rochelle Mackey,
    Editor, The Crossroads, 2001 – 2009

Almost all editors of church newsletters have one problem in common. They are desperate for talented writers who will produce good copy in a timely fashion. I found such a writer in the person of Eloise Annis. The problem was that she didn't think of herself as a writer.

Eloise and I were serving on the Stewardship Committee of Gilbert Presbyterian Church. From time to time one or the other of us was asked to inform our church family about stewardship opportunities. Not an easy task. It required a bit of research, readily available from the Presbyterian Church (USA) website, then writing a three- to five-minute essay which the author would share with worshippers at our two Sunday services.

The Stewardship Chair could always rely on Eloise to accept this assignment. To me it marked my new friend as a writer. For Eloise, however, it was a ridiculous idea which she eagerly explained: "I'm a mathematician, not a writer. I teach math. My mother always said that my brother was the writer in our family."

Somehow or other Eloise was coerced into writing her first stewardship column for the June 2002 issue of *The Crossroads*, the newsletter for our church. And she continued, producing essay after essay about stewardship as we understand God intends us to know it – a commitment of our time, talent and treasure to God's mission through our church home.

In her essays Eloise has found many topics to share her commitment to stewardship. She has used everything from foreign trips that took her above the Arctic Circle to a worship service at St. Giles Cathedral in Edinburgh, Scotland; and from the baptism of her grandchildren to wild flowers and Ta'i Chi, and so much more in between.

As you read her essays, I believe you'll agree that Eloise has eloquently and emphatically used her time and talent to build God's treasure.

Introduction

I read the article that I had written — it was boring! It was as interesting as a mathematical proof is to a non-math major. Why does Rochelle Mackey want me to write articles on stewardship every month for *The Crossroads*, the newsletter for Gilbert Presbyterian Church (GPC)? I am not a writer. I am a math major.

I quickly deleted my article — gone! "God, I can't write. I need your help." I cried. I prayed. I immediately opened my Bible and pointed to a passage. I looked down and read, "You are the light of the world. A city built on a hill cannot be hid" (Matthew 5:14). Peace came over me.

With closed eyes, I thought of that passage. It reminded me of the years my husband and I lived in Morenci, a copper mining town in the mountains of Eastern Arizona. When we returned home from an out-of-town trip at night, our children would play a game of who could first spot the lights of Morenci. From a distance, the lights shone in the night sky. They were like a beacon for the weary traveler.

Yes, a town in the mountains cannot be hid. Now I could write my article. With God's help, my fingers flew over the keyboard.

That first article was printed in *The Crossroads* in June 2002. In these fifteen years, I have always written with God's help. With encouragement from my family and friends, these articles have now become the stories in this book.

Each story is a memory — my memories as a child,

memories of my parents and where I was raised, memories of my husband and me, memories of our children and grandchildren and memories of the vacation trips I have taken. These memories are the basis for my reflections, thoughts, and ideas on service to God, church, family, and community.

Every month I wrote an article on stewardship because our love and service to God must be throughout the entire year, not just one month or one season in particular.

Sit back, read, and contemplate what you can do for God. Then in the spirit of love and thanksgiving in your heart, share your time, talents, and treasures with others.

2002

LET YOUR LIGHT SHINE

You are the light of the world. A city on a hill cannot be hidden. Neither do people light a lamp and put it under a bowl. Instead they put it on its stand, and it gives light to everyone in the house. In the same way, let your light shine before men, that they may see your good deeds and praise your name before your Father in heaven.

Matthew 5:14-16

YOU ARE THE LIGHT OF THE WORLD
June 2002

"You are the light of the world. A city on a hill cannot be hidden. Neither do people light a lamp and put it under a bowl. Instead they put it on its stand, and it gives light to everyone in the house. In the same way, let your light shine before men, that they may see your good deeds and praise your Father in heaven" (Matthew 5:14-16).

As I read the above verses, I think of our years living in Morenci, a copper-mining town in the mountains of Eastern Arizona. Whenever we went on an out-of-town trip and returned home at night, our children would play a game of who could first spot the lights of Morenci. From a distance the lights shone like a beacon in the dark sky, welcoming the weary traveler. As we drove closer to town, the lights that once seemed as one became distinguishable.

First, we saw the lights from the copper mine, then the lights from the center of town; next the lights from the church, the lights from the school, and finally our neighbor's lamp in the window. Every light, no matter how small, was very important to become that one bright beacon for travelers. Yes, a town on a mountain cannot be hidden.

The church is like a town on a mountain. Just as it takes many different lights to see a town from a distance, it takes the "lights" of everyone to operate the church.

We need many people, each one very important. We need worship leaders, ushers, musicians, Sunday school teachers, greeters, committee leaders and members, to name just a few. We also need the "lights" from the youngest, the children. Each person has a gift, a talent, to offer to God.

It is our responsibility to shine our "light" so that the church will be a bright beacon just like a town shining from the mountain. Are you letting your light so shine? You are the light of the world.

REWARDS GREATER
THAN THE GIFTS GIVEN
September 2002

Imagine a scale, the type used in the gold mining days of the Old West. Gold was placed in a pan on one side of the scale, and in another pan on the other side, weights were placed to determine the amount of gold that the prospector had mined. The scale was in balance when the weights and gold were equal.

Today, our gold mine is the church, and our gold is what we get from the church. Our gold is our spiritual growth and development as Christians, our learning about Christ and the Bible. Our gold is also our friends, good times, shared fun and laughter, a sense of belonging. We gain self-confidence by helping others through the work of the church.

The gold we receive can take on many forms. What is your gold?

To balance our gold, we give our time, talents, and treasures to the church. However, I find that the scale in this scenario is different from that of the early prospectors. My scale never seems to balance. No matter how much I give, my gold keeps increasing.

RAINBOWS
October 2002

One of the most beautiful sights I have ever seen in the desert hills of Arizona is a rainbow arching across the sky. There is nothing quite like the magnificence of a rainbow after a monsoon storm. When the rain softly falls and the sun peeks between the clouds, the most brilliant colors — red, orange, yellow, green, and blue — form an arch in the sky.

There have been times when I thought I could walk over and touch the end of a rainbow as it appeared so close on an outcropping of rocks on a hill. I have also seen two beautiful complete rainbows, one inside the other. A rainbow — peace and beauty.

When I see a rainbow, I think of the story of Noah and the Flood. "I have set my rainbow in the clouds, and it will be the sign of the covenant between me and the earth" (Genesis 9:13). A rainbow is God's promise to us. It is a symbol of all the blessings and gifts He has given us.

This month sit back, relax, and envision a beautiful rainbow stretching from one desert hill to another across the sky. That is God's covenant and promise to us. Prayerfully consider how to give thanks to God for all He has done for you. Then in November we will renew our promises and make our pledges to God and our church.

Be a rainbow!

OUR GIFTS TO THE CHRIST CHILD
December 2002

How exciting it is to read the Christmas Story! We listen in awe and vividly picture the Wise Men from the East guided by the bright star on their way to Bethlehem. We can visualize the Wise Men bowing down, worshipping the Christ Child and presenting Him with gifts of gold, frankincense, and myrrh. What fantastic treasures they brought to the baby Jesus!

Today, Christmas 2002, what gifts do we bring to the Christ Child?

The first gift we bring sparkles and glitters like gold. It is our treasure in the form of our tithes and offerings to the church. We also give to special offerings such as the Heifer Project and Christmas Joy Offering. Our gift glows like gold because its radiance is from the faces of children receiving presents through the Christmas Angel program. Share some of your treasure with those in need because that is your gift to the Christ Child.

The second gift to the Christ Child is a wonderful, sweet-smelling, highly valuable incense. Our talent we give is our frankincense. Our talents are what make each of us very special, beautiful, and unique individuals. All of us have talents — some the gift of music, others writing, teaching, caring, healing, and others the gift of building to name just a few. Using our talents for the betterment of the church and community is our gift to the Christ Child.

The third gift is a paradox — it can be bitter or very sweet. It is the gift of myrrh.

What is our gift that is like myrrh? Time is our gift of myrrh. Each of us has exactly the same amount of time every day. No one has one second more than the rest of us. But how we use our time is the myrrh of the present day. Do we vegetate in front of the TV (the bitter part of myrrh), or do we take time to help others (the sweet part of myrrh)?

Choose to volunteer some time to the church, schools, hospitals, or shelters. Practically every community organization appreciates volunteer help. Help your neighbors — the elderly, sick, or lonely. Babysit for the mother needing a little time for herself. Time can be our third gift to the Christ Child.

The Wise Men brought gifts of gold, frankincense, and myrrh. What gifts do you bring to the Christ child?

2003

WE COME TO WORSHIP HIM

After Jesus was born in Bethlehem in Judea, during the time of King Herod, Magi from the East came to Jerusalem and asked, "Where is the one who has been born king of the Jews? We saw his star in the east and have come to worship Him.

After they had heard the king, they went on their way, and the star they had seen in the east went ahead of them until it stopped over the place where the child was. When they saw the star, they were overjoyed. On coming to the house, they saw the child with his mother Mary, and they bowed down and worshipped him. Then they opened their treasures and presented him with gifts of gold and of incense and of myrrh.

Matthew 2:1-2, 9-11

HAPPY NEW YEAR!
January 2003

January 1, the beginning of a new year. Everyone is always excited about beginning something new and different. Remember the excitement you felt as a child on the first day of school? Everything was new — teacher, friends, classes, books. The new year can be like that-filled with anticipation, hopes and dreams.

Instead of making New Year's resolutions that are frequently forgotten by February, why not utilize Benjamin Franklin's plan? He made a list of thirteen items that he called "virtues," and he concentrated on only one virtue each week. At the end of thirteen weeks, the list was complete and he would start over, thereby covering the entire list four times a year.

Let's try it with stewardship. Stewardship is more than making a pledge and giving our tithes and offerings to the church. It is giving our time, talents and treasures to our home, work and community in addition to the church. Stewardship is our thanks to God for all He has given us. We should be able to think of a list of thirteen commitments, or activities, that we can commit to as good stewards. (It has to be thirteen so that our list can be repeated four times in a year.) Here are some ideas:

1. Let this be the week we clean out closets and give things we no longer use to a community organization.

2. Contribute money you have saved by smart shopping during the week to the loose offering.

3. Volunteer some of your time at a school, hospital, shelter or other community organization.

4. Learn to do something new, or improve a talent you already have. You don't know what talents you are blessed with until you try something new.

5. Share with others what you learned the previous week.

6. Give some of your time by listening to someone who needs to talk.

7. Help a neighbor who needs assistance.

8. Give the gift of life by donating blood. If you can't donate, give your time to help with a blood drive.

9. Pray for someone who has hurt your feelings or has made you angry. This will help you forgive the person.

10. Send a thank you note to someone who has helped you or someone who means a lot to you.

11. A good steward takes care of the environment. This week take care of the little piece of your environment by cleaning your yard, planting a tree, bush or flowers.

12. Spread a happy smile and a cheerful greeting wherever you go. It will only take a moment, but it may change the whole day for the recipient.

13. Children are our future. Help a child learn about stewardship by assisting him/her to do something for someone. A child can learn what stewardship is about by your good example.

Let's make the Year 2003 our year of stewardship growth. Give thanks to God by helping others.

THE LOVE OF A GOOD SAMARITAN
February 2003

Valentine's Day — we think of love, hearts, candy, our friends and family. We do special things for our loved ones — make special dinners, cookies, or cakes. Children use their budding artistic skills and make valentines for their parents and friends. Valentine's Day is the day we tell our friends and family how much we love them and how much they mean to us.

But there is another type of love we need to spread — the love of a Good Samaritan. You know the story about how only the Good Samaritan stopped to render aid, compassion and care for the stranger in need. At Christmas time our church was filled with the love of many Good Samaritans. The Christmas tree was surrounded with gifts bought and wrapped with love. We did not know the ones we were helping. We only knew that people, strangers to us, were in need. The Christmas Angel program and Heifer Project demonstrated our Good Samaritan-type of love.

There are times when entire towns come to the aid of people in need. A modern-day Good Samaritan story is The Day the World Came To Town, a book by Jim Defede. It is the most heartwarming story of the love of the entire town of Gander, Newfoundland. Gander is on the flight path between the United States and Europe. On September 11, 2001, when the planes across the nation were ordered to land at the nearest airport, 38 planes landed in Gander. They were carrying 6,595 passengers and crew. Gander's population that day literally doubled in size. That week the town opened their hearts and homes to strangers, giving them shelter, food, and clothes. Even the animals on the planes experienced the love and care of Gander.

We ourselves might experience the love of a Good Samaritan. I did in 1980. I was in the Intensive Care Unit (ICU) recovering from surgery at Good Samaritan Hospital in Phoenix. I awoke feeling very uncomfortable, restless and frightened. At that time ICU was in one very large room with no privacy between patients. A hospital employee came into the room. I had never seen her before — we were strangers. She asked if I needed anything. I whispered, "Hold my hand." We held hands — black and white together. It seemed as if time stood still. All activity stopped. I felt everyone staring at us. All I heard was the monotonous rhythm of the life-saving machines. But I will never forget the compassion, care, and energy radiating from her hands.

In those brief moments I experienced the love of a Good Samaritan, helping a stranger in need. All at once every muscle in my body relaxed. Then as quickly as she came, she was gone with tears streaming down her cheeks. I fell asleep. The next thing I knew Roy and our minister were standing beside me.

Have a wonderful Valentine's Day. Show love to your family and friends; but also help a stranger, lend a hand, help someone in need. Be a Good Samaritan!

POPPIES
March 2003

In the spring, if our Arizona desert hills have received enough moisture, the most wonderful metamorphosis takes place: The desert comes alive with poppies and other wildflowers for miles around. The colors are brilliant in contrast to the usual browns, tans, and olive greens of the landscape.

Poppies seem to spring up from nowhere among the rocks and hills. We wonder who planted the poppies, and realize it was God. Only God could have created such a beautiful sight! What can we learn from the poppies?

We have been planted at the Gilbert Presbyterian Church. Bloom, like a poppy, where you have been planted. Nurture others so they too may bloom as the rain nurtures the desert. When the wind blows, the poppies bend and sway together; when someone is hurting, we must also bend and help one another.

After pushing against rocky ground, poppies open as if to give thanks and praise to God. If there is a rocky path before us, we can be like the poppies — accepting the challenge, praying to God for guidance, and praising Him for all He has given us.

Let your face shine like a beautiful, brilliant orange poppy!

THE CROSS
April 2003

A cold wind blew across the rocky hill. The sky was beginning to show dawn's first light. A rough-hewn cross stood before me. It was empty but for a crown of thorns looped over the top. I stood there contemplating the events that led to the cross. It was cold that morning. He was not there!

It was beyond the cross, in distant mountains, where an unforgettable scene unfolded. I saw the first rays of the morning sun rise over the mountains and strike the cross. I felt the sun's warmth on my face just as people from the town's various churches and of all ages sang out with joy, "Christ the Lord is Risen Today!" Yes, indeed He has risen. Christ has risen today!

Easter morning — a time for contemplation, strength, and renewal. Jesus gave His life for us. The cross — a symbol of His suffering and shame. We have received many gifts from God. What can we do for Him? What can we do for our family, friends, and neighbors?

When we give our time, talents, and treasures, we warm our small part of the world as the sun warms the earth. Let us give with the love and strength of Christ in our hearts.

The cross — what does it mean to you?

MOTHER'S DAY
May 2003

May — a time to remember our mother, a time to honor her. May is a time to thank her for all her wonderful lessons of life. A mother is the nurturer of the family, protector, and first teacher for her children.

My mother was a teacher. She taught by example. She loved life, her family and friends, beauty around her, music, and the classics. She was a very out-going, warm person. My mother exemplified stewardship. She always gave her time, talents, and treasures to her family, friends, community, and church.

I remember my mother leading a caroling group of youth of all ages every Christmas in our neighborhood. The money collected went to a community women's organization for college scholarships. She gave her many talents to the church. The choir was enriched by her beautiful voice.

As a child I remember going with her to a care center for the elderly. My mother would play the piano and lead the residents in a hymn sing. She was one of the most popular teachers at the high school. Everyone wanted to be in her class. She taught Latin! She readily gave time to her friends, and at times provided dinner to a sick neighbor.

That is what stewardship is all about — caring for people around us and spreading love to all. In her heart were family, home, friends, church, God, and the Bible.

Yes, Mom, I learned a lot from you — compassion, love for family and friends, fondness for learning, and appreciation for the simple things of life — flowers, birds, and the sunset. But you had one last and finest lesson to teach me.

I was there when you lifted your cancer-ridden body to a sitting position with arms outstretched reaching out to some unseen force. Your face was so serene; your eyes shone as if looking at some magnificent scene. I was not privileged to see what you saw. I only saw a blank wall, but you saw more, much, much more. Yes, Mom, in your last moment you taught me the most wonderful lesson of all — there is a heaven and you are there!

Thank you, Mom, for your wonderful lessons of life.

HAVE YOU MET YOUR NEIGHBOR?
June 2003

This past semester, two of my community college students had the most incredible experience. They discovered that they are neighbors. Yes, neighbors — a block wall separates their back yards! Their paths had never before crossed. They had never met until they sat next to each other in my math class. Both have sons who attend the same elementary school, in the same grade, and have the same teacher. Their sons know each other. They are friends. Yet a block wall kept my two students from being friends. That block wall might as well have been the Grand Canyon as far as my students were concerned.

Yes, stewardship is giving our tithes and offerings to the church. But stewardship is more than that. Stewardship is taking part in church activities, assisting committees, and joyfully helping in many possible ways. But, stewardship is more than that. Not only should we be good stewards at church, but we also should be good stewards in our community and our neighborhood. We must spread love and joy to our neighbors and assist our neighbors when needed. How can we help our neighbor if we do not know our neighbor?

Our daughter, Karen, lives in Richmond, Virginia. The other day while her husband was cutting the grass, the lawn mower quit working. He went next door to solicit the neighbor's help. Another neighbor came by to lend his hand. Meanwhile, Karen came out with a plate of freshly baked cookies. A neighbor said you can't have cookies without milk, so he brought out the milk. An impromptu neighborhood gathering ensued over an errant lawn mower.

Yes, the mower was fixed, but far more important was the love, joy, and friendship spread among the neighbors. That is a neighborhood, a place where neighbors spontaneously help one another, sharing and caring for each other.

Here in the East Valley we must break through the block walls — leap over the walls or walk around our walls — connecting with those on the other side. Do not wait until you are a student in my class before you meet your neighbor. Meet your neighbor now!

THE WHEEL OF LIFE
July 2003

Wheels — we depend upon a good set of wheels on our car whether our destination is the store, work, church or a long vacation trip. Periodically we check our tires. Are the tires balanced? Is the tread worn? Are there any bulges?

I well remember our move from Ohio to Arizona many years ago. We piled everything into and on top of our station wagon. We had much too much baggage for our poor tires. None of the original four tires made the 2,000+ miles. Four times we had to unload our car to get to the spare, change the tire, reload the car, then look for the nearest town that sold tires. We can now look back and laugh at our adventure traveling west. Yes, we do depend upon a good set of wheels to safely reach our destination.

Think of your life as a wheel — the wheel of life. Our life journey is the road we take. Just as we encounter roadblocks, detours, potholes, hills to climb and descend along a highway, we also encounter such obstacles along our journey of life. At times, our life may be very smooth, just like a brand-new freeway, and other times it can be very rough like an ungraded dirt mountain road.

God is the hub of our wheel. We must be firmly connected to Him. My husband, Roy, loved to tell a story of years ago. He was at the top of a long hill when his wheel broke free from the car. There he was at the top watching his wheel bounce, bounce, bounce down the hill. God is our hub. He must be at the center of our lives; otherwise, we too will bounce along without direction.

Now divide your wheel of life into sectors. I think of six sectors only because it is easy to divide a circle into six parts. My parts are home and family, friends, health, my spiritual life/church, work, and recreation.

Is your wheel of life well balanced? Is any part of your life flat? Do you have a flat tire? Are you spending enough time with your friends and family? Are you taking care of your health? What about the spiritual aspect of your life? Are you giving your time, talents, and treasures to the church? Is there a bulge in your wheel of life? Are you devoting too much time to work? Are you doing too much — loading yourself up with excess baggage? That can cause stress, a blow-out. You must allow time for recreation, a time for yourself, to prevent such a happening.

Just as the tires on your car must be balanced, so too must your wheel of life be in balance. A balanced wheel well connected to the hub will give you a smooth ride even if the path is rough and rocky. Let God be your hub, and have a wonderful journey!

BASKETS — A SYMBOL OF
LOVE, CARING, AND SHARING
August 2003

Baskets! Baskets! Baskets! Looking down from the long walkway high above the factory floor, I saw hundreds of baskets; no, thousands of baskets of different sizes and shapes and all at various stages of completion.

Weavers were very skillfully creating baskets from nondescript strips of wood called splints. Their deft fingers flowed with a rhythm — over and under, over and under.

In July I was visiting a long-time friend of mine from childhood. One day we visited the Longaberger Company in Dresden, Ohio, where baskets are not made by machine, but lovingly and carefully created by hand. There is pride in the workmanship of these baskets. Each one is labeled with the name of the company. Siblings of the founder proudly sign the baskets bought by the visitors.

As I watched the artisans weave a beautiful basket from the thin splints, I thought how we too are like those strips of wood. Alone, we are nothing, but when we weave our lives with others, we become stronger and more beautiful. The baskets were made for different purposes — small ones for pens and pencils, larger ones for bread, some for fruits and vegetables, and

21

bigger ones for a wonderful picnic lunch. People are the same way — we all can contribute to our church and community by our many different talents. Each one of us has something to give, a different purpose, just like a basket.

As I looked over the factory floor and saw the great number of baskets, I thought that a basket is a symbol of sharing — sharing bread, sharing fruits, or sharing a picnic lunch. I heard the story of how the founder, David Longaberger, created and developed his company. Through the years, the company has substantially invested in the local schools, hospitals, parks, and roads. David Longaberger followed the practice of giving back to the community.

I then thought of the story of Jesus feeding the five thousand — a story of sharing. The baskets He used to collect the pieces of food to feed the crowd were carefully and lovingly created by someone, by hand. Today, that weaving skill is carried on in Dresden, Ohio. Baskets — a symbol of love, caring, and sharing.

GO WEST, YOUNG MAN,
AND BUILD A CHAPEL
September 2003

"Go west, young man, go west! You have only six months to live if you stay in Ohio!"

This is what a doctor pronounced to his very sick patient. That young man did go west — west by train and then by horse to the mountains of Colorado. It was the 1870's. Apparently the move was good for the young man because he thrived in the Rocky Mountains. He lived far longer than the projected six months. His life was exceptionally productive as he amassed a small fortune from his gold and silver mines near Denver.

He was an old man when he wrote his will. He had no living relatives in Colorado and instead of sending his wealth back to his niece and nephews in Ohio, he left his entire estate to his beloved church in Denver. With this gift, his church built a chapel next to their sanctuary.

I am very proud of what that gentleman did for his church. You see, I personally knew his niece and nephews as they were my grandmother and her brothers. Think of all the people through the years who have benefited by his generosity. Imagine the celebrations that have taken place in that chapel — weddings, baptisms, prayer services, concerts, memorial services, plus many other activities. That chapel is still in use today. My parents have seen that chapel in Denver. Someday I hope to see it as well.

I am not advocating that one should bequeath his or her entire estate to the church as my distant relative did. However, I do advocate leaving a portion of your estate to your church to be used for God's work on earth. You currently give a percentage of your income to the church — why not leave in your will that proportion to the church?

WHAT WILL BE IN YOUR OBITUARY?
October 2003

This month I would like to relate to you a story that I recently read in *The Arizona Republic*. Perhaps you saw it too.

Years ago no one knew how to safely blast away rock in mines, tunnels, or railroad beds. Nitroglycerin was used, but it is a highly volatile liquid. It is not safe. The slightest motion can make it explode and kill everyone who is nearby.

A chemist-inventor in the 1860's solved the problem by pouring nitroglycerin into clay. Then he molded the clay into sticks which he called dynamite. His product made him very wealthy as it was the era of extensive building of bridges, dams, tunnels, mines, and railroads.

One day the chemist-inventor's brother died. The newspapers at that time said the inventor of dynamite died, but it was his brother who had passed away. When the gentleman saw his name in the obituary and read that he died, was very rich, and had invented dynamite, he wondered if this was all the world thought of him — rich and the inventor of dynamite!

You know the rest of the story. We no longer think of Alfred Nobel as the inventor of dynamite but rather as the creator of the Nobel Prizes for Peace, Chemistry, Physics, Medicine, and Literature. Many scientists, politicians, and authors work long and hard to receive

25

that award — an award made possible by a man who did not want to be known only for inventing dynamite.

Most likely none of us will ever be wealthy enough to create a Nobel Prize or some other wonderful scholarship or award. But in our own way we can make a difference in our church, our community, and in the lives of those around us. Each of us has God-given talents to share with others.

If you could read your obituary today, is there a part you might want to change? Now is the time you CAN make that change and make a difference in your world.

THE TRIANGLE — SYMBOL OF STRENGTH, STABILITY, AND LOVE
November 2003

A single yellow rose was centered in the picture, a drop of dew on its petal caught on film, a backdrop of green leaves, the sunlight and shadows just perfect.

That was one of the most beautiful pictures I had ever seen. My father, an amateur photographer, took that picture years ago. The flowers he grew were his favorite subjects for his photography. He literally spent hours adjusting his camera, making sure the film, lens, and shutter speed were perfect. He took great pride and delight in his camera and pictures.

This was in the days long before the point-and-shoot cameras where adjustments are made automatically. Wherever my dad went, his camera went, and wherever the camera went, there was the tripod. He could not hold a camera steady enough to create the pictures he demanded. That camera had to be placed on a tripod! The tripod with its three legs forming a triangle on the ground gave the camera stability.

We know from geometry that three points determine a plane; therefore, tripods are used where stability is needed. Tripods are for cameras, for surveying equipment, and for any other delicate instrument requiring a firm and steady foundation. The triangle — a symbol of stability.

Have you ever noticed the great number of triangles engineers use in structures — buildings, bridges, and towers? Have you marveled at their design? Think of a trestle bridge with all of its triangles or the Eiffel Tower. Cranes used in construction work are designed with triangles. A triangle is the strongest geometric figure there is. It cannot be deformed as might a rectangle. Even a simple gate is strengthened by a diagonal brace forming a triangle with the horizontal and vertical bars. Engineers build with triangles where strength is needed. The triangle — a symbol of strength.

The symbol for Trinity is an equilateral triangle. The three equal sides respectively are Father, Son, and Holy Spirit. There is no love greater than the love symbolized by the Trinity. We are all recipients of that love. The triangle — a symbol of love.

In appreciation of God's love for us and the gifts He has given us, we will come forward with our pledges in November. As we dedicate our tithes and offerings, let us remember that there are two other parts to stewardship. Stewardship is not only giving our treasures but also our time and talents. Time, talents, and treasures — those three components form a triangle, a stewardship triangle.

Come. Let us give according to our abilities, a complete stewardship triangle. Our church then will continue to grow in strength, stability, and love.

Follow That Star!
December 2003

Star light, star bright,
First star I see tonight,
I wish I may, I wish I might
I wish I would be in Arizona
A year from tonight!

The year was 1962. The place, Ohio. Every evening I would look for the brightest star in the sky and say the above poem. Then I prayed that somehow my husband and I could move to Arizona. That was my evening ritual. Rain did not deter me because I knew that above the clouds there was a bright star.

To my husband and me, Arizona was the place of opportunity and sunshine. However, I knew that no matter how much we dreamed about moving, wishing upon a star would not make it happen. So, we helped our dreams and prayers along by applying for employment in Arizona. A telephone call, a math teacher needed ... then all at once we were off on an exciting adventure. Our dream came true. Our prayers were answered! We followed our star to Arizona.

Two thousand years ago the Magi from the East saw a star and followed that star to Bethlehem. Can you imagine the adventures they must have encountered on their long and arduous journey? They traveled thousands of miles to fulfill their dream of seeing the King. They knew that just by wishing upon a star would not get them to Jesus. They had to go and seek Him.

What dreams do you have for your church? Do you dream of expanding the sanctuary? Would you like to see additional programs perhaps for the youth, senior citizens or preschool children? Should the mission and evangelism programs be expanded? What are your wishes for your church?

All of these are wonderful dreams, but just wishing upon a star will not give us the desired results. We must pray for guidance, direction, and help with our dreams. We must take action. We all need to make commitments to give our time, talents, and treasures to fulfill our dreams. Then we can and will follow that star to new and exciting adventures in God's service!

2004

YOUR JOY WILL BE COMPLETE

For seven days celebrate the Feast to the Lord your God at the place the Lord will choose. For the Lord your God will bless you in all your harvest and in all the work in your hands, and your joy will be complete.

Deuteronomy 16:15

THE GOOD LIFE
January 2004

What is the "good life?" How do you define it? Is the "good life" measured by the number and value of our material possessions?

When my husband and I moved to Arizona forty years ago, we were able to put all of our belongings in our station wagon. Yes, it was filled to capacity, but all of our "stuff" was inside or on top of the wagon. On our last move eight years ago, could we have fit everything we owned in a station wagon? Of course not! Somehow, through the years our "stuff" grew exponentially. Even after a yard sale, we completely filled one very large moving van. Most likely many of you have experienced the same phenomenon—"stuff" multiplies. Is this the measure of a "good life"—the amount of our material possessions — our "stuff?"

Newsweek Magazine reported recently that for the first time in the United States, there are now more cars per household than licensed drivers. Is that the "good life" — a different vehicle for every possible occasion? Just think, a pickup for the trip to Home Depot, an SUV for vacations, a mini-van to transport the kids, a shiny clean car for church and special occasions, and finally an environmentally friendly car for that daily commute to work. And that's not counting a car for your teenager. No wonder traffic is so bad!

Nineteenth century British author, G. K. Chesterton, suggested that there are two ways to have enough: one is to accumulate more and more. The other is to desire less. Should we be desiring less? Just how much "stuff" is enough? The answer to that question comes from our love for God, neighbor, and our love for God's creation. Dream your good life consistent with your faith and values. Dream your own dream. Do not be influenced by TV advertisements for more and more material possessions.

This year make a New Year's resolution to define the "good life" for you and your family. Resolve to simplify and decide for yourself what is important. Remember, how we spend, save or give away our money, time, and talents reflects our faith and values.*

*The ideas presented above are from *Graceful Living: Your Faith, Values and Money* in Changing Times by the Rev. Laura Dunham, Certified Financial Planner. Published by RCA Distribution, Inc., 2002.

SPREAD CHRIST'S LOVE
February 2004

The rain was coming down in sheets. It was one of the worst storms ever. Already the storm drains were filled, causing the water to lap over the curb.

School had just let out. I hesitated at the top of the steps. I felt very small and scared, for I was only a first-grader. I had no protection but a light sweater. It had not been raining when I left for school, but now, the clouds were pouring out with all their fury.

A bigger child, a sixth grader, came from behind me and said, "I will walk you home for I have an umbrella." We walked together, huddled under that umbrella. She helped allay my fears. When we neared my house, I saw my mother walking toward us. I literally flew into her arms. Then my benefactor turned completely around, retracing her steps in the pouring rain to her home. Who was she? How would I ever thank her? I did not know.

Fast forward six years. This time I was the big junior high kid, trudging home from school through a snowstorm. The wind was blowing hard. It was very cold. What had been a few flakes in the early morning was now a blizzard in the late afternoon. Few people had cleared their sidewalks. That wouldn't have helped much, as the snow was accumulating fast and furiously. All I could think of at the time was sipping a cup of hot chocolate in front of the fireplace in my home. I also thought, if it keeps snowing like this, we won't have school tomorrow! I couldn't wait to get home. I had a mile to walk.

Then I met a small child, a first-grader. She was crying. I stopped and she said, between tears, that she just moved to this street and did not remember which house was hers. I had passed a house with large moving boxes on the porch. Maybe that was her home. I tried to calm her, hoping she could remember. I walked ahead, flattening the snow and making it easier for her to walk in my footprints.

After we had walked awhile, we saw her mother. She was waiting on the front porch amid all the boxes. The little girl ran to her mother. When she was safe in her mother's arms, I quickly turned around and retraced my steps into the blinding snowstorm. For the rest of my journey home, the snow did not seem so deep, the wind wasn't nearly as severe, nor the temperature as cold. My heart was warm.

Many of you have had similar experiences in helping a stranger. For the recipient of our love, the path is made smoother, clouds are lifted, and the day seems brighter. A person feels more confident knowing someone cares. When we give love, our hearts are warmed, and our own burdens are also lifted.

Let us spread the love of Christ in our hearts by giving our time, talents and treasures to others.

WE ARE LIKE KITES!
March 2004

The March wind blew across the high plateau. The sun peeked out from behind the clouds. There in the sky were kites — many kites — all hand-made by the young boy scouts.

It was quite an annual community event, the day the scouts flew their kites. Each kite was a little different — big and small, some artistically decorated. There were kites with long tails, and others had hardly any tails at all.

Some of the boys tried different shapes for their kites. Several boys were having trouble getting their kites off the ground. A few kites bumped across the desert floor landing in the brush.

Everyone helped out with quick repairs. The boys tugged at the strings and coaxed the kites high. The higher the kites soared, the greater the force between the kite and boy. Parents and siblings of the scouts cheered as the kites got off the ground.

It was a wonderful sight to see all those kites dancing in the March breeze. More clouds came, the wind picked up, and the boys brought their kites down and tucked them under their arms, safe and ready for another day.

We are like kites. God is our Maker. He made each of us a little different, but beautiful in our own way. We each have a different talent to share.

We are like kites. There is a force between God and us, an invisible string. He lets the string out, then pulls and tugs at us to keep us soaring. We are made to soar. God wants us to soar.

We are like kites. We need a little wind, challenges in life so that we can grow. The challenges help us soar. Others cheer us as we soar.

We are like kites. Periodically we need a respite from soaring. We feel God's loving arms at church, Bible study, devotions, and prayer. At times when we bump across the desert floor, land in the brush, or the winds of life become too great, others help us with a repair job so that on another day we might soar again.

We are like kites. Everything we are and everything we have comes from God. As He tugs and coaxes us to soar ever higher, let us remember our Creator and thank Him with our time, talents, and treasures.

SPENDING OUR GIFTS FROM GOD
April 2004

"Jesus went throughout Galilee, teaching in their synagogues, preaching the good news of the kingdom, and healing every disease and sickness among the people" (Matthew 4:23).

We have a gift of time. We can choose how we spend our time. Jesus filled his days with teaching, preaching, healing, and praying. How do we spend our day? What portion of each day, week, or year do we spend with Him in church, Bible study, prayer and devotion? How much time do we spend in helping others, helping the least of our brothers?

The body of Christ broken for you!

With our hands, our feet, and our body, what can we do for Christ? All of us have God-given talents. With our hands we can create beautiful works of art, play musical instruments, welcome one another, or comfort one another. With our feet we can walk/run to spread the good news of Christ. With our voices we can teach, and we can sing. With our hearts and minds we share our talents to be used for the glory of God.

The blood of Christ shed for you!

With our God-given interests and abilities, we earn a living. From those earnings we accumulate earthly treasures both in money and material goods. Christ gave His all for us. He shed his blood for us! He died for our sins! What can we do for Him? What percentage of our God-given treasures do we return to Him?

He has risen! He is not here.

This is Easter! Spread the good news! He is risen! He is risen indeed! Fill your hearts with love. Rejoice! Sing praises to Him; worship Him. Contemplate Christ's love for us, His work for us, what He has done for us. Reflect on the events that led to Easter. Renew the promises that you have made to God. Thank Him for all your gifts and grow spiritually by returning a portion of your time, talents, and treasures to Him.

WHAT IS OUR HERITAGE?
May 2004

Water from the melting snow splashed as we bounced along the wash in the jeep. We had quite a thrilling ride through water, sand and rock on a very primitive and, at times, extremely narrow road.

Jewel Nicholls and I were on a guided tour of Canyon de Chelly in Northeastern Arizona on the Navajo Reservation. The scenery was fantastic — sheer canyon walls with deeply colored stains on rock faces; each turn on the rough road through the canyon afforded another magnificent view of God's country.

Our Navajo guide told stories about the canyon. We marveled at the Anasazi cliff dwellings high on the canyon walls. We stopped at many pictographs telling their stories from many years ago. We heard about the Long Walk in 1864 when the U.S. Army forced the Navajo people to march to Fort Sumner, New Mexico. Four years later a treaty was signed, and they returned to their beloved land. The Navajo who had lived in Canyon de Chelly were able to reclaim their farms and orchards.

We learned about the Navajo heritage and culture. We stopped to purchase handcrafted silver and turquoise jewelry. We heard the melodious notes of the Navajo flute, and we ate the most delicious Indian Fry Bread that I've ever tasted.

At one of our stops we heard the echoes of children

playing, but we did not see anyone. Were the steep canyon walls echoing the sounds of past generations? Our last stop in the canyon was at the base of a very sheer cliff. There, high on the rocks stained by nature, we could see the face of Jesus looking down on us.

I frequently think of our trip to Canyon de Chelly — the supreme beauty of the land and how welcome everyone made us feel. Obviously, the goal of the Navajo people is to show their land and explain their culture and heritage to the tourists.

This year, on the 20th anniversary of the Gilbert Presbyterian Church, you will be hearing stories of our past. We are known as a friendly church. That is our culture.

Next month the school will move out of the Christian Education building. As a part of reclaiming our building, everyone's help will be needed to clean and decorate for our purposes.

It's important to involve everyone as we think about the future. What do we want to accomplish? What are our goals? We are a growing church, a giving church. That is our heritage.

As we contemplate our future, let us remember to thank God for our gifts — our culture and our heritage. We grow spiritually by returning a portion of our time, talents, and treasures to Him.

IN HIS GARDEN
June 2004

Tulips were everywhere! I have never seen so many tulips. There were large beds in front of stores and people's homes, along the highway, and on the university campus. The tulips were beautiful — tall stately green stems proudly displaying their opened blooms of red, pink, white, and yellow. The spring day was perfect — cool air with warm sunshine and a soft breeze. That is what Michigan was like when I got off the plane in Detroit last month.

I thought about the tulips, how they grew from a nondescript lump called a bulb. They take their nourishment from the soil; then gradually the small sprout pushes up. It breaks ground just as the last of the snow is slowly melting. Spring rains and sunshine help the bulbs along the way. It takes time for a tulip to become a tall and stately flower. It takes time for tulips to bloom — God's time.

We are like tulips. The love we receive from our family and friends helps us grow. We grow spiritually through our time in church, Bible study, prayer, and devotions. At times, we might feel like that small shoot pushing through a cold, hard path. As the tulips receive nourishment from God, so do we. We grow by giving our time, talents, and treasures. We must be ever patient, ever growing, and in God's time we will bloom. As He watches over the tulips, He will watch and care for us.

In God's garden there are many wonderful flowers with unique talents to share, each one nurtured by God. Perhaps God did not give you the talents of a tulip. Maybe, you are a beautiful southwestern orange poppy instead. God lovingly cares for and needs all of the flowers in His garden. God needs all of us — our time, talents, and treasures. Each one of us is a beautiful flower in His garden.

PRIORITIES — THE PUNCTUATION MARKS OF LIFE
July 2004

A panda walks into a café. He orders a sandwich, eats it, then draws a gun and fires two shots in the air.

"Why?" asks the confused waiter, as the panda heads toward the exit. The panda produces a badly punctuated wildlife manual and tosses it over his shoulder.

"I'm a panda," he says, at the door. "Look it up."

The waiter turns to the relevant entry and, sure enough, finds an explanation:

"Panda. Large black-and-white bear-like mammal, native to China. Eats, shoots and leaves."

The above joke is on the jacket cover of the British bestseller, <u>Eats, Shoots & Leaves</u> by Lynne Truss. It's hard to imagine, but the author uses a wonderful sense of humor to make a book on punctuation extremely refreshing.

Correct punctuation is essential. It provides meaning, understanding, and clarity to the written word. In the case of the panda, proper punctuation could have prevented him from firing a gun in the café!

Priorities are the punctuation marks in life. Without them, our lives would be like an incorrectly punctuated sentence — meaningless. Other people, as well as activities, call for our attention. We have difficult decisions to make on how to spend our time, money, and talents. We must prioritize. Well thought-out priorities enrich our lives and provide meaning, just as correct punctuation clarifies and enriches the written word.

For the past month, the 20/20 Steering Committee has visited many groups within the church. We have asked for your opinions concerning the direction of Gilbert Presbyterian Church. We greatly appreciate your ideas. Remember: it is never too late to contribute to this exercise. Watch for a list of the suggestions made thus far. Now, they must be prioritized. Just as each person must establish priorities to have a more meaningful life, so must a church.

Recently, at another Presbyterian church, there was considerable discussion on how to spend an endowment given to the church. According to the restrictions on the gift, they were allowed to spend the monthly interest but not the principal. Everyone on the session had his/her own idea on how the money should be appropriated. Each session member spoke fervently for the project they favored, and no two people agreed.

Finally, the youngest member of the session (a youth elder) spoke up. "The Bible teaches us that the first-fruits of our labors should be given to God. Therefore, the first check of every year should be given to a mission project." That became their priority.

As individuals, we must set priorities for our time, talents, and treasures. We must pray and ask God for guidance. As a church, we also prioritize. We must ask what God wants Gilbert Presbyterian Church to do in the next twenty years. As a church, what are our dreams, our goals, and our priorities? How can we accomplish them?

THE FRUITS OF OUR LABORS
September 2004

It was the kind of weather that fruit trees and berry bushes love — warm and humid with clouds foretelling an impending storm. The branches of the peach trees hung low with a bountiful harvest. Acres of berries grew on a slope reaching to the river. Those peaches and blackberries were the best I had ever eaten.

Wherever I went in Virginia this past summer, I saw crops of all kinds growing profusely in the rich soil. We enjoyed gathering vegetables from my daughter's small garden every evening for dinner.

The area is God's farmland. God provided the rich soil, rain, and sunshine. The trees and plants glorify God by producing their fruit in return.

What are the fruits of our labors? What treasures and talents can we share with others? Just as a plant grows, we can grow in the knowledge of God. Through prayer, God nourishes us, just as God nourishes the soil by providing needed rain and sunshine. Just as we fertilize our gardens, we must enrich our minds and souls by attending church, Bible study, and devotions.

We pull weeds from our garden, and we must also pull the weeds of sin from our lives. Just as a garden shares its harvest with us, we too must share our talents and treasures. This is our way of saying thanks and glorifying God.

LEFTOVERS
October 2004

Bills, bills, bills! Will they ever end? Time to get out the calculator, balance the checkbook, and pay the bills. Can't procrastinate much longer.

First, balance the checkbook. Yes! It balances. Next, pay the bills — mortgage, car, electric, water, gas, telephone, cable, credit cards, etc., etc., etc. Help, I'm drowning in bills!

Finally, done! No more bills until next month. Oops, forgot one — the church! I wonder how much I have left over to give to the church this time. Not much — shouldn't have bought that cute outfit.

Stop! What's wrong with that scenario? If we invite our best friends to dinner, would we serve them leftovers? Of course, not! We would buy the finest foods we can afford. Then, why are we serving our leftovers to God? If we pay all our other bills first, then give to the church a portion of what is left over, is that not giving God our leftovers?

I challenge everyone, myself included, to pay God first. Give the first fruits of your labors to God. When we pay God first, we are putting Him first — not our car, not our house, certainly not our TV. God is first.

It is a declaration of allegiance to pay God first. We are saying we belong to God. We do not belong to our creditors — those who want our money — we belong to God! It is a statement of faith to pay God first.

We are saying we trust Him. Everything we have and everything we are comes from God. God will continue to bless us. Show your trust in God with the gift of your "first fruits."

The Finance and Stewardship Committees would like to challenge everyone to increase their offering by giving 1percent more of your income. This is giving only $1 more for every $100 you earn. Start where you are and increase by 1 percent. If you currently give 2 percent, increase it to 3 percent. That way we will all grow in stewardship.

Soon you will have the opportunity to make a pledge to God through our church — a pledge of your time, talents, and treasures. Prayerfully consider all that God has given you and return the first fruits of your labors to Him.

Ideas from <u>Speaking of Stewardship, Model Sermons on Money and Possessions</u>, William G. Carter, editor, Geneva Press, 1998.

DON'T FORGET THE EGG
November 2004

"Why do you always put an egg in your stuffing?" my daughter-in-law asked me one Thanksgiving morning.

Well, on Thanksgiving some time ago, before I was married, my mother was very ill and bedridden. My dad said that we were to prepare the turkey.

"But Dad, we don't know how to make the dressing. We need to wake Mom to get her recipe." (These were the days before the easy-to-make stuffing from a box.)

"She needs her rest. We will make the dressing. You have watched her before."

"But Dad, we might know the ingredients, but not the amounts. She never measures. We need to wake her; we don't know what we are doing."

"We are not waking her. We will do it just like Mom. We won't measure either." That is exactly what happened. Nothing was measured, everything was tossed together.

"This will not taste like Mom's!" Finally, just when I thought my dad was finished, he said, "Hand me an egg."

"But, Dad, Mom NEVER puts an egg in her stuffing."

"Well, this dressing will have an egg!" Who can argue with that? So, the egg was mixed in, turkey stuffed, and into the oven it went.

At that moment, Mom awoke. My dad gave me a wink and ran into her room. "You woke up just in time. We need to get the turkey in the oven. You must tell us your recipe for the dressing. We don't know how to make it."

To continue the ruse, I went back and forth from her room to the kitchen repeating the recipe to Dad. Finally, my last trip.

"Mom, do you put an egg in the dressing?" She had a good laugh, the house resonated with her laughter — "Goodness, no!"

"Dad, no egg," I shouted.

"OK, no egg."

My brothers, Dad, and I gathered around Mom for our Thanksgiving meal. Mom was most appreciative of our dinner. She kept saying how wonderful everything tasted and that the dressing was delicious. Dad declared over and over that we never could have done it without her help. He kept telling her that it was her recipe we used and that was why it was so good. And Mom continued to laugh about the egg that almost got into the dressing. At least, that is what she believed.

To me that egg became a symbol of the fantastic love and devotion between my parents. Dad made Mom feel important and needed even when she was physically unable to care for us. And Mom was always so gracious of whatever Dad did for her. That egg was a symbol of my dad's sense of humor and my mother's laughter. That is why I always put an egg in my stuffing — to remember their wonderful love and utmost caring and pass it on to others.

What is greater than the love between husband and wife, between parent and child, or between friends? The greatest love is God's love for us. He gave us His only son. He created us.

He also has a sense of humor. There is a little

cracked egg in all of us!

Everything we are and everything we have comes from God. How can we spread that love? In thanksgiving to God, we give of ourselves to others — our time, talents, and treasures.

In November, we will come forth with our pledges to dedicate ourselves to God's work and the church. Let your pledge be your egg of love — the love of devotion, sharing, and commitment.

This year as you prepare your Thanksgiving dinner, don't forget the egg.

BE A LIGHTHOUSE FOR OTHERS
December 2004

I woke to the mournful tone of the distant foghorn. Oh how I loved that rhythmic sound reverberating in the air! I opened my curtains and could barely see the house across the street. It was veiled in white. No wonder the foghorn on Lake Erie was blaring. The sound came from the vicinity of two small lighthouses standing as sentinels marking the path into Cleveland harbor.

Another time, another place — the Outer Banks of North Carolina. There the lighthouses are tall and stately, each one painted in a different pattern. The most famous is the barbershop pole pattern of Cape Hatteras. It has a light that can be seen thirty miles out into the ocean. At night the lighthouses serve as beacons to warn the sailors of treacherous shoals along the Outer Banks. The lighthouses are landmarks by day, readily identified by their colors and patterns.

My daughter cries out, "Another lighthouse, Mom," as she drives along the ever-winding coast of Nova Scotia. The lighthouse at Peggy's Cove is one of the most beautiful I have ever seen. It stands on gigantic boulders scoured by the wind and ocean waves. How did they ever build the structure on those rocks? The lighthouse gleamed in the setting sun.

We drove along the coast to the northeastern tip of Nova Scotia. There a lighthouse stands desolate on the barren ground at the entrance to Louisbourg Harbor. The wind was bitter cold. We could almost feel ice crystals in the air even though it was late May. The North Atlantic Ocean churned wild and ominous. It was not hard to imagine ships out at sea searching for a protected harbor.

There is something spiritual about a lighthouse, the way it reaches to the heavens. Its beacon extends across the rocky and dangerous shore to the wild sea. A lighthouse is a symbol of watchfulness and helpfulness. It is a guide, lighting the way and protecting one from harm.

Two thousand years ago a star shown over Bethlehem guiding the shepherds and wise men to the stable where Jesus was born. Jesus is the light of the world. He is our lighthouse. We must allow His light to shine in our lives. His light guides us over rocky paths into safe harbors. No matter how rough the way or how many storms we encounter, he is ever there, leading us. As we travel through life, He is our light, our lighthouse to guide and protect us.

Reflect the light of Jesus and be a lighthouse for others. Every lighthouse is different in style and design, but all serve the common purpose to guide and protect. All of us have different talents to share. We are not alike, but yet we have a common purpose of helping, guiding, protecting, and loving one another.

Let your light so shine by giving your time, talents, and treasures. Be a lighthouse for others.

2005

CHILDREN'S CHILDREN ARE A CROWN TO THE AGED

Children's children are a crown to the aged, and parents are the pride of their children.

Proverbs 17:6

AN OPEN LETTER
TO MY INFANT GRANDSON
January 2005

My Dearest Little Matthew,

November 4, 2004, a little after 11 p.m. Arizona time (November 5, Virginia time), your daddy called me. "He's beautiful, he's beautiful." Your daddy was so awed by your birth that it was all he could say. He was completely speechless. In the background I heard your first cry — the miracle of birth, a baby's first cry.

What an exciting time to be born! Nothing is standing still. Science, medicine, all fields of knowledge are making fantastic discoveries all the time. So much has happened in the past twenty years. When your mommy and daddy were in elementary school, personal computers were just being developed. Now almost every home across America has access to a computer. We can instantly communicate with others around the world via electronic mail.

When I was young, a computer required 18,000 vacuum tubes and occupied an entire room. Then no one dreamed that a computer could be small enough to fit on one's lap. And when my parents were little, a computer, well that was not a machine but rather a person who computes — did arithmetic by hand.

Look at transportation — in a few hours I can fly across the country to visit you. When I was little, trains were the more common mode of transporting people from one distant place to another. And just think when my dad was a young man, he delivered mail by horseback on rainy days because his Model-T Ford could not negotiate the muddy roads.

When your daddy was born, Neil Armstrong left his footprints on the moon. Where will you leave your footprints? What leap will you make for mankind? We cannot envision the changes that will occur in the next twenty, thirty, or forty years. Yes, changes will be made, and you and your generation will be a part of those changes.

We know that the world will change. But Matthew, some things will never change. God loves you. He created you and everything about you. God's love, the love of your friends and family — that will never change. As you mature, you will discover that your life will touch others — it already has. Your circle of influence will grow ever wider. You were conceived in love, born in love, and you will be raised in love. Continue spreading God's love to others.

God gave you many talents. As you grow you will discover more about those talents. Your talents are what make you special — make you unique. Use your God-given talents to make your corner of the world a better place in which to live. Find your passion and go for it.

I am sorry to say that there will always be hurting and sorrow in the world. That will not change. Help those who need help, those who are less fortunate than you. You were born into the Presbyterian Church. Support your church and its mission programs. Support community programs that help the needy, the children, and the elderly.

The length of a day will never change, 24 hours

every day, today, yesterday, and tomorrow. But what will you do with your day? That is the important question. Prioritize your time wisely. Spend time with your family and friends. Help others. Spend time in studies, devotion, prayer, and worship. Devote each day to learning, ever questioning. Do not lose your childlike wonder for the world around you. Keep asking why.

You are richly blest by God. Appreciate what He has given you by giving thanks to Him. As you grow in body and mind, grow spiritually by giving of your time, talents, and treasures. Pass on that love of Jesus Christ to others.

With lots of hugs and kisses from your loving grandma,

Eloise Annis

HOW DO WE HONOR GOD?
February 2005

A magnifying glass! I wondered why I was given a small magnifying glass as I entered the gallery of Albrecht Dürer's work, "A Renaissance Journey in Print," at the Virginia Museum of Fine Arts in Richmond.

I stared in disbelief at the prints on the walls. In the background of one was a flock of birds circling a castle on a high mountain. With the naked eye, the birds were just specks in the sky. But with the magnifying glass, I could see their outstretched wings catching the breeze.

In another print a galloping horse, with flying mane and tail, showed the ripple of every muscle. The print of Adam and Eve displayed them in the Garden of Eden surrounded by animals, plants, and trees of all kinds. Yes, the serpent was there tempting them with the forbidden fruit.

I had never seen such exquisite and minutely detailed work. One could spend hours studying each individual print. Yes, the magnifying glass was needed to examine the lines, curves, and crosshatches. Dürer was a master at creating the perfect shadows and shadings. His people and animals came alive with great emotion and intensity.

Four rooms were filled with Dürer's prints, many of which depicted stories from the Bible: Adam and

Eve, at least a dozen prints on the birth and life of Christ, quite a few on Mary the mother of Jesus, and fifteen prints illustrating the Book of Revelation and the Apocalypse.

Other prints looked like scenes from his homeland (Germany) and his period of time (early 1500's). Amazingly, these were not ink or paint drawings but prints from woodcuts. In a woodcut, the artist draws on a block of wood and then cuts away the space, leaving the design elevated. The woodcuts are then inked and pressed against paper. Dürer was the first to use printmaking as a major form of art.

Much of the art from the Renaissance period is of religious nature. Perhaps it was the artist's way of teaching the Bible to others. Or perhaps it was his method of honoring God. Renaissance artists have left a special legacy in their paintings, frescoes, prints, and woodcuts.

What will be our legacy? How do we honor God? How do we thank Him for all He has given us? No, we are not artists like Michelangelo, Leonardo Da Vinci, or Dürer. But, we too can honor God. All of us have talents. We must develop our God-given talents to be used in the work of the church and community. We can help others. We can spread the love of Jesus Christ to others. We can learn. We can teach. We can grow spiritually. We can leave a legacy for future generations. All of us have gifts to give — our gifts of time, talents, and treasures.

THE CROSS OF JESUS
March 2005

I walked into a small Scottish shop in Williamsburg, Virginia, intending to buy a cross — a Celtic cross like the one in our sanctuary. But first I had to look at everything else: the tartans, plaid neckties, scarves, kilts, beautiful wool skirts and sweaters, toy sheep and dogs, and even a six-foot tall teddy bear dressed in full Scottish attire.

It was a very interesting shop, but I was off to buy a cross. I picked out a small, sterling silver Celtic cross — made in Ireland. Paying for it was the easy part. But to wear a cross — that can be difficult. What does it mean to wear a cross? Am I worthy to wear the cross of Jesus?

Simon was forced to carry the cross for Jesus. Can we assist others as they carry their cross? Do we give of our time, talents, and treasures to help others? Do we joyfully serve the church? Do we find a need and fill it? Are we generous with our kind words to our family and friends? Do we stop for a moment in our busy lives and listen to others? Maybe that is all a person needs — someone who will listen.

I have an uncle in Ohio with Alzheimer's disease. His wife calls me late at night when she can't sleep, knowing that because of the time difference I am still awake in Arizona. What can I do, 2,000 miles away? I can listen; listen to her and the many difficulties she encounters, her cross that she must bear. Yes, giving of our time can be so important to others.

What does it mean to wear the cross of Jesus? Jesus said, "Father, forgive them, for they do not know what they are doing" (Luke 23:34).

Is not forgiveness the first step to stewardship? How can we help others if we do not first forgive? How can we have love and compassion in our hearts and minds if we do not rid ourselves of dislike, hostility, and revenge? Yes, forgive! Forgive seventy times seven.

In my first year of community college teaching many years ago, I had a student who on the first day of class constantly interrupted me by asking questions that had nothing to do with the course. On the second day of class he was even worse. Why was he doing this to me? What was wrong with him? He was an adult, older than I, and he should know better. Did I dislike him? Yes! Want to get even? You bet. Flunk him!

The following Sunday, the sermon was on forgiveness. I will never forget it. The minister stopped and asked us to think of someone who had recently wronged us, then forgive and pray for him or her. Thinking of someone was easy — my student, but to forgive and pray for him! I was a skeptic at first, but I did try in my heart to forgive and pray.

A few days later I walked to class with much trepidation but with prayer and forgiveness. Something amazing occurred.

My student wasn't interrupting — not even once. All of his questions for the rest of the semester were very pertinent to the lesson. He became one of my best students in that class — the power of prayer? Divine intervention? forgiveness? — maybe all three.

How can we help others if we do not first forgive?

The cross around my neck is empty. He is not here. He is risen! Go and spread the good news.

It is Easter! Rejoice! Wear the cross with pride. Know what it means to live as Jesus lived — to forgive, to help others, to serve our church, to give of our time, talents, and treasures.

Yes, wear that cross — a guide and inspiration!

ARE WE GOOD STEWARDS?
April 2005

A soft spring breeze blew across the desert. Wildflowers waved to the rhythm of the breeze and earth. The wind caught an empty plastic grocery sack and carried it aloft. Its desert adventure was short lived as the arms of a cactus seemed to reach out and snatch it. There the plastic sack remained, caught forever.

A few yards away, an empty plastic bottle lay beside a boulder. It had once contained water, quenching the thirst of some hiker. In a dry wash was an old rusted car, wheels long gone, doors skewed, and windows missing. Once it was a new, shiny piece of steel proudly carrying people from place to place. Now, however, it was a forgotten, useless piece of junk. And there it lay among the rocks and desert brush.

Is there any place not desecrated by man? Pieces of rubber from tires can be seen along our freeways. The other morning on a city street, drivers dodged a large box. Around the corner near the curb was what looked like pieces of linoleum. And an empty soda can rolled across two lanes of highway. Even the man in the moon, ever smiling down on us, is not immune to the refuse of modern society.

Where is there a place of natural pristine beauty not disturbed by man? A quiet, serene place, a place made by God?

Randy Tufts and Gary Tenen discovered such a place in 1974 when they first ventured into Kartchner Caverns. They were the first people ever to set foot in that cave. Man walked on the moon before any man walked in Kartchner.

Randy Tufts and Gary Tenen knew that a cave so accessible could easily be destroyed. They decided the best way to preserve and protect it was to have the state buy the land and develop it as a state park and tourist attraction. In April 1988, Kartchner Caverns became a state park.

Recently my friend and I toured the Big Room of Kartchner Caverns. We entered through air-lock doors that keep the cave at constant temperature and humidity. As we entered, everyone in our tour group became very quiet, awed by the beauty of the cave formations. It was the most wonderful sight. Kartchner Caverns is a living cave — its stalactites and stalagmites growing ever so slowly with each tiny drop of water. It is an underground cathedral made by God.

Considerable time, money, and energy were spent to keep from harming any cave formations during the construction of a path that winds through the cave's most beautiful sections. Every evening after the last tour group has exited, the path is washed down and water is recycled outside to the thirsty desert plants.

Kartchner Caverns has become a living scientific laboratory — a study in keeping the cave in its pristine state, yet allowing visitors to behold its beauty. The number of visitors in each group and the number of tours each day are strictly regulated. The Big Room is closed off for six months of the year to allow its original residents, the bats, to return home and give birth to their young.

God created beauty in the earth from the deepest cave to the highest mountain, from the sun during the day to the moon and stars at night. That is God's handicraft, God's work, God's gift to us. But with these gifts comes responsibility. God has made us the stewards of the land. He has given us the responsibility to care for the environment — the plants, animals, earth, and sky. How are we doing? Are we preserving and protecting God's work? Are we good stewards of God's world?

UPON THIS ROCK
May 2005

"Daddy, Daddy, do it again! Make the rock skip across the water. Show me how!"

When I was a child, my family frequently took Sunday afternoon drives to a nearby river. Invariably we would stop, walk along the shore, and toss rocks into the water. To my youthful eyes, my dad was the best rock skipper. He would carefully choose a flat stone perfect for rock skipping, and then give it just the right flick with his wrist.

Off it went — skip, skip, skip, six or seven times across the river. I was fascinated watching the rock create ever-widening concentric circles of ripples generated from each point of contact with the water. Soon the circles were overlapping one another. As much as I tried, my stones would only skip once or twice. Most of the time my rocks went kerplunk!

This month, as I think of Pentecost, the early Christian Church and the apostles spreading the news of Jesus across the land, I am reminded of Peter, the Rock. "...On this rock I will build my church..." Jesus said (Matthew 16:18). How appropriate — a rock — a solid foundation to build a church, but also a rock skipping across from city to city creating ever-widening circles of love and understanding.

The apostles were the chosen ones, carefully selected by Jesus to bring the Good News to all people.

They were the rocks, and from these rocks a ripple of believers began to spread out teaching, helping, and loving others. These early ripples generated a wave, a wave stretching from countryside to countryside, town to town, city to city, and nation to nation. In this way Christianity spread throughout the world.

What does Pentecost mean to us? Can each of us become a rock, create a ripple, spread the Good News? Do people know us by our love and actions? Are we giving of ourselves and our time to help others know Christ as we know Him?

We are chosen, chosen by God to do good in His world. Spread the Good News; be thankful for what God has given to each of us. Be thankful for those first Christians who created ripples across the land. We too can create ripples by giving our time, talents, and treasures to do God's work in His world.

Be a rock! Create a ripple!

BIRTHDAY GREETINGS,
GRANDDAUGHTER
June 2005

Happy Birthday, Desireé,

You are now thirteen years old — a teenager — the years between childhood and adulthood. These are the years when friends at times are more important than family.

The teen years are when confusion reigns — who am I? what will I do when I grow up? The teen years, when at times you want more responsibilities, but at other times shy away from responsibilities, asking, "Do I have to?" The teen years, when decisions are made that may have long-lasting consequences.

I remember when I was your age — spring semester of my 7th grade. At that time I was not the good student that you are — I was just average, really never caring about school. Geography was my nemesis.

Every Friday our teacher (who I thought was "old") gave a ten-question quiz, and every week my grades... well, let's just say they weren't the best. Then one day my friends said to me at lunch time, "Here are the answers to the quiz. We got them from the morning class. All you have to do is memorize them and get an A." Every week my answer to them was the same — I tossed the answers into the nearest waste paper basket, never really looking at them. Of course, every

Friday I got the same old dumpy grade.

Well, guess what Desi? The cheaters were caught! I never was implicated because my quiz grades were too low for anyone to think I was cheating.

When report cards came out, there was the grade I earned in Geography, a D. "Wait a minute; I'm an average student — C, not D. I can no longer get the answers from my friends. What do I do? Study? Me? I'll study just a tiny bit, just enough to make a C." Well, I overdid it.

There was a B in Geography on my last report card for the 7th grade. My teacher went on and on about how much I had improved. I had the entire summer to think about what had happened and to make perhaps the most important decision I made as a thirteen-year old: I decided to take school seriously, study, and do it without cheating. I became a conscientious student for the rest of my life.

There is a funny ending to this story. Later in high school as I was planning for college, the guidance counselor was looking over my past grades. She did not believe that my grades prior to 8th grade were correctly recorded in my permanent record file. According to her, major errors were made. I could not convince her otherwise.

Desi, you are an excellent student and your grades are great. We are all very proud of your accomplishments. But Desi, there are decisions you will be making as a teenager, and some of these decisions may be of great significance.

There will always be decisions on how to spend your time. (Many adults have trouble with this one.) Time is the great equalizer. You have no more or less time than anyone else. It's how we use time that makes the difference. Invest your time wisely. Spend time studying; use your time to explore, investigate, and pursue new knowledge. Take time to stop and smell the roses, look at the sunset, or search for a rainbow. Commit time with your family and friends to help them and to love them. Finally, spend time with God in prayer and devotion.

Now in your teen years you will be making decisions as to the courses to take in high school and college. You will decide what career to pursue. Now is the time to explore your many God-given talents. Be open. Do not have a closed mind about any subject. Have fun exploring. Find your passion and go for it. Reflect on how you can use your talents to help others.

You will have decisions to make concerning your treasures. Since you occasionally earn money by babysitting, make a decision now to give a portion of your earnings to the church or a community program that helps the less fortunate. Why not begin now to save part of your money to buy a gift for a Christmas angel? It is not the percentage or amount you decide to give that is important but rather the fact that you are giving. That decision will become a habit for the rest of your life. In thanks to God, we return to Him a portion of what He has given us.

Happy Birthday, Desi. You are very fortunate to be truly blessed with many talents, a loving family, and many friends. When you need to make those difficult decisions, seek out your parents, grandparents, aunts, uncles, teachers and friends.

Ask God for help — pray for guidance, pray for strength to make the right decisions that are so important in your life. Desi, enjoy your teenage years.

May God continue to bless you.

Love from your Grandma, Eloise

A STORY OF LOVE
July 2005

Congratulations! Ann Annis and Mark Emeott — July 2, 2005 — the most important day of your lives, your wedding day.

I remember the day I first met you, Mark. I just knew, as you walked through the door of Ann's apartment, that you were the one for my daughter. Maybe it was the twinkle in your eyes, your pleasant smile, or maybe just mother's intuition, but I knew that you and Ann were made for each other.

As both of you know, I have a rock garden. Come into my garden and listen to the rocks tell a beautiful story, a story for you as you embark on your life together. Every rock in my garden represents a time when your father and I hiked the hills, arroyos, and mountains of Eastern Arizona.

The rocks, composed of a rainbow of colors, represent your wedding vows — promises — that you made to each other. A rainbow is God's covenant or promise to us. Several of my rocks are completely spherical but otherwise nondescript. Are they the geodes that hold a hidden treasure inside? Geodes represent hope — hope for the best possible life together.

Some of my rocks have streaks of blue and/or green — a sign of the minerals azurite and malachite. They can be transformed into copper — copper wire, cable, tubing, pans, coins, and copper decorations. Azurite

71

and malachite, the rocks of faith to represent the trust you have for each other. Trust molded into love.

The beautiful bright agates represent the sunny days the two of you will have together. The fire agates with the iridescent red symbolize the spark in your lives. The dazzling white crystals are the ones to light your path. And let us not forget the black rocks — the Apache tears. Yes, you will have some difficult days, time of concerns and problems — the Apache tear days. But hold an Apache tear to the light — God's light — and the rock becomes very beautiful and translucent.

My rocks represent the time that you will spend together. My rocks are faith and hope. My rocks express the happy times and difficult times. My rocks were made by God. Taken all together, my rock garden is a symbol of love — the love between husband and wife. And the greatest love of all — the love that God has for us.

The two of you are now embarking upon the most wonderful and exciting journey — your journey of life together. Your plans, hopes, and dreams for the future will entail the two of you — no longer just one. You will need to make important decisions together — decisions concerning your time, talents, and treasures. Spend time together, develop interests that both of you can enjoy. Spend time together in worship, prayer, and devotion.

God gave both of you many talents. Work together and use your talents. Put love into whatever you do. Use your talents to help others. Use your talents in a church where both of you can worship. Everything you have comes from God. Together, make the decision to return to God a portion of that with which He has so richly blessed you.

I have in my kitchen a small figurine, a girl stirring perhaps flour, sugar, eggs, and butter in a mixing bowl with her puppy dog looking up at her. The inscription reads "The secret ingredient is love!" Yes, Ann and Mark, the secret ingredient to a long and wonderful marriage is love. Whether the two of you are mixing muffins, engaged in mundane tasks of cleaning house or doing laundry, or making exciting plans for the future, add the ingredient of love — love that is as beautiful and solid as a rock, the love of a married couple blessed by God.

Congratulations!
With much love and happiness.
Your Mom

THE POWER OF WATER
August 2005

The Niagara River rushed to the brink of the falls; then, with a roar, spilled over with cascading beauty. The water pounded the rocks and boulders below. A cool mist sprayed in my face as I contemplated the scene before me. At times a rainbow could be seen across the falls. Such power, strength, and beauty created only by God.

A few days before my excursion to Niagara Falls, I was at Headlands Beach in Ohio. That day Lake Erie was so peaceful and calm. The water gently lapped against the white sandy shore. The water felt refreshingly cool on that hot summer day. At one end of the beach was a pile of driftwood as a reminder of more turbulent and stormy times.

The previous week I was in Midland, Michigan, standing on a footbridge spanning two rivers. It was a beautiful bridge with its three arched sections coming together directly above the confluence of the two rivers. I was there at that point looking down on the water. The rivers, now one, slowly meandered through trees and meadows on their way to Lake Huron. It was a scene of peace and quiet.

Are our lives like the waters of the Great Lakes basin? We come together with others, and we share our feelings and thoughts just as the rivers come together and flow into the lakes. Our lives are enriched by others as the lakes are enriched by their rivers. We enrich others by the love we share. Sometimes our days are like the calm cool waters on a hot summer day. Other times we may feel we are like the Niagara River rushing toward some unseen falls. In the midst of turmoil there is a rainbow in the sky, there is peace, there is power, and there is God.

Just as the beauty and power of the rivers and Great Lakes come from God, everything we have and everything we are comes from God. Can we return to God a portion of our treasures, our time, and our talents that He has given us? That is our power, the power that He has given us, to be shared with others.

JUST PLANE TALK
September 2005

The engine roared as the plane gained momentum, racing down the runway. As I was thrust back in my seat, I imagined, like a child, that I was flapping my arms helping the plane get off the ground. It is a marvel of science how these gigantic machines ever fly.

As the plane started to climb, the cars and buildings took on the appearance of children's toys and building blocks. Soon the cityscape was gone and now out the window were the mountains just north of Phoenix. I looked down and saw raging brush and forest fires. It is impossible to imagine the depth of the fires until one actually sees the thick smoke. God's beautiful creation was being devastated.

I always enjoy looking at the changing topography on my flights back East — the Rocky Mountains and dry rivers of the West, the large irrigation circles of crops in the central states, and finally the green trees, lakes, and rivers of the East. Invariably the beautiful fluffy clouds in the West change to a complete stratus cloud cover in the East. Now my view of earth and a final destination are completely hidden. I have no idea where we are, but the pilot knows the airport ahead. Then, all at once, the plane swoops down from the clouds and again the tall city buildings, cars, freeways, and homes become visible ahead.

When I fly, I have complete trust in the pilot to get me to my destination safely. I have faith in the aircraft and the workmen behind it. Because of my trust and faith, I can sit back, relax and enjoy my flight even if I cannot see the ground below.

Who is the pilot in our lives? Who knows our destination and makes sure we arrive there safely? God is our pilot — have faith and trust in Him. Just as we cannot see through the dense clouds, we cannot see the future or the times or events ahead. We must have faith in God and trust Him.

Enjoy your journey through life. Observe His wonders around you. Stop and thank God for all that He has done for you.

But having faith and trust in God requires responsibilities from us. In our journey in life, we cannot sit back and do nothing like a passenger on a plane. We have responsibilities! Everything we have really belongs to God! We are the stewards of His gifts! As stewards of His land, we are responsible for its care. As stewards of the treasures that God has given us, we have the responsibility to designate them in the manner that He wants.

Our talents? Yes, God has given all of us talents. We must first discover our talents, and then utilize them to the best of our abilities for God's work. Enjoy life's journey, and enjoy the scenery, but remember we all have responsibilities as stewards of God's gifts to us.

A RAINBOW OF OPPORTUNITIES
October 2005

The ray of light from the sun shone on the triangular prism in my hand. I shifted it ever so slightly so that the refracted light produced the most beautiful rainbow of colors — red, orange, yellow, green, blue, and violet. Our children squealed with delight as they tried to catch the rainbow in their hands. Each little hand grabbed at it and each little foot stomped on it as I made the rainbow dance on their hands, shirts, sidewalk, and a wall of our home.

Somehow through the years the prism must have been dropped on its corner, for now it has a flaw — an internal crack about one inch long. Even with its imperfection, that prism produces the most radiant colors when sunlight strikes it.

Just as the sun shines into a prism, so does God's light shine into us. The white light from the sun refracts within the prism, and color emerges according to its wavelength. We reflect God's light. Each of us is on a slightly different wavelength, reflecting a different color, but taken all together, we can make a most beautiful rainbow.

Some of us might reflect the color red. When I think of red, I imagine the color of power and strength — the strength it takes to be a leader in the church or community. Orange follows on the spectrum. Are these the people who joyfully serve and are willing to help no matter what the task? Yellow is a happy, sunny color. These are the people who always greet others with a smile. They make others feel welcome.

Calm, cool green — is that the color of scientists, mathematicians, and engineers asking why and creating order out of chaos? Blue is the color of love — the love of parents, the love of teachers, and the love of those caring for others. What is violet — a mix of blue and red? Is that the color of music? Music to get us moving, music to celebrate, or music to soothe the soul.

Just as my prism has an imperfection, so do we. God does not care if we have a few sharp edges. He still shines His light on us. My prism still creates a beautiful rainbow, and so can we.

On Sunday, October 30, there will be a Ministry Fair providing you with a rainbow of opportunities to explore the many different ministry and mission activities at Gilbert Presbyterian Church. Where do you fit in the rainbow of GPC? What color do you reflect? What color are you? Come, explore and be a part of the beautiful spectrum of colors reflecting and honoring God's light — the light He shines on each one of us.

SIGHTS AND SOUNDS OF AUTUMN
November 2005

The early morning air was dry and crisp as I walked in the neighborhood. I knew by the feel in the air the monsoon rains of summer were now over. Yes, no more oppressing heat! I love the cool days of autumn — my favorite season.

On my walk I saw the Arizona trees — palo verde, mesquite, and palm — but visualized in my mind the oak, elm, and maple trees of my childhood. There I was back in time, skipping off to school. The tall trees lined the walk, their branches reaching out like giant umbrellas. I loved the trees in the autumn with their full array of colors — gold, yellow, orange, red, and browns. The dry leaves that had already fallen now crackled beneath my feet. What a neat sound! I stopped to admire a leaf or two or perhaps gather a few pretty ones to give to my teacher. In the next block, squirrels were scampering about gathering nuts for the winter ahead.

I loved the fall — a time when my family would take a Sunday afternoon drive to the orchard to buy fresh apples and cider. In those days we had "real" apple cider — cloudy in color, the type that would ferment in a few days.

I loved the fall — Thanksgiving — family and friends gathering, surrounded by mounds of food. I loved the smell of freshly baked pumpkin pies, homemade breads, and turkey just coming out of the oven. As a child there was nothing better than fall with the anticipation of Christmas around the corner.

My favorite time of year is still fall when we reflect on what God has given us — a bountiful harvest, friends and family, beautiful countryside, and autumn trees. It is also a time to look forward to Christmas, the celebration of God's greatest gift to us — the birth of the Christ Child.

I love the fall — a time for gratitude and thanks to God. It is a time to make a promise to God to give back to Him a portion of the riches he has given us. Everything we have and everything we are comes from God.

This month make a pledge to God through the church to give a portion of yourself — your time, your treasures, and your talents.

Just as it takes many different trees ablaze in color to create a beautiful autumn scene, so does it take all of us — all of our talents, treasures, and time — to create a wonderful growing and welcoming church. How are you using your time, talents, and treasures to serve Christ?

A LETTER TO MY INFANT GRANDSON
December 2005

My Dearest Little Nathan:

November 8, 2005, the phone rang — I dashed for it — I had been anticipating your birth since yesterday morning — maybe this was the news. Your daddy's voice, shaken and worried, said, "It has to be an emergency C-section. The baby's heart rate is dropping. He is in distress. Eloise, pray."

I felt so helpless and alone — 2,000 miles away. I could tell by your daddy's voice that he was very concerned. What could I do? Yes, Mark, I can pray. I immediately called our family in Arizona and Virginia and then I called my church family.

"For where two or three come together in my name, there am I with them" (Matthew 18:20). I found solace in reading the Bible. Just think, Nathan. At the moment you were born, friends and family in Michigan, Arizona, and Virginia were praying for you and your mom for a safe delivery.

An hour later, your daddy called again — good news this time. "Baby weighs 6 pounds, 13 ounces and is 20 inches long. He is fine, beautiful, cried at birth. Mom — tired and exhausted."

"And how is Mark? I asked.

"Still a little shaky — more than what we bargained for," he said.

Yes, Nathan, there will be times in which life will

present you with a few punches — more than what you bargained for. There may be times when you will feel alone and helpless. But Nathan, God will always be with you. You are not alone. Go to Him in prayer. Pray that He will give you strength for life's challenges. Surrender your worries and concerns to God. He will listen. You are not alone. Find comfort in reading the Bible.

As you grow in wisdom and maturity, you will learn that prayer is communication with God. But communication is two-way, both listening and talking. As we talk to God, we must listen to His responses. You will learn that God sometimes answers our prayers immediately, as He did the day you were born. Other times, He will say, "Not at this time. Wait," or "No, it is not for you." Pray that you can accept His will. He knows what is best for you.

Ask God for guidance to make the right decisions: decisions that will affect your life, decisions regarding how you will spend your time, decisions pertaining to your talents — what courses you take, what profession you enter.

What will be your path in life? Then decisions related to your treasures — how will you spend your money? Remember, God has given you many talents and treasures. Ask for God's guidance as you ponder how best to serve Him.

Finally, let us not forget there are prayers of thanksgiving and prayers of joy, and they will probably be the first type of prayer you will learn as a small child — thank you God for our food, for daddy and mommy, for friends and family, for toys, and home.

Nathan, you were surrounded in prayer at the time you were born. Continue that path of prayer in life. Pray without ceasing, pray for guidance, pray for strength, pray for others. Give thanks to God! May you grow in communication with God, knowing Him, loving Him, and serving Him.

With lots of hugs and kisses from your loving grandma, Eloise Annis

2006

THE WAVES OF THE SEA WERE HUSHED

Then they cried out to the Lord in their trouble, and he brought them out of their distress. He stilled the storm to a whisper; the waves of the sea were hushed. They were glad when it grew calm, and he guided them to their desired haven.

Psalms 107:28-30

T'AI CHI – A STEWARDSHIP SYMBOL?
January 2006

I watched in silence, mesmerized. Such grace, beauty, and precision exhibited by the instructor and two of her students. In silence they gently flowed from one position to another. They did the identical steps — the three of them in perfect unison, never missing a beat. I was watching T'ai Chi. It was beautiful, rhythmic, so calm and peaceful. Could I ever do that?

Last August, I enrolled in the T'ai Chi class, unsure what lay ahead. It looked easy, but it wasn't. Could I ever understand how to do the postures? I felt frustrated; I could not remember. My teacher said to practice, but how could I practice? As soon as I walked out the door, I could not remember anything I was taught.

Very gradually I was learning, but it felt so slow. I was impatient. I wanted to understand now! If only I could relate it to something I already knew, perhaps I could understand. Is it possible to take an ancient Chinese martial art form and relate it to a twenty-first century Christian message — a message of stewardship?

The first posture in T'ai Chi is called preparation — standing quiet, relaxed, still, calm. Yes, prepare to listen to God; hear His message. Feel your inner strength that is coming from God. Feel His presence, bask in His glory, and remember that all you have and all you are He has given to you.

Next, the hands are slowly lifted up, and then they gently float down like the tides on the ocean. That posture reminds me of God's time. We cannot rush God's time — it is gentle, ever flowing, in and out like the ocean tides or autumn leaves drifting down from the trees.

T'ai Chi is built on balance, an ever-shifting of one's weight from one foot to the other. It was Solomon in Ecclesiastes who said, "There is a time for everything...A time to plant and a time to uproot, ...a time to tear down and a time to build..." A time to shift on the left foot and a time to shift on the right? Yes, our lives must be in balance.

There must be a time to share with others, a time to give to others and a time for renewal — quiet meditation with God.

The hands form a ball — a moving circle. Is this the circle of love, the circle of our family and friends, as well as a circle of love that we pass on to others?

In T'ai Chi there is ward-off left and ward-off right. Is this not warding off temptations? Roll back, press, and push — push away our sins, and press toward our goal. Next the fingers of the right hand come together and are held up and over the left hand. This posture looks as if something is flowing from the right hand to the left. Then the hands are separated. Is this not our treasure flowing from our hands, then reaching out to give to others?

A salute is formed in T'ai Chi — a salute to all who use their talents and gifts for the work of God. There is even a posture called "play guitar." Yes, "Make music to the Lord with the harp," (Psalm 98:5). Sing praises to Him!

In T'ai Chi the first section is completed with the

arms reaching up, generating a flowing arc. A rainbow is an arc — a symbol of God's covenant to us. But when we make a rainbow, it then becomes a symbol of our promises to God — our promise to return a portion of our time, talents, and treasures to God; our promise to ever seek, find, and maintain a balance in life; our promise to spread love to others.

Finally, T'ai Chi is closed with the arms crossed in front of the chest — a cross, a symbol for Jesus, Jesus close to our heart. Now I understand — I understand T'ai Chi.

LET THE LITTLE CHILDREN
COME TO ME (Matthew 19:14)
February 2006

The wind blew, and snow was dusting the ground. The sky was gray and gloomy — typical for Michigan in January. Outside it was cold and freezing, but inside I was a part of a scene of warmth and love.

I was holding my two-month-old grandson, Nathan. Our eyes met. We stared at each other. He was so beautiful with his fine blond hair and dark blue eyes. His little hand reached up toward my chin. His face seemed to radiate a hint of a smile. He continued to study my face. I wondered what he was thinking. He is so trusting. Nathan already knows that Mom and Dad care for his every need. He is safe and secure.

It was just a year ago, when my grandson, Matthew, from Virginia was that tiny infant staring at me. Now he is a curious fourteen-month-old getting into everything. He investigates the kitchen cabinets, tosses toys out of the toy box, wrecks grandma's block towers, and giggles as the cat runs by. When I was there last month, Matthew was excellent at cruising around the furniture but unsure of himself about letting go and walking alone. Since then I have heard that now he toddles with arms outstretched into Mom or Dad's loving arms.

The day after I returned home, I watched my

almost-five-year-old grandson, David. He builds towers instead of wrecking them. He is no longer that wobbly toddler. He walks, runs, jumps, plays ball, and even does Tae Kwon Do with confidence. David wants to help — he helped me with my laundry. We made cookies together — cookies that he took home to share with his family.

Do we have faith like a child? Do we trust God as a small child trusts us? What is our relationship with God?

Do we reach for Him when we are unsure of ourselves or when we feel like we are falling? Do we go forth in confidence knowing that He is always with us, that He cares for our needs, that we are safe and secure in His arms?

Are we enjoying the simple things of life? Do we still have the curious and inquisitive nature of a child?

Do we continue to seek more knowledge and understanding of God? Do we fully appreciate everything that God has given us? Are we looking up and smiling at Him and saying "thank you?"

Do we help others and give our time, talents, and treasures for the work of God?

Do we have faith like a child and believe, "...for the kingdom of heaven belongs to such as these" (Matthew 19:14).

BLUEPRINTS FROM GOD
March 2006

"Where is my bedroom?" I was excited about the prospect of a new home, a home that my dad would soon be building. I was eight years old, trying to make sense of the many lines carefully drawn on a large sheet of paper before me.

My dad had the tools of an architect spread out — T-square, triangles, compass, pencils, and eraser. He patiently explained every detail in his drawing. "This is the living room, dining room, and kitchen. Upstairs are the four bedrooms — this is your bedroom. Here are the windows, doors, and fireplace, and this is how our home will look on the outside."

Of course, at the time I was more interested in my bedroom, a bedroom just for me. "Can it be painted pink?"

"Of course, your bedroom will be painted pink."

I well remember those drawings of our home. Before my dad laid a single brick, cut a piece of lumber, or strung the electric wiring, there he was, checking his blueprints. He was always measuring to make sure every brick was in the right location, all walls were correctly placed, and doors and windows perfect. Later, when I was twelve, my dad allowed me, under his tutelage, to draw the plans for the connecting breezeway and garage. This time I was able to think beyond a pink bedroom, and now I pretended to be the architect.

Behind every home, office building, skyscraper, bridge, and dam, there is a plan, a design, and a set of blueprints. Blueprints — a standard, a set of specifications, a means to compare and measure the actual construction. Is the project being built according to the architect's design, his blueprints? Will it serve the purpose for which it is constructed? Will the dam hold water? Will the bridge carry the traffic? Will the home be a pleasant and safe place for the family? Will the skyscraper be strong and reach high to the heavens?

God is the supreme architect. He designed the world. He created us.

God has given us a standard. He has given us a set of specifications, something to measure our lives against. He has given us blueprints. He has given us the Bible and Jesus Christ. Do we as the engineers and builders of our lives, check against the blueprints God has given us? How do we measure up to His specifications?

Jesus taught us to love, be forgiving, and be compassionate. He taught us how to pray. Through His parables, Jesus taught us to be good stewards.

Are we giving as He taught us to give? Are we serving Him? Are we following the blueprints from God? Are we guided by them as a builder is guided by his blueprints?

Are we thanking God for all that He has done for us? Let us thank Him for the set of blueprints He has given us — the blueprints for our lives — the Bible and Jesus Christ.

BY FAITH WE CAN MOVE MOUNTAINS
April 2006

The road went ever steeper, turning and twisting up the canyon. Off to the right was the former road to old Morenci, now blocked by a gigantic pile of rocks. The original high school was there, but it too is now buried. The car climbed higher. Another sharp turn and, once again, we saw a side road completely blocked by a tremendously high pile of dirt and rock.

My husband Roy and I lived at the bottom of that road thirty-six years ago. Where is the hillside that was explored by our oldest son? It is now under immense copper leaching ponds. Where is the mountain that was the site of the first underground copper mine in Eastern Arizona? Gone! Moved!

Where is that narrow-gauge railroad that hung precariously on the steep slopes as it carried the ore of long ago? Gone! And where are the early miners who had the faith and dreams to build the largest copper mine in North America? Gone, but their faith and dreams live on.

In March my friends and I stood on a high lookout above the Phelps Dodge open pit copper mine in Morenci. We were transfixed by the immensity of the operation, three miles by five miles in size. There is beauty in that open pit — the natural blues, grays, tans, and yellows of the rock.

We looked far below and saw the electric shovels

and trucks that move mountains. From our location, they looked no bigger than toys, or perhaps bugs scurrying back and forth for another load of rock. Can they truly move mountains? Of course they can.

Scoop by scoop the shovels dug into the mountain and filled the waiting trucks, each carrying 270 tons of ore on tires 12 feet in diameter. Little by little the mountain was moved — off to the dump or to the leaching ponds for the extraction of copper. Each year about 840 million pounds of copper are produced at Morenci, Arizona. Yes, man moves mountains in Morenci.

Do we have a mountain that needs to be moved? Do we have the faith to move that mountain? Do we look to Christ for the faith? Are we for some reason afraid to reach out to others with love and compassion? Do we hide our God-given talents or perhaps not utilize the talents we have? Do we have a mountain in our home, namely a TV or computer, that takes precious time away from family, friends, and devotion to God? Is that our mountain?

As a church family, what is our mountain that needs to be moved? Do we pray and seek God's guidance? Just as the miners of long ago had a dream in Morenci, what is our dream for our church? Think of the mountains that we can move together if each of us by faith contributes more of our time, talents, and treasures to the work of God. Let us be thankful for what God has done for us and move those mountains for Him.

"I tell you the truth, if you have faith as small as a mustard seed, you can say to this mountain, 'Move from here to there' and it will move. Nothing will be impossible for you" (Matthew 17:20).

A LINK TO THE PAST
May 2006

Grandma Robinson gave me a quilt, a quilt she made just for me. She intended the quilt to be for my crib, but somehow Grandma kept making it bigger and bigger until it was the size for a twin bed. My mother called it a Dutch doll quilt. I'm not sure where she got the name, as the dolls look more like nineteenth century girls with long, full dresses, large sun bonnets, and high-button shoes. There are 56 large blocks in all, each with a seven-inch girl in the center.

Oh, here is my favorite girl, the one with a purple floral dress, slightly darker purple bonnet, with matching embroidery on the bottom of the dress, long sleeves, and a bonnet. The embroidery stitches are so delicate, made to look like little flowers. The girl is a side-view, so only one little hand and one shoe are visible. The buttons on the shoe are a perfect circular knot of embroidery thread. The face is completely hidden by the large bonnet.

Wait! That is not my favorite — here is another beautiful one. The pattern on the dress is pink and yellow flowers with green leaves. She has a matching pink bonnet with yellow flowers embroidered on it.

Here is a pretty one — white daisies against a blue background and again intricate embroidered stitches on the blue bonnet and skirt.

This is a cute one — tan and yellow with little white

anchors on the dress. That is one of the few without flowers on the dress.

I give up. I can't make up my mind which one I like the best. The quilt is so beautiful — each girl completely different — each one unique — all with exquisitely embroidered designs on the dresses and bonnets.

As a child I loved to examine that quilt; I still do. That quilt is my link to the past. I got to know my grandmother through that quilt. The girls' dresses were made from scraps of material my grandmother had accumulated after making her daughters' dresses.

My dad said that his mother raised beautiful flowers in her garden. Looking at all the floral patterns in the quilt, I can easily understand she loved flowers. The embroidery designs are so perfect, very artistic.

Yes, that was my grandmother, Frances Mae Robinson. I look at the quilt and remember that she raised nine children on a farm in Southern Ohio with neither running water nor electricity. She made everything for the family by hand — clothes and quilts. My dad said she attended Normal School and then taught in the elementary grades before she was married.

My grandmother loved music — violin was her instrument. I look at my quilt and remember the stories my dad told me about her. I look at that quilt and think of the lessons she now is teaching me — love for beauty, hard work, creativity, perfection, achievement, and the wonderful love for a grandchild. Grandma, you must have spent hours making my quilt as intricately embroidered as it is. And all of it was stitched by hand.

Yes Grandma, you gave me a wonderful legacy — a legacy that tells a story — a beautiful quilt.

As Christians we have a link to the past — the Bible. As my quilt can teach me about my grandmother, the Bible teaches us through stories of the past. We read about the life of Jesus, His parables and we learn about love, service, sharing, obedience, forgiveness, and thankfulness. We read of the followers of Jesus and the early Christian Church. We read the Old Testament and the stories of Noah, Moses, David, Daniel, Ruth, and Esther to name just a few.

I look at my quilt — each girl different and yet each so beautiful. We are like the girls on my quilt. Each one of us is very important and beautiful. God has given us talents and the responsibility to share our talents with others. We are unique like the girls on my quilt. Yet we can all come together for a common goal, a beautiful pattern of service, friendship, and love.

Let us give thanks to God by sharing our time, talents, and treasures.

GOOD ADVICE FOR THE ROAD
June 2006

Passport ✔
Plane tickets ✔
Clothes ✔
Shoes ✔
Jacket ✔
Camera ✔
Sudoku puzzles for the long plane rides ✔

What I am forgetting? All my friends and family are giving me advice concerning my vacation trips this summer. My kids gave me a new digital camera so I can take lots of pictures. My friend has loaned me travel books. Even my banker is giving me advice.

Maybe I'll ask some experienced travelers what they would pack and if they have any helpful hints to share. I wonder what the seasoned travelers from the Bible would say.

"So make yourself an ark..." (Genesis 6:14). Noah, I don't need to build an ark! But Noah, my first trip is a cruise on the Hudson River, Erie Canal, and Lake Ontario to the St. Lawrence River.

My voyage won't be as long as yours, Noah, but did you or your family or any of your animals, well you know, get seasick from those rough, stormy waves?

I'm not sure how the motion will affect me, so maybe I need to get some Dramamine, just in case.

"And rain fell on the earth forty days and forty nights" (Genesis 7:12). Noah! I don't expect that much rain! But, maybe you have a point there. My second trip is to Scotland, and I have heard they have more rain than Arizona. Thanks, for the tip, Noah. I'll pack a poncho for the rain.

Moses, you and your people wandered around the desert for forty years. My trips won't be that long, but do you have any advice for me?

"So the people took their dough before the yeast was added..." (Exodus 12:34). Good advice Moses, I'll get some crackers and other munchies for my long plane rides.

Jesus, you sent your disciples out to preach, teach, and heal. What advice did you give them? Anything I can use? "Take no bag for the journey, or extra tunic, or sandals..." (Matthew 10:10).

Jesus, I'm a woman — I need lots of extra clothes, shoes, and luggage! I've got to have my walking shoes besides my sandals! This is the 21st century!

But, you have a good point, Jesus. Even on short trips I always take along much too much stuff. I must limit myself. How can I truly enjoy my vacation if I am weighed down by too much from home? Maybe, packing less can equate to more fun and joy.

"It's like a man going away: He leaves his house and puts his servants in charge..." (Mark 13:34). I don't have a servant, Jesus, but my next door neighbor will watch my house. Also, my sons live close by. I know they will occasionally stop by my home. Yes, Jesus, I'll stop the newspaper, have the post office hold my mail, and my neighbor will pick up those flyers from my door.

Paul, you did a lot of traveling. My friend from church is going with me on my journeys. I know, Paul, you always took a friend, a believer like yourself. Also, you wrote letters to everyone. What I will do is keep a journal and take pictures so that when I return home I can tell my friends and family all about my trips. Paul, you visited churches on your journeys. Wouldn't it be great if my friend and I could visit a Presbyterian Church in Scotland?

"For I testify that they gave as much as they were able, and even beyond their ability" (2 Corinthians 8:3). Paul, I am not going on a missionary trip, like you! The churches you visited gave money to the churches in Jerusalem. I am not collecting money. My journeys are vacation trips, not missionary trips.

"Each man should give what he has decided in his heart to give, not reluctantly or under compulsion, for God loves a cheerful giver" (2 Corinthians 9:7).

Oh, now I understand what you want me to do, Paul. You want me, while I am on vacation, to remember my home church and send them my offering. I'll be having so much fun that I'll forget to do that, Paul. How about if I, before I leave, write a check to the church to cover the weeks I will be gone? I know even if I am not present, my church still has to pay the electric, water, and telephone bills, mortgage, the pastor, and others on the staff. Thanks for reminding me, Paul.

"May the grace of the Lord Jesus Christ, and the love of God, and the fellowship of the Holy Spirit be with you all" (2 Corinthians 13:14).

Why, thank you Paul for the blessing. And thank you everyone — Paul, Jesus, Moses, and Noah — for your helpful tips and advice. Now to pack.

HE STILLED THE STORM TO A WHISPER
(Psalm 107:29)
July/August 2006

It was cool, breezy, and drizzling, but my friend and I did not care. We were standing on the top deck of our cruise ship taking pictures and enjoying the scenery of Narragansett Bay. A little rain was not going to dampen our spirits. We were from Arizona. We loved the cool rain.

I was excited. This was my first cruise. I was planning to savor every moment of our voyage. The beautiful homes on the water's edge were shrouded in mist. Soft colors, gray skies, mist — this was fantastic!

"Without warning, a furious storm came up on the lake, so that the waves swept over the boat. But Jesus was sleeping" (Matthew 8:24).

We had just passed the wonderful sights of Newport, Rhode Island, when all at once the storm and rough seas hit us. We were no longer in the protective bay but in the open Atlantic Ocean. The waves immediately increased in size, rocking our ship from side to side. Her bow plunged up and down in the sea. Now the wind was blowing. It was raining harder. We landlubbers had a difficult time standing or walking, but somehow we made it to the dining room below. There we could see the waves slam against the windows, completely covering them.

What looked like a good-sized ship docked in the harbor now felt like a small boat against the Atlantic Ocean — only 183 feet long by 40 feet wide — a speck in the vast waters.

"The disciples went and woke him, saying, 'Lord, save us! We're going to drown!'" (Matthew 8:25). All evening long into the black night, the storm and waves tossed us about. Now I understand how the disciples felt that day, and how our ancestors felt as they made their way across the ocean in tiny wooden ships taking them to the New World. Yet, there is no comparison.

We were in a much larger and safer ship with modern electronic equipment to tell the crew where we were and to tell someone on land if we were in serious trouble.

"He replied, 'You of little faith, why are you so afraid?' Then he got up and rebuked the winds and the waves, and it was completely calm. The men were amazed and asked, 'What kind of man is this? Even the winds and the waves obey him!'" (Matthew 8:26-27).

I could not sleep that night because of the ship's tossing, plunging, rocking, and pitching into the stormy sea.

At last, peace and calm prevailed when we entered Long Island Sound. Once again there was land on both sides of us — the mainland to starboard and Long Island to port. The land was like two arms reaching out protecting us from harm. I finally drifted off to sleep but awoke in a few hours when the first rays of the morning sun streamed through the clouds and into our cabin. We made it through the black of night, safe and secure. We docked right below the Brooklyn Bridge at Pier 17, South Street Seaport, Manhattan.

"He stilled the storm to a whisper; the waves of the

sea were hushed. They were glad when it grew calm, and he guided them to their desired haven" (Psalm 107:29-30).

All of us have encountered storms in our lives. Our storms are not necessarily storms of the wind, rain, and waves. Any circumstance that causes great anxiety is a storm.

Do we worry unduly? Or, do we go to God with our cares and concerns? Can we feel His loving embrace? Do we allow Him to be our buffer in life's storms as the land was a buffer against an angry sea during my cruise? God will calm our troubled waters, light our blackest night, and guide our paths.

Reach out to others and help others in their storms. Thank God for the sunrise, the bright new day, a new beginning. In appreciation for what God has done for us, let us give of ourselves — our time, talents, and treasures for the work of God.

ST. GILES', THE FIRST
PRESBYTERIAN CHURCH
September 2006

A crown! A crown for a steeple! A large beautiful crown rises high from the center tower of St. Giles' Cathedral. It is easy to recognize. No other church tower is like St. Giles'. Look up and there is the crown of St. Giles' Cathedral — the landmark of Edinburgh, Scotland.

My friend and I could not help but wonder what the cathedral looked like inside. The outside was so beautiful with its massive stone blocks that were customary in early cathedrals. A church has been on this site since 1124. Since then St. Giles' has been rebuilt, remodeled, and restored. St. Giles' is a living church — services have been held here for over 800 years.

We walked a short distance up the hill from our hotel. We climbed the old stone steps. What treasures would we find behind those doors? We entered the sanctuary and immediately gazed upon the mammoth columns supporting the high, vaulted cathedral ceiling.

In the center of the church was the communion table. Near the table a large brass eagle held the Bible in its outstretched wings. A small green stole was draped around the eagle's neck.

It was Sunday morning. We were ushered to a pew with a little door on the end. We sat down, looked up, and saw the most beautiful stained glass window depicting the Crucifixion and Resurrection of Christ. Another window showed Jesus in the boat stilling the storm. Other stained glass windows were just as magnificent.

In a connecting chapel was a wood carving of an angel playing the bagpipes. Toward the back of the church was a larger-than-life statue of John Knox, seemingly looking over his church and giving his approval. Yes, this is John Knox's church, the leader of the Scottish Reformation. He was minister here from 1559 to 1572.

St. Giles' Cathedral is the Mother Church of Presbyterianism.

The music was as grand as the cathedral. The organ (4,000 pipes) with its rich sounds resonated into every corner. The choir and minister processed in. Because the communion table was in the center of the church, the congregation sat on both sides.

Communion is served every Sunday. At the appropriate time, people were invited to come forward to form a large circle around the table. The minister passed out four small loaves of bread to various sections of the circle. We then in turn tore off a piece and handed the bread to our neighbor. In like manner, four large silver cups containing the wine were passed around the circle. Everyone drank from the silver cup.

The organist softly played chimes after all partook of the elements. We greeted our neighbor and returned to our seats. Three times a circle was formed in order for everyone to receive communion. To me, this was worldwide communion.

St. Giles' Cathedral is located on the Royal Mile

in the heart of Old Edinburgh surrounded by hotels. There had to be many visitors to the church that day like my friend and me, from other countries.

Taking communion in the Mother Church was the highlight of my vacation to Scotland.

The Cathedral is named after St. Giles', the patron saint of lepers. I thought of the story of Jesus healing the ten lepers in which only one returned to thank Him. Let us remember to thank God for all that He has done for us — giving us courageous people of the Reformation, a wonderful heritage, beautiful churches in which to worship, and their heavenly music.

Let us give our time, talents, and treasures to the work of God.

THE POWER OF CONNECTING
October 2006

Look Dad! Look Mom! Look what I built! A child excitedly calls for his parents to admire his "Tinkertoy" building. The child's structure looks beautiful with many brightly colored sticks, each one connecting to another through the use of the wooden spools. He has carefully secured the connections so that the structure stands straight and tall.

Every day a colleague and friend of mine carefully places a beautiful pendant around her neck. A delicate silver chain holds the pendant. Each link of the chain is intertwined with another link. She tells me her grandmother gave the pendant to her years ago. That pendant means a lot to her. It is a symbol of her faith. My friend is a Buddhist.

I look under my desk and see a mass of cables and little electronic boxes. Are they the mark of modern technology? A cable from printer to computer, a cable to a little black box for the Internet, another cable to the surge protector, wires to the speakers, a wire to the mouse, plus two more little boxes with their corresponding cables and wires.

The purpose of those last two boxes? I don't know. The whole jumble of cables and wires somehow come together to be connected by one cable to the wall socket—the source of power! Thanks to the magic of technology, my computer is a tool in my work and a

107

connection to the outside world.

I hold my infant grandson in my arms. I look down at his soft delicate face, and he in turn stares intently into mine. Our eyes connect and love flows between us.

I look at the Celtic cross I wear. A circle connects the vertical and horizontal parts of the cross. That circle surrounds the center. I look at the symbol for the trinity — three circles interwoven with one another.

One of the connections in the child's "Tinkertoy" structure becomes loose. The connection is now broken. The building begins to sag at its weakest point. The extra stress of uneven weight pulls at other connections. They in turn also break apart. What once was a tall "Tinkertoy" building is now a pile of sticks and spools.

One day my friend came to me with tears in her eyes. Somewhere on campus she had lost her beautiful chain and pendant. One link was weak and broke. The entire chain and pendant fell ever so softly, ever so quietly to the ground. When did it drop? Where did it fall? My friend did not know. She retraced her path, but the beautiful pendant was never found.

I have been working on my computer for several hours now. Just a little more work and I will be done. I feel a need to stretch. Feels good — feels great to stretch the legs! Oops! I accidentally kicked the power cord and plug. The screen goes black! My connection to my source of power is gone! Nothing!

By loving our children and grandchildren, we teach them to love and connect with others. We build relationships with others as a child builds a tower. We bond with others. We strengthen our connections. We cannot stand alone. All of our connections must be solid and secure. There can be no weak links. Our source of strength and power is God. We connect with Him, through Him, and by Him.

Come to church and explore the many opportunities for stewardship by connecting with others in the church and community. Come help strengthen our links with one another, and connect in joy, peace, fellowship, and love.

In appreciation for all He has done for us, let us pledge our commitments to God.

EVER RECEIVING, EVER GIVING
November 2006

It was cold and foggy that morning in July as our cruise ship entered the region called the Thousand Islands where Lake Ontario empties into the St. Lawrence River. It is beautiful — fish in the water, birds flocking overhead, deer and other animals by the tree-lined shore. It was peaceful and relaxing, drifting along with the current.

The water is dotted with islands, both big and small. I was on the upper deck enjoying the scenery — some islands are very tiny, with rocks jutting out and a tree or two. Other islands are barely large enough for a small house and single tree.

The fog created a feeling of mystery — what lay ahead around the bend? Would we spot another island with a house? Oh, look, there is a lighthouse on that island! And on another island, a castle!

I was amazed — the homes literally were on the water's edge. There are no tides here. The water stays at a constant level. Homes can be built on the shore without danger of flooding; yet, this region has its share of storms. Wind, rain, and snow come, but Lake Ontario is always the same. It is in perfect balance — water flows into the lake and then out by way of the St. Lawrence River and finally into the sea.

Lake Ontario is a fresh-water lake, vibrant and alive because waters are ever flowing in, mixing, and then flowing out to sea. Lake Ontario — receiving and giving — ever a balance created by God.

What can we learn from Lake Ontario? Can we emulate the lake? We too are richly blessed. Treasures from God flow into our lives.

Can we create a wonderful blend of our treasures and talents with one another? Can each of us individually give generously to the church so that collectively our dreams for it will be fulfilled?

Lake Ontario receives water and gives water — a balance of always receiving, always giving. Jesus said, "Freely you have received; freely give" (Matthew 10:8). He gave His disciples very simple instructions as He sent them out. That one sentence can be our guide.

God has given generously to us. Let us freely return a portion to Him. Make a commitment to grow in giving, to grow in faith and grow in trust. Yes, storms will come, but trust Him to provide your needs and provide that balance in your life.

THE GIFT
December 2006

Here it is only a few weeks before Christmas and my to-do list keeps getting longer and longer. I have presents to buy and wrap, cards to send, cookies to make for the bake sale, and choir practice. Also, I can't forget a present for my angel from the Christmas tree.

My house — it needs cleaning. My one-year-old grandson is coming! I must baby-proof the house! And somehow, I will find time to grade the students' finals and average their semester grades. I'm getting tired just thinking about all that needs to be done. I'll just sit here for a few minutes, turn the lights down low, get comfortable, put my feet up, and relax.

Oh, what was that? The doorbell — at this hour? Nobody is at the door! Look a package — someone left a package. My name is on it. But, who is it from? There is no return address. Who could have sent it? This is a mystery. I'm not expecting anything. Maybe if I open the box, I'll find out who sent it.

Look, there are three brightly wrapped gifts inside the box. I'll open the biggest one first. It is a lighthouse — I love lighthouses! It is hand carved from a piece of wood! I wonder who created this wonderful piece of art — it is very beautiful — so realistic.

Look, the lighthouse is magical — there is a light shining at the top and a little path to the door. It seems to beckon me to come. Someone must know me — know that I like lighthouses, but, who is it from? Oh, here is a note — "I am the light of the world" (John 8:12). Still, there is no name. Who could have given me this beautiful gift?

The second package is smaller than the first — I'll open that next. It's heavy — I wonder what it is. A rock! It looks like a type of agate. A band of different colors arcs across its surface like a miniature rainbow. The rock reminds me of the beauty of the Arizona desert, a sunset, and a rainbow after a storm. It brings back wonderful memories of Roy and I hiking the desert looking for beautiful rocks like this. Look, another note — "...and on this rock, I will build my church ..." (Matthew 16:18).

Again, no name. This is truly a mystery. Who is giving me these wonderful gifts?

The last package is small. In it is a cross — a small simple cross, but meaning so much. Again, a note: "... If anyone would come after me, he must deny himself and take up his cross and follow me" (Matthew 16:24).

My hands shook. Tears fell from my eyes. Have I forgotten what Christmas is all about? Now, I understand who sent me this gift. It is from Him who knows me, knows my thoughts and ambitions, from Him who has given me a light and a path to follow. It is from The One who has given me life, He who gave me my family and friends.

My gift is from the One who created the beauty of the earth. It is from Him who gave me my church and my church family. My gift is from Him who has given me salvation, grace, forgiveness, and love. It is from Him who has given me His only son. Everything I am and everything I have comes from Him.

Oh, what can I give Him, not only at Christmas but

every day throughout the year? I must return to Him a portion of my time, talents, and treasures that He has so richly given me!

Did I doze off! Was this a dream — my gift of a lighthouse, rock, and cross! I glanced over to the corner of the room and saw light beaming from a lighthouse. Yes, it is handmade from wood.

A smooth, colored rock lay nearby. I reached up and felt my cross around my neck. Then my eyes gazed upon the Infant Jesus lying in the manger.

"Today, in the town of David a Savior has been born to you; he is Christ the Lord" (Luke 2:11). The ultimate gift of all!

2007

There is one body and one spirit – just as you were called to one hope when you were called – one Lord, one faith, one baptism, one God and one Father of all who is over all and through all and in all.

Ephesians 4:4-6

IT'S GOD'S MONEY!
January 2007

"Doesn't that make you nervous to spend thousands of dollars of other people's money?" my mom asked my dad. I was in junior high, but I well remember that day of their conversation at the dinner table. My dad was a civil engineer for Alcoa (Aluminum Company of America) and was responsible for purchasing equipment and materials for construction projects at work.

I will never forget his answer: "I just pretend it is my money and use the same principles of good money management at work as I do at home."

Through my dad's actions and behaviors, I learned his principles of money management. He continually looked for bargains without sacrificing quality. He always paid cash. To my dad, paying interest was a needless waste of money.

I remember one year, on the day before Christmas, when he and mom came home with a brand-new Oldsmobile. To him that was the ideal time to purchase a car and get the best deal because everyone else was shopping for Christmas gifts, not cars. Of course, he paid cash that he had been carefully saving for several years.

That car was our Merry Oldsmobile. If he could not afford an item, he simply did not buy it. Of course, along with buying only when he had the money saved, he took very good care of everything he owned.

My father was a firm believer in doing the work himself. If he was capable of doing a task, then he did not believe in paying someone else to do it. That concept even applied to his building our home when I was in elementary school. He laid every brick and did all the carpentry, electrical, plumbing, and roofing with only Mom's help.

The only thing Dad did not do related to the construction of our home was dig the hole for the basement — that he could not do.

My dad's beliefs stemmed from his childhood. He was one of nine children raised on a small farm in Southern Ohio. Of course, money was in short supply, so Dad's family, just as many others in that generation, either did without, made do with what they had and repaired it, or made it themselves.

Dad went to college during the depression, and he was able to get his four-year degree by working his way through school. I am sure those years sharpened his money management skills.

Times are certainly different now. It seems as if every day the mail presents us with another offer for a credit card. Pay no interest for the first nine months, and after that, pay "only" 18% (in small print). Goods just don't last like they used to, or they are out of date within a year of their purchase. This seems to be a throw-away society. We are forever tempted with products that are screaming "buy me!" Life was so much simpler in our parents' and grandparents' generations.

Yet, I keep going back to my dad's answer of long ago — "pretend it is my money." His answer is not quite complete. Let's make a slight correction. Pretend it is God's money, because it is God's money! Through our

117

God-given talents and abilities, we earn money.

Now, how are we going to take care of God's money?

What does God want us to do? Spend wisely, do comparative shopping, pay with cash or debit card, limit credit card expenditures, keep our belongings in good repair, do work ourselves according to our abilities, and give to our church and other non-profit organizations. Is it not good stewardship to act responsibly with what God has entrusted to us?

Let this be our resolution for the New Year: To become a better steward of God's money.

If we could limit our eating in fast-food restaurants and buying snacks and trendy coffee and soda drinks, just think how much each of us could save. Coupons for food and other items can help us save as well. If it were possible for each family to save $10 per week and add that amount to their weekly offering, the church would benefit by an extra one thousand dollars.

With 100 giving units, an additional $52,000 would be available for the church during the year. It's exciting to think how many more of God's plans we could fulfill.

Yes, pretend it is God's money. Because it is His money!

Now what does God want us to do with His money that He has entrusted to us?

ONE BRICK AT A TIME
February 2007

This was the weekend that I was going to see our new home! I could hardly wait. I was eight years old and my dad was constructing the house by himself. We lived in a rental duplex several miles away so it wasn't very often that my brothers and I had the opportunity to see dad working on our home.

On this visit, my dad was laying the bricks for the outside walls. Mom passed him the bricks one at a time so that he could work more productively and efficiently. He developed a rhythm — receive brick, slap on mortar, press brick into place — repeating the sequence again and again.

The bricks were of different hues — some a darker red than others and some with even a bluish tinge. I liked the blue bricks. They looked neat. My dad was very particular about the placement of the bricks — those laid next to each other had to be of slightly different color. This made our new home more beautiful. With each visit, I saw our home steadily grow, brick by brick, layer upon layer, reaching ever higher.

It took many bricks to build our two-story home — bricks in the fireplace and chimney, concrete blocks in the basement, then bricks for the outside walls. One by one the bricks were laid carefully, diligently, and lovingly. Each one was just as important as another.

I enjoy going to an art museum. I especially like gazing at Claude Monet's paintings. How many dabs of paint did he use for his garden scenes? How many dabs of paint did it take Leonardo da Vinci to paint the Mona Lisa or The Last Supper? Many, of course — each dab just as important as another and each one a little different from the others.

I also enjoy listening to music. How many notes did it take for George Frederic Handel to compose the Messiah? Many — each note thoughtfully placed. And, how many grains of salt does it take to season our soup?

Likewise, how many people does it take to build a vibrant church? Many, of course — all with different talents working together for God's plan.

And how many dollars does it take to fulfill our dreams for Gilbert Presbyterian Church? Many, but remember my dad built our home one brick at a time, Leonardo da Vinci created The Last Supper one dab of paint at a time, and Handel composed the Messiah one note at a time.

One dollar every day set aside by everyone to add to their weekly offering will fulfill our dreams — God's dreams — for Gilbert Presbyterian Church. An additional dollar per day from all can grow into at least an extra $50,000 for the year.

What dreams do you have for Gilbert Presbyterian Church?

STOP! BE SILENT AND LISTEN!
March 2007

Hmm...What words can I make with these seven letters — E, N, T, Q, I, S, and L?

I was playing Scrabble and had just picked my little wood tiles. Can't do much with that Q so I will put it aside until I have a U to go with it. Spelling never was my strong point, so maybe I should peruse the dictionary.

Oh look! I can spell LISTEN with six of my seven letters. Wait! Another word — SILENT with the same six letters! SILENT — LISTEN, LISTEN — SILENT! I cannot spell listen unless I spell silent. I cannot listen unless I am silent. How true!

The other day as I was entering Ta'i Chi class, a classmate stopped me. She wanted to talk. At that time I was still thinking about my class — my mind was not silent. I had no idea what she was trying to say. I was too engrossed in my own thoughts. After class she again approached me. This must be important! Now I stopped, was silent, and listened. She desperately needed someone to talk to.

A few days before, a good friend of hers tragically passed away. How many times do we walk away from friends or family just at a time when they need us most? This time I was lucky; she did not allow me to walk away. Until we are absolutely and completely silent in mind and body, we cannot listen.

"The Lord came and stood there, calling as at the other times, 'Samuel! Samuel!' Then Samuel said, 'Speak, for your servant is listening'" (1 Samuel 3:10).

Do we listen for God's voice? Can we hear Him speak? Wait, God. Wait until I turn off my TV, cell phone, iPod, and all other electronic noisemakers of the 21st century.

Can God get our attention over the din of modern society? Stop, be silent. Only then can we say as Samuel said, "Speak, for now we are listening."

And, what is it God, you are trying to tell us? "The earth is the Lord's, and everything in it, the world, and all who live in it" (Psalms 24:1).

Yes, the earth is the Lord's. Everything we have and everything we are comes from God. He has entrusted us to be the stewards of His creation.

God has given each one of us time — time to pray, time to honor Him, time to worship Him, and time to listen to our family and friends. Use your time wisely.

God has given each one of us talents — talents to be developed and used for His will.

God has given each one of us treasures — treasures for His kingdom. Be responsible in all that He has given you. "For where your treasure is," (and talent and time) "there your heart will be also" (Matthew 6:21).

Stop, be silent, and listen! Listen to your family and friends! Listen to God! Seek His help and guidance. Hear Him speak through the Bible, through prayer, worship, and devotion.

Be silent and listen!

AMAZING GRACE—AMAZING STORY
April/May 2007

I sat there, unable to move. I was speechless. The story was enthralling. The movie was over, the credits rolled by, the lights came on, but I did not want to leave. I wanted to reflect upon what I had just seen.

"Amazing Grace" is a powerful movie about an uncompromising politician from the late 1700's to early 1800's in England. As a young man, William Wilberforce became attracted to the politics of Parliament. While he was a member of the House of Commons, he converted to evangelical Christianity. At that time William Wilberforce contemplated leaving politics for the ministry. His friends convinced him that he could fulfill his calling from God by continuing his work in the House of Commons.

When he was ten, William Wilberforce became acquainted with the teachings and ministry of Reverend John Newton. Here was a sea captain who had given up a lucrative career as a slave trader for the ministry. John Newton composed many hymns, including "Amazing Grace."

It was God's amazing grace that influenced the lives of John Newton and William Wilberforce. For years they worked together for compassion, justice, and human dignity. John Newton encouraged his friend to take on the campaign to abolish slavery. Year after year, William Wilberforce spoke and presented anti-

123

slavery bills to the House of Commons. Again and again these bills were defeated.

William Wilberforce became discouraged and his health declined, but through encouragement from all his friends, he persisted. Finally, twenty years later on February 23, 1807, the House of Commons overwhelmingly voted to abolish the slave trade in the British Empire.

John Newton died a few months after that historic vote. William Wilberforce continued dedicating his life to the problems of poverty and caring for the poor. He generously gave away a quarter of his income every year.

Is there not a lesson for us in this movie and story? Everything we are and everything we have is from God's amazing grace. William Wilberforce made his secular politician's job a sacred vocation. Can we do the same? Can we make our secular job a sacred vocation?

God took two ordinary men, men with weaknesses, John Newton and William Wilberforce, and accomplished great tasks. If we allow God to work in our lives, what might we be able to accomplish? God's amazing grace! Yes, how sweet the sound! I will never again sing that hymn without thinking of two men, John Newton and William Wilberforce, who experienced and lived God's marvelous grace.

"My grace is sufficient for you, for my power is made perfect in weakness" (2 Corinthians 12:9).

Information and ideas for this article are from the movie, "Amazing Grace," opening day, February 23, 2007, and the book, Finding God in the Story of Amazing Grace, Kurt Bruner and Jim Ware, 2007.

A JOURNEY
June 2007

I read my e-mail over and over again — a trip to Scandinavia! It sounded interesting — visits along Germany's Baltic coast and then into Denmark and Sweden.

My e-mail was from the Science History Tour group, the one that I went with last summer to England and Scotland. Their plans this summer include tours of science museums, study of famous scientists including Linnaeus, Celsius, Bohr, and Nobel, a tour of Hamlet's castle of Elsinore, plus many other places of interest.

Should I go? The trip sounded wonderful! I asked my kids — immediately they replied, "Go, Mom, go!" This past semester I even had a student whose parents were born in Denmark. She likewise encouraged me to go.

OK, I'm going. Now, to plan for the trip. Passport — got it. Next, I must read about the places I will be visiting. Money — each country has different currency. I need plane reservations as the tour begins in Luebeck, Germany. Oh, another e-mail — an alternate way to Luebeck. Sounds interesting.

Go to Google, maps, and get directions from Phoenix to Luebeck. Take I-17 to Flagstaff, then I-40, but I don't want to drive across the country. I'll continue reading anyway: I-90 Massachusetts Turnpike; take

125

exit 24; merge onto Atlantic Avenue; right at Central Street; right at Long Wharf; swim across the Atlantic Ocean 3,462 miles.

What? Swim across the Atlantic Ocean? No way! I'm not swimming! I'll get my plane reservations now!

Gilbert Presbyterian Church is embarking on a journey even more exciting than my Scandinavia tour. The Session has heard you — you want an associate pastor for our church. The next step is to plan and prepare for our journey. What do we need to do?

In many ways, our journey to call an associate is no different from any personal trip we might take. We need to thoroughly investigate and learn about calling an associate. There will be challenges along the way. Some of our challenges may even look like we are swimming across the ocean.

We must get our passport in order. It won't look like our personal passport, but it is a passport to an associate. Our passport will be a description of our church, our dreams and plans, and how we anticipate an associate will fit into our programs.

Before anyone can embark on a journey, money must be considered — how much will we need? Yes, to fund a position for associate pastor, it will be necessary for everyone's giving to be above and beyond their regular giving.

Finally, we all can help by praying. Pray that this is God's plan for Gilbert Presbyterian Church. Pray for God's guidance along the way. And pray that we all have a part in achieving the goals for our church.

The Session has heard you; now prayerfully respond with, "Yes, here I am Lord. I can help on our journey to call an associate pastor."

YES, IT IS GOD'S WORLD!
August 2007

No matter where you travel — it is still God's world!

I saw God's world in Alaska where the snow-capped mountain peaks reached up to the sky. The glaciers towered over our small ship. With a roar, chunks of ice broke free, then dropped and splashed into the bay. I have never seen a more brilliant blue than the color of the icebergs in Tracy Arm, Alaska.

I saw God's world in the majestic bald eagles soaring in the sky. God's world was in the lumbering sea lions. I saw the playful puffins, spouting whales, seals resting on icebergs, and the big bears walking on the rocky shore. High on the steep rugged slope, I saw the white woolly mountain goats.

I saw God's world in the many waterfalls created by the melting ice and snow. God's world was in the beautiful sunset at Glacier Bay. I saw God's world as the native Alaskans shared their dances with us. Yes, it is God's world!

I saw God's world in Scandinavia where fields of brilliant yellow mustard grew. I saw the rivers, lakes, streams, bays, and Baltic Sea. I marveled at Stockholm, a city built on islands. God's world was in the gentle rain bringing life to trees, grass, and flowers.

I saw God's world in the people of Scandinavia as they proudly showed us their heritage and culture. I saw God's world in the cathedrals with their towering

127

spires.

And inside those cathedrals were the most amazing astronomical clocks built in the 1400's. Besides telling time, the clocks were an intricate calendar marking the church holidays for several centuries. At the very top of the clocks was a procession of small wooden figures bowing to Jesus as the clock struck noon. The craftsmanship that it took to construct clocks like these 600 years ago was truly unbelievable. That was the work of man inspired by God!

One does not have to go to Alaska or Scandinavia to see God's world. God's world is here in the eyes of my family and friends as they welcomed me home. It is God's world in the flitting of the hummingbird moving from flower to flower in my back yard. It is God's world at our church as we work and pray together for a common goal, a united goal.

It is God's world as we give of our time, talents, and treasures to the work of God. Yes, it is God's world at home and away!

A LETTER TO LUCAS AND AARON
September 2007

My Dearest Little Lucas Emeott and Aaron Wilson,

Summer 2007 was a wonderful summer for your grandma. It began with your baptism, Aaron, on May 20 and ended with yours, Lucas, on August 5.

You were so funny, Aaron, when your mom dressed you in a beautiful baptismal gown lovingly made by your grandmother, Brenda Wilson. You scrunched up your little face and seemed to say, (that is if you could only talk), "You are not putting me in that dress, are you?"

Mom whispered in your ear, "I promise, this is the last time you will ever have to wear a dress."

Someday, I know you will appreciate all the work and effort that your grandmother spent in making your gown. It was beautiful white satin with two little butterflies on the front. The butterflies are a symbol of new life. She had problems making the pleats, so her neighbor helped her — neighbor helping neighbor.

You were so pretty dressed in white. Your tiny white shoes had crosses on their soles. Your daddy baptized you at his church, Appomattox (Prince Edward) Presbyterian Church, in Virginia. Mommy, two grandmas, and one very proud grandpa held your big brother, Matthew, and watched as your daddy sprinkled you with water.

Lucas, your baptismal outfit was not the traditional

gown but rather a very pretty and very soft white knit romper. A small blue cross was on the front of your outfit. Your Aunt Karen sent it to your brother Nathan to wear for his baptism. Now it was your turn.

You also wore tiny white shoes with crosses on their soles. Your mom added a very special touch to your baptismal outfit: She hand-crocheted a little frame around tiny pictures of your grandpa, Roy Annis, and grandma, Barbara Emeott, and pinned them to your outfit. Yes, they were there smiling down from heaven. Your family gathered round — Mommy, Daddy, big brother Nathan, Grandpa Dale, and I intently watching the minister sprinkling you with water.

Lucas and Aaron, you are very special little boys. In your baptisms, your parents have made a wonderful commitment and promise. They have promised to raise you to know and love Jesus Christ. They have promised to nurture and guide you on your spiritual path. Not only did your parents make their commitments but also the congregations were asked to assist in your spiritual upbringing.

What an exciting time it is for everyone to share in your journey to become the people that Christ intends you to be.

This is your first step to a wonderful life knowing and loving God. Later, when you both are older, you will profess your faith and become active members in your church.

Baptism is just the beginning of your life journey, a journey of commitment, a journey of giving of your time, talents, and treasures to the work of God. You are touched by the love and grace of God.

Lucas and Aaron, you are very special in the eyes of your family. Your moms are sisters, which means you are first cousins. You were born a month apart

— February 28 and April 2. You were baptized during the same summer. You both have big brothers.

You have a lot in common — I hear reports about you two all the time — smiling, laughing, rolling over, sitting up with support, and first teeth.

Next it will be crawling and walking. What joy it is to watch you grow and mature in your love for one another, your family, your neighbors, and God!

With lots of hugs and kisses to both of you from your loving Grandma.

BONJOUR, MES AMIS
October 2007

Parlez vous français? Do you speak French? Moi — I'm trying to learn.

As I leave the classroom, my head is spinning — more vocabulary words to memorize, adjectives must agree with the noun both in gender (masculine or feminine) and number (single or plural), and verbs to conjugate. Plus, the pronunciation — that is something!

Some words run together and then there are letters at the end of words that are not pronounced. How can I ever remember everything! What am I doing in a French class at my age? What have my kids talked me into?

The Science History Tours is planning a trip to France in the summer of 2008. I have already been on tours with them — this past summer to Scandinavia and the previous summer to England and Scotland. It was a wonderful experience to tour the countries of famous scientists and learn about their work. Just think of the French scientists the group will study next summer — Louis Pasteur, Pierre and Marie Curie, the mathematician René Descartes, plus others. What an exciting trip it will be — visiting the Louvre, Eiffel Tower, and many other places of interest. Immediately my kids said, "Go, Mom, go. But you better take a French course first."

Yes, my kids are right. I need to learn the French

language and culture before my trip. I need to be able to read signs, ask basic questions, and communicate at least on an elementary level. I know whatever I can learn now will make my trip so much more meaningful and enjoyable.

We are all on a journey, maybe not to France, but on a journey of life — a journey to know Christ. It is a journey of working with others, giving of our time, talents, and treasures to the work of God. Come, find out and learn about God's work at your church.

Have you wondered about the committees in your church? Come and find out. Have you ever wondered about the Presbytery? Ask and I am sure your questions will be answered. Agencies in your community can also provide you with information about their work in God's world. Come, explore and learn about the opportunities to connect with others in your church and community.

Make your journey of life more meaningful by discovering how to serve and work for God.

LET THE SERVICE BEGIN!
November 2007

A few Sundays ago, one of our members was telling me about her trip to the World Mission Conference for the Presbyterian Church U.S.A. (PCUSA) held in Louisville, Kentucky, in October 2007. She said that it was an awesome conference. Each worship service ended with the statement, "The worship has ended, let the service begin."

Yes, let the service begin! Why should we serve? Jesus came into this world to serve others. He held children in His arms, He healed the sick, He taught us to love and pray, He washed the disciples' feet, and He died for our sins. To Jesus, greatness comes from serving.

Let the service begin!

How do we serve? Each of us has been given special gifts. Pray to God for guidance in discovering these talents and looking for opportunities to use them. Let God give you the strength needed to use your gifts. As we help others, even by carrying out the most mundane tasks, we are serving God.

Yes, let the service begin!

Who and where do we serve? We serve our church. We serve our home. We serve our community. If there is a need and we are able to fill it, with God's help, we do it. Ask for His guidance in serving others.

Let the service begin!

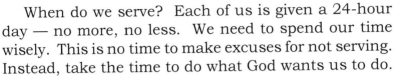

When do we serve? Each of us is given a 24-hour day — no more, no less. We need to spend our time wisely. This is no time to make excuses for not serving. Instead, take the time to do what God wants us to do.

November is Stewardship month. Grow in love, faith, and acts of service by dedicating a portion of your talents, time, and treasures to the work of God. Come forward with a pledge of your commitments to God in appreciation for all that He has given to you.

Yes, let the service begin!

SILENT NIGHT
December 2007

The sanctuary was aglow from the light of candles. It never looked as beautiful as it did Christmas Eve. Our friends, our neighbors — young and old — gathered to celebrate the birth of Jesus. We held our candles carefully while singing as one big choir the lovely carol, "Silent Night."

We blew out our candles, hugged one another, and wished each other a very Merry Christmas. We walked outside into the clear, cold mountain air. The luminarias lit our path to and from the sanctuary door. The stars shone bright in the sky. Yes, it was easy to imagine that they were guiding the way to the Christ Child.

It was ever so beautiful. It was a silent night. It was a holy night. It was midnight. It was Christmas.

As a family, what were we thinking about that Christmas Eve some thirty years ago? Roy and I probably were thinking of our four children, how proud we were of them, and wondering what the future would bring.

At that time our youngest was just a toddler asleep on her daddy's shoulder. Our two middle children were probably thinking of Santa.

Our oldest child was proudly beaming because he had spent several hours that morning filling the luminaria sacks with sand and candles. He also helped set up the candles in the sanctuary to be ready for the evening service. He started a family tradition at the Shepherd of the Hills Church in Morenci, Arizona. That was our children's service to the church for some fifteen years until our youngest graduated from high school. To them it was an honor and privilege to help make the sanctuary beautiful for Christmas Eve. What wonderful memories they have!

I love to sing and hear the carol, "Silent Night." I am reminded of my mother leading a group of neighborhood children caroling every year at Christmas time. It was a lot of fun for my friends, my brothers, and me. My mother's hot chocolate and cookies tasted ever so good after our evening of caroling in Ohio's cold and snow. That is a wonderful memory. It was my mother's service to the community. She was a member of a local women's club, and the money collected during the caroling went toward a college scholarship for a high school senior.

"Silent Night" brings back cherished memories of my mom's service to the community and my children's service to the church. It makes me wonder how this lovely Christmas carol came about. What is its story?

In 1818, Father Joseph Mohr at the Church of St. Nicholas in Oberndorf, Austria, was preparing for the midnight Christmas Eve service. But the beautiful organ in the church was broken, and he feared that the evening service would be a disaster — what to do?

A major problem became an opportunity — an opportunity for Father Joseph to write a new song. He quickly wrote a poem and asked his organist to set it to music — a very simple tune that could be sung without an organ.

"Silent Night" was sung for the first time that night accompanied by a guitar. From there it spread throughout the country and eventually around the world. A beautiful carol, so common, known by everyone, came about because of a broken organ. A major problem became an opportunity! Without a broken organ, we would not have this beautiful carol.

What do we do when we encounter problems and disappointments in life? Can we too turn them into opportunities? Can we ask God to guide us on a different path when stuff happens and things get in our way? Can we create our "Silent Night?"

What memories will we create for our children this Christmas? Will we create memories of family tradition that include service to God, the church and community? Will we stop our busy lives for just a little while this Christmas and think about the gifts we may bring to the Christ child?

Sing "Silent Night" and thank God for what God has given to each of us and say a prayer of thanks for our problems. Yes, thank God for our problems because through our challenges there are opportunities. Remember, because of a broken organ, the world was given the beautiful carol, "Silent Night."

The story of "Silent Night" is from the book, <u>Come Let Us Adore Him, Stories Behind the Most Cherished Christmas Hymns</u>, Robert J. Morgan, 2005.

2008

REJOICE WITH ME; I HAVE FOUND MY LOST SHEEP

Then Jesus told them this parable: "Suppose one of you has a hundred sheep and loses one of them. Does he not leave the ninety-nine in the open country and go after the lost sheep until he finds it? And when he finds it, he joyfully puts it on his shoulders and goes home. Then he calls his friends and neighbors together and says, 'Rejoice with me; I have found my lost sheep.' I tell you that in the same way there will be more rejoicing in heaven over one sinner who repents than over ninety-nine righteous persons who do not need to repent."

Luke 15:3 7

THE PARABLE OF THE LOST LUGGAGE
February 2008

Fog was all around us. A blanket of white hovered over the ground. It looked beautiful as we gazed into the distance — soft, muted colors. The snow from a week ago was practically gone — melted by the previous day's rain and warmer weather. Now, fog had sneaked in during the night. Despite the weather, morning traffic flowed steadily and smoothly on the freeway.

My daughter, Ann, was driving me to the Detroit Airport that morning. I was on my way to visit her sister, Karen, in Virginia. What a wonderful Christmas vacation I was having — spending a week with each daughter and her family!

Oh, great! What long lines! Well, I should expect that; after all, it was the day after Christmas. Finally, made it through security. Now I must look at the board to check my gate. Oh no — delayed, delayed, delayed. All the flights in and out of Detroit were delayed that morning — mine by two hours. No wonder I had neither seen nor heard any planes taking off or landing as we drove toward the airport — delayed because of the fog!

Here it is almost noon — the fog is finally lifting. Now, maybe my flight will be announced. Yes, it was announced all right — Northwest, direct flight to Richmond, cancelled. Another line to stand in, wait my turn, and "How do I get to Richmond?" I asked.

"A later flight, Northwest, is completely booked but you can go to Richmond on Delta with a layover in Cincinnati."

"I'll take it, but what about my luggage?"

"Don't worry; we will take care of that," she said as she poked a few computer keys.

Some twelve hours after Ann had dropped me off at the Detroit Airport, I finally was at the Richmond Airport watching and waiting at the carousel. All sizes, shapes, and colors of luggage came out of the chute except one olive green suitcase with bright red and orange pom-poms on both handles.

Another line to stand in — the missing luggage line. "Name, address, phone number, describe it... Now, according to the computer your luggage was transferred to the Delta flight that you were on. It is there on the carousel."

"I know my suitcase. It is not there. It is olive green with bright red and orange pom-poms. It is very easy to spot."

Later that evening, I arrived at my daughter's home sans luggage. For the next two days, we made telephone calls to Delta — no luggage. December 28, we called Delta again. They reported, "We do not have your luggage. We have notified Detroit, Cincinnati, and Northwest but as yet no response."

Finally I said to my son-in-law, "Let's call Northwest ourselves — their Lost and Found here in Richmond."

Ten minutes later, Northwest replied, "We have it. It will be delivered to your home this evening."

There was much rejoicing that evening: "My luggage has been found! Yes, see the bright red and orange pom-poms, they are there! Everything is here!"

I called my daughter in Detroit and my sons in Gilbert to tell them the good news: "My suitcase that was lost is now found." I was celebrating!

My lost luggage is a 21st century equivalent to the parable of the Lost Sheep or the Lost Coin of Biblical times. We all can relate to those stories — our initial emotions of worry and anxiety when we realize we have lost or misplaced something of value to us. Frantically, we search and look everywhere. Perhaps it is our cell phone, our keys, our luggage, or maybe even a scrap of paper with an important message written on it.

When we find our lost article, we rejoice and call our family and friends — the lost is found! Through the centuries the story has not changed.

God knows us. He recognizes us. We do not need to wear bright red and orange pom-poms for God. God knows our thoughts, feelings, and abilities. God knows when we stray onto the wrong path. God knows when we are lost in a fog. God doesn't need a computer to know where we are or where we are going.

Let God guide your way. The heavens rejoice when we come to God in prayer, praise, and thanksgiving. Let us work toward becoming more like Jesus by demonstrating His love and concern for everyone, including those that are lost and troubled. Share God's love and share the talents and treasures God has given you.

THE SAINT JOHN'S ILLUMINATED BIBLE
March 2008

I stood before the painting in awe. It was divided into seven long, narrow panels, each one depicting a day in the Story of Creation. The painting was magnificent. The first panel was that of darkness with brilliant splotches of red and blue bursting forth. Other panels showed the moon and stars, the seas, and man. A large black bird, a raven, flew across the middle panels. Small gold leaf squares tied the panels together.

The Story of Creation was the first of many illuminated paintings in a special exhibit at the Phoenix Art Museum. Another painting depicted a vertical shaft of light (gold leaf) which rose from the manger. Angels (also in gold leaf) were in a horizontal line across the shaft of light, producing the image of a cross. A donkey, sheep, and ox were in front of the manger with Mary, shepherds, and one king looking down into the crib.

It was impossible to choose my favorite painting. Was it Jacob's Ladder, the Genealogy of Christ depicted by a Menorah, the Parable of the Sower and the Seed, the Crucifixion, the Transfiguration, the Life of Paul, or was it the Story of Creation, or the Birth of Christ? I cannot choose — they are all so beautiful.

The Saint John's Illuminated Bible is a 21st century work of art created in the style of the hand-

143

written medieval manuscripts. Every page of the Bible is meticulously written using hand-made quill pens. It takes one day to produce a page of manuscript. Gold leaf is used extensively in the paintings. The illumination is what makes the pictures come alive.

Donald Johnson, one of the world's leading calligraphers, is the director and illuminator of the Saint John's Bible. He has scribes, artists, and craftsmen working with him on the project. From childhood he dreamed of creating a handwritten illuminated Bible. Now his dream has become a reality.

Do you have a dream — perhaps a dream from childhood? Have you prayed to God about your dream? Is there a special legacy you want to leave your family and your church? We do not have the talents that Donald Johnson has to create an illuminated Bible, but God has given us gifts to use. Perhaps our talents are to create beautiful quilts for the wounded veterans, cook and serve in the shelters, teach Sunday school, take part in the Worship Service, or help others in our church and community.

Ask God to help you discover your talents so that you may use them for the betterment of His kingdom. Let us praise Him and give thanks for all He has given us by giving of our time, talents, and treasures.

A LESSON FROM THE POPPIES AND HAWK
April 2008

Every morning as I eat breakfast, I read my newspaper. And every morning there is depressing news — more workers laid off, many families without health insurance, death toll of Americans in Iraq now at 4,000, and homes depreciating in value. Television is no different — the same news. I fill up my car with gas — over $3 a gallon! Will there ever be any cheerful news related to the economy or the hostilities in the Middle East? People are worried. They want answers.

Then I think of the Sermon on the Mount where Jesus gave us a lesson on worry. Do not worry about your food or drink — think of the birds — God provides for them. Do not worry about your clothes — think of the lilies — how beautiful they are. "Therefore I tell you, do not worry about your life..." (Matthew 6:25).

My friend, Grace Mossman, and I decided one day to get away from the worries of the modern world and see God's world — the wildflowers. It was slightly overcast that morning. As we left the Valley traveling towards Superior, there were a few wildflowers along the roadside — blue ones, white ones, and a couple of my favorite — the orange poppies. The ground was very rocky. It looked barren except for the cacti. Where were the poppies? Are they not yet in bloom? We were wondering.

Somewhat disappointed, we turned around in

145

Superior and headed back home. As we were driving down the mountain, the sun peeked out from behind the clouds. There they were — we saw the poppies — hundreds of them — no thousands, clinging to the steep mountainside! It was like a resurrection. Out of this barren and rocky ground, the brilliant orange poppies opened up and came to life. All it took was a little sunshine to bring the poppies out and create the most wonderful scene.

Then we looked up and saw a hawk with wings outstretched, soaring high in the sky. He went with the flow of air currents. It was beautiful.

Can we go with the flow like the hawk? Can we open up, shine, and praise God like a poppy? Can we honor God by creating beauty and love around us?

Further, what does worry do for us? Nothing! Does the hawk worry about his flight? Do the poppies worry that their home is in rocky ground? Of course not! Worry takes us away from God. It takes us away from thanking and praising Him for all that He has done for us. It takes us away from creating solutions to our challenges and problems of life. Worry takes us away from loving others and giving to others. Worrying about tomorrow takes away our joys of today.

Worrying takes away our faith in God. Trust God and give Him your worries and concerns! Pray to Him for guidance and help.

OUR VALUES, OUR MONEY, OUR TIME
May 2008

Take a sheet of paper and fold it into three parts as if you were mailing a business letter.

These instructions were simple enough, but we wondered what was next as we sat around the table. Pastor Terry Palmer, John Paterson, Grace Mossman, and I were at a Stewardship Workshop in Casa Grande last month conducted by the Synod of the Southwest. Rocky Mackey was one of the leaders.

Now, what were we to do with our paper?

Title the first section, "The Ten Things I Value Most," and list those ten things in order.

My first ones were easy — God and church, family and friends, and my country and freedom. Good start. Now, what is next? I continued my list — education and learning, my health, my travels, and yes — nature. I love God's world — the moon and stars at night, mountains and desert, oceans and flowing streams, flowers and trees.

It seems like the things I value most are intertwined. I want to learn; therefore, I teach and travel. Through my travels I see more and learn more about God's world. I can worship, praise, and serve God through my church. Because of my health and the fact that I live in the United States, I am free to choose my values and act upon them accordingly. Behind me and encouraging me in all that I do are my family and friends.

Next, title the middle section of your paper, "The Ten Things I Spend the Most Money On."

I am sure the first one has to be my home — mortgage, utilities, plus all other expenses related to it. After that I am not sure of the order. Church and other contributions are there someplace. My family is certainly on my list, since I would be including my plane tickets to visit my daughters. Taxes must also be near the top — income tax, sales tax, and property tax. Then for me, vacations and books would be among my top ten.

For the last third of the paper, title it, "The Ten Things I Spend the Most Time On." Well obviously, the first one for me is sleep because I need eight hours of sleep each night. After that my work is high on the list, even though I only teach part-time. It seems as if I am always writing tests, grading papers, or answering e-mails related to work in addition to my actual teaching.

My friends and family are on my list — phone calls and semiannual visits with my daughters, lunches with my son and brother, days at the mall with my daughter-in-law and granddaughter, and lunches, dinners, and conversations with my friends. I also try to fit in time for leisure reading — newspaper, magazines, and books. Of course, the time I spend on church and spiritual activities is near the top of my list — church services, choir practices, Session, Stewardship Committee, and my personal time for devotional readings including the Bible. My vacation trips are among the top ten things I spend time on. My exercise time — walking, fitness center, Yoga class — is on my list. And television — I hope it doesn't make my list.

Our next challenge was to look at our three lists and compare them. Do the lists correspond? Are we spending the most time and money on the things we value the most? Are there parts of the list that are inconsistent? Are we spending time and/or money on things we do not value? Or, the reverse, are we spending little or no time and money on things we value the most?

There is also the possibility one could value something that is free. I value God's world. It costs me nothing to stop and look at a beautiful sunset, feel the rain, or smell a rose, and those things have great meaning to me.

I invite you and your family to do this exercise. What do you value the most? Where do you spend the most money? What takes the most of your time?

Within your family, you could have some interesting discussions. If you wish to share your lists and your thoughts on this exercise, please respond. Perhaps, in this column next month I can include some highlights of your answers and your reactions to this activity. If you desire, you may respond anonymously.

Now, take a blank sheet of paper and fold it into thirds...

PLAN FOR STEWARDSHIP NOW
June 2008

"Mommy can we have a puppy?" Four sets of little eyes were looking up at me and pleading their case.

"And who will feed the puppy?" I asked.

"Me, me, me, me."

"And who will walk the puppy?"

"Me, me, me, me."

"And who will brush her?" Again, four more "me's." Who can resist that?

"OK, kids. We will get a puppy, but not just any puppy. First, we will go to the library and read about dogs, read about the different breeds, and read about their care. The dog we choose must be good with children, gentle, and large enough for four kids to love and hug at the same time."

Our children were involved in our decision-making process. From our reading, we decided that a collie would be a good match for our family. So, on a Palm Sunday, many years ago, a very cute little bundle of fur which, of course, we named Lassie, came home.

Within a week, Lassie's pleasant disposition was tested. Our youngest, then two, patted Lassie on the head and said, "Nice doggy, nice doggy" while the dog was eating. I held my breath, but Lassie completely ignored the pestering of the toddler. Our family could not have asked for a better and more gentle dog. And yes, she was big enough for four kids to love her, hug her, and brush her all at the same time.

I always thought that Lassie was perfect for our family because of the time we spent in reading about dogs, then planning and preparing for our pet before we purchased her. It seems as if the better prepared we are for an event, the more likely it is that everything will turn out well.

I cannot imagine taking a vacation without considerable preparation. Likewise, I spent time planning for college — where to go, what to study, and where to live. Then there were wedding plans, plans to move to Arizona, plans for jobs; and of course, all the preparations made before our children were born. All our lives we spend time in planning and preparing — preparing for future events.

The Stewardship Committee recently devoted two weekends at a Bi-Presbytery workshop in Casa Grande. We were involved in planning our stewardship goals and activities. As individuals, we too must make plans — plans for stewardship. What are your personal stewardship goals for the year?

Evaluate what you have done so far in terms of giving of your time, talents, and treasures. Are there any changes or additions to your activities that you would like to make? Is there a committee that interests you? I am sure they would love your help. Do you have a talent that you would like to develop? What better place than in your church to pursue that gift — a gift from God. And your treasures — what goals do you have in your giving?

Everything we are and everything we have comes from God. Plan now to return a portion of those gifts to God and become an active part of the work of His kingdom.

TICK, TICK, TICK
July 2008

Tick, tick, tick. "Hurry, get the time bomb — it's going to explode." Tick, tick, tick. "Hurry, it's not in that room — the other room."

I was on the edge of my chair screaming at the TV. The entire half-hour program was about finding a bomb in a building. Not much of a plot that I can remember, but I do remember it was an Alfred Hitchcock show late at night.

It was 1949, and my dad had just purchased our first television set. To my brother and me, TV was really wonderful. The screen was all of twelve inches across, if that. The set had a huge vacuum tube in the back with grainy black and white pictures; but wow, the pictures were sent right into our living room. It made me feel as if I was hunting for that time bomb myself.

The bomb was found. The ticking stopped. Thank goodness! I turned off the TV and climbed the stairs to go to bed.

Tick, tick, tick. "What? Is there a bomb in our house?" With every step, the ticking got louder. Tick, tick, TICK. "It's coming from my bedroom!" TICK, TICK, TICK. "Who is after me? I'm only a 10-year old kid!" "It's under my bed."

Half afraid, I got down on my knees and peeked under my bed. TICK, TICK, TICK. Oh no! My brother's

old wind-up clock was loudly ticking. And my brother
— he was in the hallway laughing hysterically.

How many minutes did it take my brother to run
up the steps, locate the clock, wind it up, and then
place it under my bed? Obviously, not very many.

Tick, tick, tick. How many ticks of a clock does
it take to be good stewards of our environment? Not
many. We can pick up a piece of trash and put it
where it belongs very quickly.

I have a neighbor, an elderly gentleman, who on his
daily walks takes along a sack and fills it with empty
soda cans, water bottles, and any other trash he finds
along the street.

Tick, tick, tick. How many minutes does it take to
pray for someone — someone who is hurting, someone
who has a difficult decision to make, someone whose
family needs help, or for someone who is sick? Not
many minutes.

Tick, tick, tick. How long does it take to say thank
you God for all that you have given us and for the
beauty of the earth? Not long.

Tick, tick, tick. How many minutes does it take to
greet someone with a happy smile? Not minutes —
only seconds.

Tick, tick, tick. How many ticks of a clock does
it take to stop and listen to someone, really listen to
what they have to say — listen to their problems? It
does not take many ticks of a clock to tell them we
care. I have a friend who one day telephoned me at
1 a.m. and wanted to talk. I do not remember our
discussion, but she has never forgotten that I did not
hang up on her.

Tick, tick, tick. How long does it take to visit a
person in the hospital and hold their hand? Not long.

Tick, tick, tick. How long does it take to tell a parent

you are concerned for their sick child? Not long.

Tick, tick, tick. How many minutes does it take to make sandwiches for the needy and serve them? Not many.

Tick, tick, tick. How many ticks of a clock does it take to give of your time to love and serve others? Not many. Yet, the recipient of your love and care will never forget those moments.

God gave us all 1,440 minutes every day. Time is not a commodity. Time cannot be bought or sold. Time cannot be stored. Time cannot be saved. At the end of our day, 1,440 minutes have gone by. Some minutes may be hardly noticeable and others may be loudly ticking, but 1,440 minutes are gone every 24 hours.

Therefore, each day, let us joyfully use a portion of those minutes in service to God, church, and community. Tick, tick, tick.

IT TAKES THE TALENTS OF ALL
August 2008

Where were we going? To a classical concert, and that is all we were told. We followed our tour guide up a very steep and narrow spiral staircase. The stone steps were well worn, which was understandable since they were centuries old. We were wondering how much farther we would need to go. Finally we walked into a large room, a chapel — a chapel made for a king!

I was breathless — from the climb or from what I saw, or perhaps from both. Wow, the colors — an explosion of colors — reds, blues, greens, and yellows! We were surrounded by fifteen 50-foot-tall stained glass windows and one rose window. There was very little spacing between each window, and there were no supporting pillars in the room to break the view. It looked like there were windows and no walls. It was as if we were surrounded by heavenly light.

The windows depicted stories from the Bible, both the old and new testaments. It was magnificent! Yes, I was in the upper chapel of Sainte-Chapelle in Paris, France, on an Elderhostel tour.

The concert by a string quartet — two violins, a viola, and a cello — was fantastic. They performed music by Pachelbel, Bach, Mozart, and Schubert (some of my favorite composers). The first violinist directed the group with nods from his head without missing a single note. It was fascinating to watch the four communicate with their eyes. The music came alive as they played their instruments with expression and love. I am not sure who had the more enjoyable evening — those of us who were listening or the quartet itself.

I will never forget that evening of June 6, 2008, in Paris, France — sitting in a 13th century chapel, completely surrounded by exquisite stained glass windows, listening to music composed in the 17th, 18th, and 19th centuries being played by professional musicians of the 21st century. The talents and skills of everyone, from the initial builders, glassmakers, and composers to the present-day musicians, blended together for one memorable evening!

Creating a vibrant church is no different from creating an unforgettable evening. God gave each one of us talents to be used for His work. We do not all have the same talent. We are not all builders, we are not all composers, we are not all musicians, but each of us has unique gifts to share. When we blend everyone's gifts and work together, we can build the most wonderful, enthusiastic church of joy and love.

LET IT RAIN!
September 2008

I like clouds. I love to look up, study the sky and try to predict the weather. Will those clouds drift by or will they billow and cluster ever larger? Is there a storm coming? Will it rain?

I like clouds. When I fly across the country, I enjoy looking down on the clouds. At that angle, they appear to be like big fluffy beds and pillows where I might take a nap or climb and leap from one to another. Blue sky above and clouds below — am I in heaven?

I like clouds. When we lived in Eastern Arizona, I loved watching the clouds accumulate and tower over the mountains. During the monsoon season, the clouds kept building until finally they could hold no more water. The wonderful rain fell to the ground with thunder reverberating from mountain peak to mountain peak and lightning flashing.

In the evenings, after the storm passed, we would take a walk or sit on the porch and watch our children ride their bikes and play. Then we said, thank you God for the refreshing rain.

I like clouds. I remember one time looking out the window and seeing rain but no clouds. That is not possible — there have to be clouds to have rain. I ran outside and saw one little cloud amid a bright blue sky. Thank you, God, for that one little cloud causing the rain.

I like clouds, but sometimes they disappoint me. It seems all too often, in the East Valley, I hear the thunder, see the lightning and feel the wind. I pray to God for rain. God, we need rain. The desert needs your rain. The trees and plants need your rain. However, my prayers are not answered. The clouds disappear. Perhaps, another day it will rain.

I like clouds. As a child, I enjoyed watching clouds drift by. To me, clouds took on the forms of animals or other objects. That cloud looks like a horse, and a dog is over there. There's a castle — is God living in that castle?

I imagined that heaven was in the clouds and God was high in the sky looking down on me. Thank you, God for watching over me and taking care of me.

I wonder what God would say if we were the clouds, and the rain was our gifts and offerings. God might say, "Thank you little cloud for your gift. I know that you have only a few treasures but you are giving your all. You are giving with love in your heart and with compassion and gratitude for everything that has been given to you. I know you would like to give more."

And to another cloud God might say, "You have many treasures; consequently, you give more. You are very generous with your gifts and offerings."

Then to all the clouds God would say, "Thank you for working together and creating a wonderful and loving rain. Your rain of treasures, for my church and my people, will pay the bills, create new programs, and bring joy to those in need."

Let us unite like the clouds billow in a summer monsoon storm. Just as rain refreshes and renews the earth and creates new life, our gifts and offerings likewise will refresh, renew, and create new life for our church. Let it rain!

GREETINGS FROM FINCASTLE, VIRGINIA
November 2008

I am looking out of my daughter's sunroom at the beautiful Southwestern Virginia countryside. I have a wonderful panoramic view of her neighborhood. It is hilly with hardly any flat land.

In the distance are the Blue Ridge Mountains, and yes, they do look blue. The grass is still green, a few flowers are in bloom, and the trees are beginning to change colors.

A month ago when I first arrived, all the trees were green. A week later, the deep cranberry red and brilliant gold leaves began to appear. Every day there are more colors in the leaves. Now as I look outside, some trees are still green while others are yellow, orange, red, and brown.

A few days ago we drove into the mountains and hiked to a waterfall. At that higher elevation, leaves were already falling and covering our trail. The trees were beautiful. They made the most fantastic kaleidoscope of color.

Autumn is here in Virginia. Down the highway are apple orchards with trees heavily laden with fruit. Roadside markets are selling pumpkins, apples, homemade jams and cider. One farm not far from here has a corn maze for children to venture through. Matthew, my almost-four-year-old grandson, loved it as he guided grandma through the maze.

Changes are in the air. A week ago the temperature was still in the 80's, but yesterday it rained. Today is cold and windy. The clouds are low, stratus, blue and gray in color. These are not the summer clouds of a few days ago. The trees are not the trees of summer — the leaves are changing color. Yes, the season is changing — summer to fall. And with the change in the season are the preparations for winter — squirrels gathering nuts and people getting out their warm clothes and jackets and checking their heating systems.

Change is a transformation process. Change is growth. With change, there are challenges and decisions that must be made. Gilbert Presbyterian Church is going through a transformation process. What changes do you want to see made? What challenges will we encounter and how will we solve our problems? How will we prepare and plan for the future of our church?

Let us pray to God for help and guidance as we take the path to growth and change. Just as it takes many different trees in full color to create a beautiful autumn scene, it will take the time, talents, and treasures of everyone to create a wonderful, vibrant, and growing church that is welcoming to all.

ALL ABOARD!
December 2008

It was cold that morning. The wind was gusting off Lake Erie, bringing a few snowflakes in the air. The tall buildings of Downtown Cleveland failed to block the blast of cold air.

However, I was oblivious to the weather because I was engrossed in watching a display of model trains in the May Company store window. The little trains chugged along throughout the miniature village and countryside to the tune of Christmas carols. The railroad cars were filled with tiny Christmas presents.

Every year from the time I was a child through my college days, my mother and I would go shopping the day after Thanksgiving. Every year my mother would say that the Christmas display at the May Company was the most elaborate and fantastic one ever. For years our tradition was to enjoy the sights and sounds of Christmas in downtown Cleveland.

Christmas 2007, my daughter in Michigan along with her husband and their two little sons took me to a large exhibit of model trains. A retired gentleman spends the entire year enlarging and improving his display.

In December and January the public is invited to watch the gentleman's little electric trains go over bridges, through tunnels, up and down hillsides, and passed towns. His elaborate miniature railroad yard is designed to look like the Chicago yard with even city skyscrapers painted on a wall. He has over one mile of track in a building devoted entirely to his hobby. My toddler grandsons were completely enthralled to see the exhibit. They did not want to leave.

In January, I was in Richmond, Virginia, with my younger daughter and her family. One evening we visited the Lewis Ginter Botanical Garden. Every Christmas the plants, shrubs, and trees are decorated with sparkling lights in the shape of flowers and animals. It was beautiful walking around the gardens, but the highlight of the evening for my little grandsons was the model train display. The little engines chugged through a miniature winter wonderland of small villages, hillsides, tunnels, and bridges.

For my family and me, one of the traditions of Christmas is enjoying electric toy trains. When I was a child we always had a Lionel train circling our Christmas tree. Years later my children also played with a Lionel train. And today, yes, I have a battery-operated train tooting out carols while circling my Christmas tree. It has become a tradition for my Arizona grandchildren to help grandma decorate her tree and set up the train.

Why are we so fascinated with model electric trains? What do they represent? Can they be a symbol for our lives? Do we at times feel like we are racing down the track? Can our church and Bible study be a station for a much-needed rest?

Does our track we take in life split into different paths? How do we determine which way to go? Do we ever get derailed? And, are there difficult times in our lives when we feel like we are chugging up a long, steep hill?

When we operate our model trains, we use electricity

to make them run. We work the switches to allow the train to change to a different track. If our train is derailed, we are there to get it back on track.

Who is our power? Who guides us on our way? Who helps us with our decisions? And who keeps us on track? It is God!

Let us thank Him for His love, guidance, and for all He has given us. Then as we watch a display of model trains merrily chugging along, bringing little Christmas gifts to a toy village, let us think about the gifts we bring to the Christ child.

Can we bring gifts of love, gifts of ourselves, and gifts of our time, talents, and treasures?

2009

I CAN DO EVERYTHING THROUGH HIM WHO GIVES ME STRENGTH

I know what it is to be in need, and I know what it is to have plenty. I have learned the secret of being content in any and every situation, whether well fed or hungry, whether living in plenty or in want. I can do everything through him who gives me strength.

Philippians 4:12-13

WITH CHANGE WE GROW
January 2009

I stared at the picture in my Weekly Reader. It was unbelievable! There was a picture of a gigantic computer occupying an entire room. Its name was ENIAC, and it had 18,000 vacuum tubes. Yes, in elementary school I knew what a vacuum tube looked like. Vacuum tubes were inside our radio. They made it work.

The year was 1946. I am sure at the time I did not fully comprehend the significance of that computer, but I have never forgotten the picture.

Later, in ninth grade, while my classmates and I were studying different occupations, our teacher, Miss Campbell, made a profound statement. She said that many of us would be working in jobs that at that time did not exist. We stared at her. What was she talking about? What jobs? The year was 1953.

Four years later I began my summer employment in the cost accounting department of Glidden Paint Company. I learned to operate a comptometer (a large, clunky, noisy, completely mechanical type of calculator). However, my principal job at Glidden each summer was to make the inventory book. It had to be handwritten on special paper. For some reason it could not be typed.

Yes, every day for six weeks each summer, I wrote by hand all the names of paints, prices, and other information needed for Glidden's inventory. To keep myself from boredom and to not think about my aching hand, I pretended to be a medieval monk painstakingly copying the Bible. In August 1961, as I said my good-byes at Glidden and headed to my new adventure in teaching, I was told that I would be replaced by a computer.

In 1965 I began working as a statistician for the Arizona Department of Health. I was hired for a special project. We collected so much data that it became unwieldy using the department's equipment. We needed a computer for our study. This time I did not want to be replaced by a computer — I wanted to learn how to program one.

I was off to Arizona State University for a programming class in FORTRAN. Computers were still quite large, occupied an entire room, had blinking lights and used punched cards for their input. I had to use a key-punch machine to type my programs. Beginning students were not allowed to operate the computer. We stood in line with our deck of cards waiting for a technician to place our cards on the computer.

If by chance someone had a continuous loop in his/her program, the computer would grind on forever until noticed by the operator. A bent or mangled card or one out of place would cause the program to stop. And if the cards were dropped, that was a disaster.

In the summer of 1981, we purchased our first home computer — Radio Shack TRS-80. I programmed math games for our children. Instead of punched cards, we used cassette tapes as a means to store our programs. A few years later we upgraded to an Apple IIe that had word processing capabilities.

When our children were in high school, our home

became a very popular place as most families did not yet have a computer. At that time, very few professionally made computer games were on the market. Our children and their friends had to program their own games.

Now practically every home has a computer. The computer is our source of knowledge — encyclopedia, newspaper, and dictionary. Our computer is our road map. We buy goods on the computer and make plane and hotel reservations. We pay our bills by computer. We send and receive messages miles away by computer. We use word processing, spreadsheets, database, and PowerPoint. And of course, we play games on the computer.

Computers have changed. Our lives have changed because of computers. Would we want to return to the 1980's and have to program our computer before we could use it? No! Would we want to return to the 1950's where only government and universities had computers? Of course not! And yes, Miss Campbell you were right, many jobs today did not exist in 1953!

Change can be disturbing. What we do not know and understand can make us apprehensive, but change can be wonderful. With change, we grow and learn. With change we move forward.

Gilbert Presbyterian Church is initiating a transformation process to determine our vision for the church. You have taken the survey, the results are in, and now is the time to look them over. Are there changes you would like to see? Pray to God for guidance and direction for Gilbert Presbyterian Church. Let us all work together, bringing our talents, treasures, and time to develop a vibrant and friendly church for all.

SNOWFLAKES
February 2009

The early morning air was bitter cold — only 11 degrees. A layer of fresh snow had fallen during the night. It was beautiful. There were no footprints yet on the snow — it was too early or too cold for people to be about.

The street lamps were still on. The snow reflected their light. Peace, quiet, beauty — that was the scene as my daughter drove me to the Detroit airport early New Year's Day.

The morning reminded me of growing up in Ohio. When I was a child I loved to watch snowflakes hit my coat. They were so delicate, so beautiful. Would I ever see two snowflakes alike?

My teacher in elementary school had said that snowflakes are all different. She taught us how to fold a piece of paper a certain way and cut out snips from the creases. When we opened the paper, there was our snowflake. We decorated the classroom with the paper snowflakes. It was a snowstorm! Our snowflakes were so beautiful and all very different.

Yes, no two snowflakes are alike. However, they all have the same basic hexagonal crystalline shape. The different temperatures and water vapor in the clouds create the variations we find in snowflakes... snowflakes are different because of their environment.

We are like snowflakes — no two of us are alike.

God has made each of us unique with our own talents and abilities. God has shaped us and has touched our lives. Because of our Creator and our environment, we are all different. Our diverse nature, talents and skills all help to make us beautiful.

We are like snowflakes — working together we can create a wonderful scene. Sharing our time and talents, caring for one another, and by sharing a generous spirit we can do the work that God wants us to do in His world.

We are like snowflakes — we reflect the light of Jesus, God's light. That light is our faith, love, joy, and the compassion we show to one another.

Yes, we can be a snowflake, a beautiful unique snowflake reflecting light, the light of Jesus, the light of God.

OUR INVESTMENTS ARE GROWING!
March 2009

I wonder what is in today's mail — a report of my investments! No, I don't even want to open it. I know what it will say. Stocks and mutual funds have been on a down-hill slope. They are melting faster than a snowball under the hot summer sun.

I remember the time not long ago when people were advised to buy a home, as its value would keep increasing. Not anymore! Today's newspaper said that the Valley's median home price is at an eight-year low. There goes my investment in my home. I need to quit reading the newspaper — too depressing!

More companies are laying off workers or forcing them to take days off without pay. People have invested their time and talents into their job and what do they get — a pink slip! Is there not any good news? Are all of our investments evaporating?

I glanced over to last Sunday's church bulletin. It was still on the table amongst the mail. I read the list of opportunities for the week at Gilbert Presbyterian Church (GPC) — Christian education, Bible study, orchestra and choir practices, Boy Scouts, prayer shawl knitters, Presbyterian Women, and Contemporary Youth Worship.

Other weeks it is the quilters, Men's Fellowship, Good News Gathering, patio project, plus all the committee meetings. That's it—there is the good news, right in front of me in Sunday's bulletin! Our investments of our time and talents in the activities and programs at Gilbert Presbyterian Church are not disappearing. These investments are growing!

I thought of our mission programs — East Valley Men's Center, Paz de Cristo, Christmas Angels, food baskets, the Presbyterian Women's offering, special Presbyterian offerings, and the latest — the Honduran project. These are all fantastic investments of our time, talents, and treasures!

I have been at GPC long enough to have seen our youth grow from little children to self-assured teenagers conducting the Contemporary Youth Worship Service. There is no better investment than to spend time with our children, teaching them the Bible and God's love. The children respond by sharing their time and talents with us. Our investments are growing through our youth.

Can you imagine the thrill of the recipient of a prayer shawl or a quilt or an angel tree gift, or a food basket? Oh, what a wonderful investment of time and talent. Think of those who benefit from our time and assistance at the East Valley Men's Center or Paz de Christo. This is how our investments are growing — when we give to others and share the love of Christ. What a wonderful act of stewardship.

Yes, we do have a concern in this troubled economy. The number and amount of pledges are down from last year. Last year 83 families pledged a total of almost $170,000. So far this year 74 families have pledged $146,000.

The amount pledged provides a guide for program planning. If you haven't pledged this year and you plan to, please do so. And if you have personal financial concerns that have kept you from pledging,

171

we understand, as these are difficult economic times. With prayer and faith, the members of the Stewardship Committee believe that pledges and loose offerings will come in to cover our programs and expenses for 2009. (This is how it has worked in the past.)

Thank you all for investing your time, talents, and treasures in the work of our church and community! Our investments grow as we do the work of God.

A LETTER TO MY NEWEST GRANDSON, AIDAN MICHAEL ANNIS
May 2009

My Dearest Little Aidan,

"I have someone here who would like to speak to you." That was your daddy on the phone. Then I heard your first cry at 8:02 p.m., Tuesday, April 7, 2009. Tears of joy and happiness filled my eyes — the miracle of birth.

The next day I saw you with mommy and daddy. You were so little, very beautiful and precious, a gift from God. Your little hand and fingers were encircling your daddy's finger. Yes, Aidan, take hold of your daddy's finger. Let him teach you and help you as you grow.

What will your little hands do? What will they explore? With your little hands will you someday build a sand castle, draw a picture for mommy, or throw a ball? Later will you play a musical instrument — a drum, trumpet, or piano? I wonder what talents God has given you. With your hands, will you build or operate a computer or other equipment? Will you be skilled with using very fine instruments? With your hands, clasp them in prayer to give thanks to God.

Then I held you — you were lightweight but very strong. You kicked off your blanket, and I saw your cute little feet move. "Let's go, Grandma, take me places," you seemed to say. Where will your little feet go? By this time next year you will be toddling to mommy and daddy. Later you will be hiking the mountains with daddy and exploring God's world. What paths will you take? I wonder what places you will visit and see. Remember, wherever you go, walk with God and let Him be your guide.

I heard your voice, your strong first cry. Soon you will be babbling and then saying "Mama" and "Dada." Next will be the questions — Why? Why? Why? What will you ask, what knowledge will you impart, and what prayers will you say? With your voice, praise and honor God.

When I first held you, you blinked at me. I wonder what you were thinking. What will your mind create, what books will you read, and what will be your interests? And with your heart, what gifts will you give and what treasures will you share? With your heart and mind, do the work of God.

You must have felt safe and secure in my arms as you fell back to sleep. You are a very lucky little boy — loved by your mommy and daddy, grandparents, aunts, uncles, cousins, and family friends. But best of all, you are loved by God.

With lots of hugs and kisses, Your Loving Grandma

THE STORY BEHIND MY STORIES
June 2009

"Rocky, I can't write. You write the articles on stewardship."

Rocky would not listen to me. She walked away. She wanted me to write an article every month for *The Crossroads*, the Gilbert Presbyterian Church newsletter, to remind everyone that stewardship was for the entire year rather than for just the Fall Stewardship campaign.

"Good idea, Rocky. But don't look at me. I'm not a writer."

With that, all my bad memories of writing experiences came over me. When I was 9 years old my older brother laughed at my writing. He was 13 — his writings were good and he liked to write.

Throughout my junior and senior high school years, my mother would say, "You must let me help you with your essays and correct your mistakes before you hand in your papers."

Then my high school English teacher said, "You must be having a bad day. I know you can write better than that. Your brother wrote so well." Yes, whenever I had to write, it was a bad day.

College was no better. I just barely squeaked by getting C–'s in Freshman English. I chose math because I like math. In math I don't have to write. For over 50 years I have avoided writing — I have avoided writing like the plague. What is Rocky doing to me?

"Rocky, I can't write!" If Rocky wants a short paragraph, then that is all she will get.

A few days later I sat at my computer. Well, here goes. It sure isn't going to be very long. One paragraph later I was finished — that's it. The next day I thought I would give my little article one last look before giving it to Rocky. I read it. It was awful! It was horrible! It was very boring!

If I can't stand to read it, why should anyone else want to read it? I can't write. I cried. "Oh, God, I can't write. I need your help. Help me God. I can't do this." I quickly deleted my entire article. Gone, gone, and gone — never to be seen again!

I reached for my Bible and turned to my favorite part, The Sermon on the Mount. I read Matthew 5:14 — "You are the light of the world. A city built on a hill cannot be hid." I closed my eyes and thought about that verse.

Yes, God, a city built on a hill cannot be hidden. That verse reminded me of the years Roy and I lived in Morenci, a copper mining town in the mountains of Eastern Arizona. When we had been gone and were returning home from an out-of-town trip at night, our children would play a game of who could first spot the lights of Morenci. From a distance, the lights high on the mountain shone like a beacon in the night sky. As we drove closer to town, the lights that once seemed as one became many. First we saw the lights from the copper mine, then the lights from the center of town. Shortly we could see the light from the church, the lights from the school, and finally our neighbor's lamp in the window. Every light, no matter how small, was very important to forming that one bright beacon for weary travelers. Yes, God, a town on a mountain cannot be hidden.

With my eyes still closed, I thought of Gilbert Presbyterian Church. Yes, God, a church is like a town on a mountain. Just as it takes many different lights to see a town from a distance, it takes the "lights" of everyone to operate a church. We need many people, each one very important. We need worship leaders, ushers, greeters, musicians, Sunday school teachers, committee leaders and members, to name just a few.

We also need the "lights" from the youngest, the children. Each person has a light to shine, a gift, a talent to offer to God. With all working together, our church will be a bright beacon for everyone just like a town on the mountain. That is it! That is my article!

My fingers flew over the keyboard. Oh thank you God, for helping me. I have written my article on stewardship. Oh, thank you. That was my first article printed in the June 2002 issue of *The Crossroads*.

I have learned many things writing these articles for *The Crossroads*. I have learned how much God is a part of my articles. I believe He speaks to me through you, my friends and my family. He speaks to me through the sunset, clouds, moon, stars, mountains, rocks, and wildflowers. There is no burning bush; but yes, I believe in my heart that God speaks to me and touches me. It is He who gives me the ideas and the guidance I need.

Before I write, I pray, "Oh, God, what little story do you want me to tell this month? Please, God, help me write your message." Then when I am finished, I thank God for helping me. It is like a partnership — He gives me the ideas, He tells me what to write, and I do the typing. I know that God is in my heart when I write my articles for *The Crossroads*.

When I write, I think of John 15:5, "I am the vine;

you are the branches. If a man remains in me and I in him, he will bear much fruit; apart from me you can do nothing."

Yes, without Christ, without God, I can do nothing. Immediately my favorite Bible verse comes to mind (Philippians 4:13), "I can do all things through Him who strengthens me."

The above article was read during the Contemporary Service on Sunday evening, March 29, 2009.

ARE WE PLUGGED IN TO GOD?
July 2009

With my cursor, I hit "Send" on my computer screen. There goes my e-mail to my friend. I wonder if she will receive my message. Maybe I will phone her to be sure. That should not be necessary.

Even though I do not completely understand the science behind computers and the internet, I have faith the system will work. I am continually amazed about how messages on my screen are sent to my friends and family. I can receive and send not only letters and numbers, but also pictures, music, and speech. Computers are the wonder of modern technology.

One day my friend asked me if I had received her e-mail. No, simply because I had not turned on my computer that day. Her message was still out there somewhere waiting for me. All the marvels of modern science are for naught if we are not plugged in.

Do we exhibit the same faith in God that we do in our computers? Computers can and have let us down, but God will never abandon us. Believe in what God can do and will do for you. His omnipotence is far greater than the power of any computer.

Are we plugged in to God? If we are not attuned to Him, we cannot receive His messages. Perhaps His message is somewhere out there waiting for us to listen. Amid all the noise and confusion of modern life, I wonder what God is trying to tell us. Ask Him and then listen to His response.

Maybe God is saying, "Stop and look at all the wonders and beauty of the earth. Take care of the earth as you are the stewards of the land." Other times He might say, "Open your hearts and help those who need your assistance, for you have been given abundantly. Reach out and listen to the sick, hurt, and lonely. Share your time, talents, and treasures with others."

And finally, I believe God says, "Let the children come, love them, and teach them about Jesus and the Bible. Teach them to pray."

Plug in and listen to the messages from God.

THANK YOU, GOD
August 2009

The plane descended through the clouds as it came into Calgary, Canada. Was that a few sprinkles of rain on the window? I did not care. I'm from Phoenix. I like the rain. I was off on an exciting Elderhostel adventure to the Canadian Rockies. But first I would be visiting Ward and Dixi Mackenzie on their farm north of Calgary.

I heard my name. Dixi was calling me. Here I am in a busy airport a long way from home and greeted by friends from Gilbert Presbyterian Church. I was not sure who was more excited about my visit — the Mackenzies or me. For me — it was wonderful. I was going to see this part of Canada for the first time.

Thank you, God, for a safe flight. And thank you for my friends.

Momentarily, we heard an announcement over the PA system: The airport was closed due to the storm and lightning. I just made it. I had my luggage. What had been a few sprinkles on the windows of the plane a few minutes ago had become a deluge.

It was pouring, and thunder and lightning seemed to be close-by, but we drove over to a brand-new store, Bass Pro Fishing Shop. The Mackenzie kids were already there waiting for us. The place was huge with all kinds of outdoor sporting equipment — hunting, fishing, camping, and boating. There was even a

24,000-gallon freshwater aquarium.   As we were looking at the fish, we heard an announcement that everyone had to go outside — the store was closed. In this rain! Someone lifted the cover off a drain inside the store and water came gushing up like a geyser.

Outside, the rain was still coming down in torrents. When we reached our vehicle, we learned that the main highway was flooded; but with the Mackenzie's truck, we were able to get through.   The storm gradually subsided as we left Calgary. There was only sunshine when we got to their farm.

Thank you, God, for the refreshing rain, the rainbow, and sunshine after the storm. At times our challenges in life are like your storms. Sometimes, there are only a few sprinkles, but other times it feels like we have a deluge of problems. Yet, we need to remember that you are in control and will help us through our challenges. Thank you, God, for your guidance and for providing the rainbow after the storm. The rainbow is a symbol of your promises to us.

Their farm is in the transition zone — between the flat plains of Eastern Alberta and the high Rocky Mountains in the west. The land is beautiful — 500 acres of green fields of canola and barley. Behind their home is a vegetable and flower garden. A red barn over 100 years old is off to one side. This is the farm where Ward was raised. This was his parents' land. Dixi is from a farm just six miles away.

Thank you, God, for the beautiful farmland, the grain in the fields, vegetables in the garden, and flowers all around. This is your rich land. Thank you for the many generations of farmers who have cared for your land.

Dixi drove me around the farm. We went across the road in front of their house and down a very steep dirt road into a coulee (deep ravine). At the bottom of the coulee was a lake filled with water. Green grass and marsh-type plants were along the water's edge, and trees were across the lake. It was very beautiful there, so peaceful and quiet. The occasional car or truck on the road above was hardly noticeable. This was wonderful — only the sounds of nature. A fox crossed in front of us and then stared at us from the hillside. Her den probably was close by. We also saw ducks, birds, and the neighbor's black cows. The coulee is part of their farm.

Thank you, God, for a place of peace, tranquility, and beauty; a place to enjoy nature, and a place to truly feel your loving presence.

After dinner we sat outside warming ourselves by a log fire and watching the kids play soccer. We then walked behind their home, a little past the garden and gazed at the sunset. It was beautiful. Beyond their farm and rolling green fields, we saw the jagged snow-capped mountains of the Canadian Rockies. And setting behind those mountains was the sun. What a spectacular view! A fantastic close to the day! Yes, a few days later, I would be there in those mountains.

Thank you, God, for your magnificent creation, the beauty of the mountains, the sunset, and your promise of tomorrow. Thank you, God, for a wonderful beginning to my Canadian journey.

God has given so much to us, what can we do for Him? We can take care of His land and give of our time, talents, and treasures for a brighter tomorrow!

A FITNESS PROGRAM FOR STEWARDSHIP
September 2009

Just one more rep — I can do it! The first few repetitions were easy, but they got increasingly more difficult. By the time I was lifting that last weight, my muscles were beginning to burn. Afterwards, I felt great. I did it! I was at Freestone Recreation Center going through my exercise routine.

Once a week I meet with my trainer to review my exercise program. She encourages me and makes necessary corrections and additions to the program. During the week I follow her written instructions. She has divided my exercises into three parts: cardio, weight resistance, and core strengthening, stretching, and balance.

In a similar manner, there are three parts to stewardship. In our personal stewardship fitness program we give our time, talents, and treasures to God, church, family, and community. When we give our treasures, it is like lifting weights. Yes, the first few dollars are easy to give, but the last ones are more difficult. At times our stewardship muscles may begin to ache, but we may be able to give just one more dollar — we can do it!

Sharing our talents with others is giving a gift from our heart — that is our cardio exercise. There are many different exercises for the heart, such as walking, jogging, running, biking, or using a treadmill or elliptical machine. Likewise, each one of us has a different talent to share, a gift from the heart. Some people have a gift of music, others a gift of teaching, speaking, or leading, and some a talent for making quilts or serving in community shelters. A friendly greeting, happy smile, and active listening are gifts we all can give. The gifts from our heart: that is our cardio exercise.

We need to exercise balance in our lives in order to give the gift of time. We all have the same number of hours in every day, but what is important is how we use our time. Can we share a part of our time with our church, family, and community? We can if we balance our commitments.

Our stewardship muscles will grow, strengthen, and stretch as we share our time, talents, and treasures with others. Just as we feel good after physical exercise, we will feel great knowing we are working with God.

And who is our stewardship trainer? The one who can lead us and encourage us is Jesus Christ.

Where are our instructions for our stewardship exercises? In the Bible.

MY FATHER'S GARDEN
October 2009

"You can't grow anything in that dirt," said our neighbor to my dad, years ago. "That is clay, not good soil. And furthermore, your corner lot was the neighborhood dump."

My dad ignored our neighbor's pessimistic view. My dad was not discouraged with the amount of work that needed to be done in order to have a garden. He cut and pulled weeds and scrub brush, removed rocks, and carried off truckloads of trash from the land.

Yes, it was the neighborhood dumping ground. But the first year he grew vegetables and the second year he built our home on that corner lot. After we moved into our new home, we always had a garden.

My father was raised on a farm in southern Ohio. He loved the feel of dirt in his hands. He loved planting seeds and nurturing them to grow. He could raise anything. My dad grew sweet corn, tomatoes, potatoes, lettuce, green beans, carrots, onions, and strawberries.

Our home was surrounded by his flowers. Dad built miniature greenhouses in the basement window wells so that his seeds could germinate and grow during the cold winter months. As soon as the weather was warmer, he would transplant the small shoots outside. Since our home was on a corner lot, everyone in the neighborhood walked by and marveled at his garden.

I remember my brothers and me hoeing the garden and pulling the weeds. And yes, we were still tossing out rocks that somehow worked their way to the top. I remember my dad testing the soil to determine the correct fertilizer to apply. My dad used his knowledge of science and farming to grow the vegetables, strawberries, and flowers in his garden.

Harvest time was wonderful. There is nothing that tastes better than freshly picked sweet corn. Strawberries were so tasty — we walked out to the garden and popped berries into our mouths. Many years we had a bumper crop of freshly grown foods. We shared our strawberries and veggies with our neighbors. My mother made the best strawberry jam. We took home-grown foods to our church's potluck events. I remember my father's garden.

"No wonder your garden is so great," said our neighbor to my dad. "That is virgin soil."

When God looks at us, He sees the good in us, not the rocks or weeds. He sees how we can lead productive lives — caring and helping others. He sees the virgin soil in us where new ideas can take root and flourish. He sees us blossoming and blooming under His care.

Everything we are and everything we have comes from God. Let us thank Him by spiritually growing and sharing our time, talents, and treasures with others.

BRING IN THE HARVEST!
November 2009

The air was crisp and cool. The sun was peeking out from behind the clouds. Autumn leaves were turning — red, orange, brown, and gold. We were on our way to the apple orchard. I loved apples — my favorite fruit.

A trip to the orchard was a thrill for me when I was a child. I was a Northern Ohio city kid. Nothing tasted better than a freshly picked apple or just-pressed cider.

The trees are laden with apples, bring in the harvest! Big pumpkins are on the vine, bring in the harvest! Squashes are ready, bring in the harvest! Squirrels, hurry — gather your nuts for the winter, bring in the harvest!

Even in Arizona we can feel when autumn is here. Finally, our early morning and evening air is no longer stifling hot. Cool breezes are blowing; get the sweaters or jackets out. The citrus on the trees are getting bigger and ripening. In another month, we will be bringing in our harvest of oranges, grapefruit, and lemons.

On Sunday, October 25, the congregation symbolically brought in the first fruit of the harvest by placing a fruit or vegetable on the communion table. These gifts were taken to Open Arms Food Bank in Gilbert to help feed the less fortunate in our community.

In the evening many of our church family came together to make the Harvest Home Dinner a wonderful success. The youth presented a meaningful program on stewardship for the contemporary worship service. This is what stewardship is about — giving the best of our talents and time, sharing with others, and expressing our love for one another. What a wonderful day of Stewardship!

On Sunday, November 8, you will have the opportunity to promise God the first fruits of your harvest of time, talents, and treasures by bringing forth your pledge card for 2010. God has given you many talents. Promise God that you will share your time and talents with others.

Everything we have comes from God. Promise to return to God a portion of your treasures. Perhaps consider writing your first check each month to God's work at Gilbert Presbyterian Church. That first check is symbolic that God is first in your heart — that Jesus is Lord of your life.

May God guide you as you make your pledge for 2010. Pray for guidance and direction as to how you can become a part of God's work at Gilbert Presbyterian Church.

Consider how Gilbert Presbyterian Church will grow with everyone's support of time, talents, and treasures. Come forth with your pledge, your promise to God, with love, joy, and thanksgiving in your heart on Sunday, November 8. Let us all look forward to a wonderful year working with God.

"I THINK I CAN"
December 2009

"Please Daddy, read me the story again." I loved the book, <u>The Little Engine That Could</u>. I wanted to hear it over and over. Only the little blue engine was willing to take the load of toys over the mountain to the good little girls and boys. All of the other engines kept making excuses as to why they could not help. The little blue engine huffed and puffed and slowly made it over the mountain as she repeated the words, "I think I can. I think I can. I think I can."

Santa brought me <u>The Little Engine That Could</u> one Christmas during World War II. Years later my mother said that at that time it was nearly impossible to find toys in the stores as raw materials were used for the tools and machines of war, not toys. So, my brother and I received books. I was too young to understand or comprehend the problems of the adult world, but I loved my book.

I will always remember the story of <u>The Little Engine That Could</u>. Throughout elementary school and years later whenever I faced a difficult task, I would repeat to myself, "I think I can. I think I can." When I finally made it over my mountain, I would say to myself, like the little blue engine, "I thought I could." What a wonderful message of optimism and perseverance for a child.

At times it is a challenge to find a meaningful gift

like <u>The Little Engine That Could</u>. It seems as if our children are inundated with toys and other material things. We adults are no different.

For this Christmas can we find gifts that will have a deep meaning for the recipient? Can we give a gift from the heart, one that always will be remembered? Perhaps the best gift of all might be a gift of time for our family and friends. Also, let us not forget our gifts to the Christmas Tree Angels. Can they receive from us something they will never forget — something they will always cherish and that will brighten their lives?

Not only is <u>The Little Engine That Could</u> a story of optimism and perseverance, but it is also a story of stewardship.

Can we be like the little blue engine, willing to help others in need? The other engines made excuses — too busy, too tired, and can't be bothered.

Our neighbors need us — our time, talents, and treasures. Let us not forget what Christmas is all about — the birth of the Christ Child and love for our fellow men. Take the time for worship, prayer, and devotion.

In the coming year, let us expand our acts of stewardship to something individually we never before tried. Perhaps we can serve in a shelter, lead the worship service, quilt, or play a musical instrument.

Be that little blue engine and say, "I think I can. I think I can."

2010

I WAS HUNGRY AND YOU GAVE ME
SOMETHING TO EAT

For I was hungry and you gave me something to eat, I was thirsty and you gave me something to drink, I was a stranger and you invited me in. I needed clothes and you clothed me, and I was sick and you looked after me, I was in prison and you came to visit me.

Matthew 25:35-36

MOVING FORWARD
January 2010

"Aidan, you can do it. You can crawl. Just lift your little hand up and forward." He seemed like he wanted to crawl. He kept eyeing a toy just out of his reach. He was on his hands and knees rocking his body back and forth. But the balance and coordination wasn't quite developed yet for crawling.

I was watching my little grandson roll, twist, and turn. He was constantly on the move. Nothing discouraged him. He kept trying to crawl. In a few days he will make it. Next he will be pulling himself up to a standing position, and soon after that will be his first step.

Babies seem to be programmed to develop and learn new skills. Before they completely achieve one goal they are working on the next. They are always on the move. Nothing stops them. Babies are persistent. They do not become discouraged. A little tumble will not deter a baby. And, if one should laugh at a baby, the baby will simply join in the fun.

Why is it as adults, we become leery of trying new skills? So many times we become discouraged if we can't succeed on the first try. We are worried about what other people might say. We are concerned that we might fail, so we don't even try. Yet, we were all babies once with the inherent persistence and desire we needed to develop essential skills.

This is a new year, a new decade — 2010. Now is the time to set a goal — to try at least one thing that you have never tried before. Is there a skill that might interest you? Try it — go for it. Is there an activity that you think you might like? Do it. Is there a committee that interests you? Yes, go and take part. When we learn new skills, we grow. With growth comes a fresh new outlook on our daily experiences.

Change makes life more interesting. Let this be the year to learn, develop, and achieve a new skill, a God-given skill.

Gilbert Presbyterian Church is celebrating its first twenty-five years. This year, 2010, is the beginning of our next twenty-five years. What an exciting time for GPC. Think about the goals for the church for this year. Envision the church in twenty-five more years. What changes would you like to see now and in twenty-five years from now? The decisions we make today will affect those in the future.

Happy New Year 2010 — a new year, a new decade.

What do we hope this year will bring? The same? Or, are we willing to move forward in both our personal lives and in the life of the church? What new skill can you bring to Gilbert Presbyterian Church? Let's carefully consider how we can serve God, church and community!

JOYFULLY GIVE
February 2010

A child clutches the candy bar tight in his hand. He does not want to share with his brother. "My brother can get his own candy," he shouts. His grip is so strong that the candy begins to melt from the pressure of his hand. He looks at his hand. What once was a well formed candy bar is now a gooey chocolate mess. He has nothing.

Another child gladly shares his candy bar with his brother. He carefully divides it, and his brother delights in the gift. Both children have a piece of the yummy sweet candy. Both are happy.

Are we not like a child with a candy bar? God has given us many talents and treasures; that is our candy bar. To some of us, God has given a Hershey bar, others Snickers, and perhaps some get a Milky Way or M & M's. Some might get the ultimate Millionaire Bar. These are God's gifts to us.

What are we doing with God's gifts? When we share our talent with others, that talent becomes better and stronger. It does not matter what that talent might be, whether it is planting seed and growing crops, working on computers, singing, playing an instrument, sewing quilts, leading worship or teaching a Sunday School class, greeting people, or serving in shelters.

With practice, we become more competent and skilled. Not only will others delight in our gifts, but we also will be joyous knowing we are serving God with our gifts. A talent not shared becomes weak and deteriorates with inactivity just as the child's chocolate bar melts when he holds it tight.

All that we are and everything we have comes from God. God has given generously to us; let us return a portion of that gift to Him. Allow God to guide and teach you when, where, and how to give. We grow spiritually and show the love of Christ when we joyfully share our talents and treasures with others.

"FAITH AS SMALL AS A MUSTARD SEED"
(Luke 17:6)
March 2010

I sat there in trepidation wondering what my ophthalmologist would say. I was in her office anxiously awaiting the results of my tests. A review of the month's events was running through my mind. At my annual routine eye exam my optometrist discovered hemorrhaging in my left eye. I had not noticed anything — no loss of vision.

I was referred to one eye doctor and he in turn sent me to another — one who specializes in glaucoma. Finally, she returned with the results. Yes, I have glaucoma, the progressive, non-curable eye disease.

Now the good news — glaucoma can be arrested with the application of eye drops. It only takes one small eye drop every evening, not much bigger than the proverbial mustard seed, to keep glaucoma in check. I must have faith. I have so much to be thankful for — my glaucoma was caught early.

We routinely exhibit faith in our medications. There are pills to lower our blood pressure or cholesterol and pills that help us get well if we are sick. There are vaccines to keep us from getting the flu or other diseases. Many of these medications are "packaged" as capsules or pills that are not much larger than a mustard seed.

Ideas as small as a mustard seed can germinate,

grow, and blossom into wonderful activities and programs. Greg Mortenson wrote of his ideas in his books, <u>Three Cups of Tea</u> and <u>Stones into Schools</u>.

Mortenson started with the idea to build one school in the mountains of Pakistan. He has now established, in the past sixteen years, more than 130 schools in Afghanistan and Pakistan in the heart of Taliban country.

Don Stephens had a dream to own and operate hospital ships that travel to the poorest countries needing medical care. He tells his story in the book, <u>Ships of Mercy</u>. Both men have faith in their ideas, ideas as tiny as a mustard seed.

What ideas do we have for Gilbert Presbyterian Church? Do we have faith as small as a mustard seed to make our plans grow and bloom?

Twenty-five years ago our church was founded on an idea. That idea has blossomed. Now where do we go from here?

With everyone working together, our ideas will continue to grow. Let us give thanks to God for all He has done for us by giving of our time, talents, and treasures. Help that mustard seed grow!

PASS IT ON
April 2010

The parents admire their newborn baby — so beautiful. He is a precious gift from God. Love flows from parents to child but the baby is too young to reciprocate their love.

The newborn is totally self-centered, completely me, me, me. "I want to be fed now! I don't care if my parents are tired. My tummy hurts, I want comfort now, and I will cry until I get it!" The parents give their little one unconditional love.

A month or so later the baby begins to respond to his parents' smiles, funny faces and noises. "Look, come quick, the baby has learned to smile." Two years later the toddler will share a piece of his cookie with his parents. The child is learning to love and share. The parents continually give their child unconditional love. They nurse the child through hurts and illnesses, encourage the child in his learning and development, and clothe, feed, and educate their child. The parents make personal sacrifices, but they don't mind because they love their child.

The child is now an adult and on his own. He comes to his parents and says, "How can I ever repay you? You have done so much for me. You have always been with me and encouraged me."

The parents reply, "We have all we need. Rather than repaying us, pass it on. Do for your children and love your children as we have loved you."

Years go by, and mom is now a widow. Each child comes and helps mom according to his or her abilities. The garage door will not open — son immediately comes over and the problem is solved. Difficulties with the computer — "Don't worry, I will help you Mom." Daughter says, "I will make you a necklace to match your new outfit."

"Come visit us, Mom, and we will take you to new places." "Come over for dinner and we will prepare the food." Her grown children help her because they love her, not because of what they might get from her. Mom might live alone, but she is never lonely for she has her children and grandchildren.

The above scenarios are repeated in many homes throughout the world. They have occurred in my family.

The love we show our children and what our children do for us is minuscule in comparison to what God has done for us. He has given us unconditional love and unconditional grace. He has given us His son, Jesus Christ, the ultimate gift of all.

"Oh, God, what can we do for you? Everything we are and everything we have comes from you. What can we give you?"

"Nothing. You cannot earn a star on a chart or work your way up to heaven. My grace and love to you are unconditional."

We cannot out-give God. However, we do have a tremendous responsibility to respond to God's love by sharing our time, talents, and treasures with others. Jesus is our mentor and guide. The Bible contains our instructions. Pass it on to others — God loves you. Christ loves you.

A LETTER TO MY GRANDDAUGHTER, DESIREÉ
May 2010

Dear Desi,

Congratulations on your many school achievements! Soon you will be walking down the aisle to the sound of "Pomp and Circumstance." Your very proud family — parents, brother, and grandparents — will be in the audience. Yes, your high school days are quickly coming to a close.

These last few years, I have watched you pour over college catalogues, reading course descriptions. You have visited several campuses.

Last November you flew to New London, Connecticut, and came home declaring Connecticut College was the place — your choice. The college is located in New London along the banks of the Thames River. Your pictures are very beautiful, but I cannot help but wonder why someone from Arizona would choose a college in the cold, snowy part of the country and so far away. You are drawn to Connecticut College like iron is attracted to a magnet — that is your school. And were you ever excited when they accepted you!

Upon hearing your good news, your Uncle Rodney said that our ancestor, Robert Morey, moved to New London, Connecticut, shortly after the Revolutionary War. His son, Ephraim, moved to Ohio in 1832. As you already know, your grandpa Roy and I moved from

Ohio to Arizona in 1962. Desi, you will be completing the circle when you leave Arizona for college in New London, 178 years after Ephraim left New London for Ohio.

It is difficult for us to imagine what it was like for the early pioneers to travel from one distant place to another. Perhaps Ephraim moved by using a wagon pulled by oxen or horses or maybe by a boat on the Erie Canal, or perhaps he used both modes of transportation. However he got to Ohio, he had to have a plan, a goal. He did know where he was going because he settled in that area along Lake Erie called the Connecticut Firelands.

In 1832, Ohio was still very much a wilderness. Can you imagine the hardships and challenges he must have endured? Ephraim persevered, though, letting go of the past and following his dreams on the rugged path to Ohio. What an inspiring story for you to follow!

Desi, you soon will be heading for Connecticut College. Even though your trip across the country by plane will be nothing in comparison to Ephraim's journey, the traits that served him well can inspire you as you begin college. He had to have a goal. He knew where he was going.

As you begin your studies, you too will need a plan. Decisions will have to be made as to your desired field. Test your goals — are they correct for you? As you progress in your studies you may need to make some corrections to your original plans. Many college students discover their goals change as they mature.

In college you will have challenges. At times it may seem like a rugged path. But remember the difficult days will pass and you will persevere. Just as Ephraim let go of his past and followed his dreams, you too will let go of your high school days and follow your dreams to the future.

From stories I have read, the early pioneers took their Bibles with them to their new homes on the frontier. Their spiritual life was very important to them. In 1620, 212 years before Ephraim's journey to Ohio, William Brewster led the Pilgrims on the Mayflower in worship and prayer. Yes, Desi, William Brewster, the spiritual leader of Plymouth Colony, is also our ancestor.

Take your Bible to college. Read it, pray for guidance, and thank God for all that He has given you. Remember, everything you are and everything you have comes from God.

Find time to help others and share your many talents when and where you can. Just as God led our ancestors safely across the ocean long ago, he will guide you on your up-coming journey.

With lots of love and best wishes for wonderful and successful years at Connecticut College, Grandma Eloise.

OUR BODIES BELONG TO GOD
June 2010

My kitchen table was stacked high with finals to be graded — the bane of a teacher. What a pile — will I ever finish? I felt stressed — I need chocolate. I have to have candy or cookies! An hour later, I had a sugar crash and needed more sweets.

That was the scene in past semesters, but not this year. Of course there are just as many papers, but I had no desire to eat sweets. Why no stress this year?

A day later after the grades were posted, I had to sort papers — some to be filed and others to be tossed. I looked around — no clear place for sorting. Yes, the floor! So I quickly sat on the floor, sorted, then without difficulty got back up again. I had not used the floor as a work space in years.

My granddaughter's high school graduation ceremony was coming up in two weeks. The family graduation dinner was at my home. Of course, that meant I had to clean the house, go to the store, cook the food and have everything ready by 4:30 p.m.

That evening, after a very busy day, I had no difficulty walking quickly from the parking lot up the ramp to Wells Fargo Arena on the ASU campus. From there, I climbed steep stairs to our seats.

In past years I would have been out of breath, but not this year. Why was I able this year to do the above activities without difficulty when in past years I would have been exhausted with an aching back? Why am I physically stronger and feel great? After forty years, how have I finally been able to lose weight?

The answer to all of the above questions is very simple — this year I exercise and eat a healthier diet.

In 1 Corinthians 6:19-20, Paul says that our bodies belong to God. "Do you not know that your body is a temple of the Holy Spirit, who is in you, whom you have received from God? You are not your own; you were bought at a price. Therefore, honor God with your body."

If our bodies belong to God, we must care for them with good diet and exercise.

My grandparents lived on a farm. Their foods were fresh fruits and vegetables. We rarely ate candy, and when we did, it was considered a special treat.

Their exercise was working the land and caring for the farm animals. I, like many others today, lead a more sedentary lifestyle. I have to search out my exercise. It is at the fitness center.

Today we are surrounded by an abundance of foods and drinks. The choices can be overwhelming. I must choose wisely.

Our bodies belong to God. We are to follow the teachings of Christ and practice good stewardship by sharing our time, talents, and treasures with others. Each of us has only a certain amount of discretionary income. If we are spending our hard-earned treasures on fast food, candy, cookies, sodas, and other high-calorie, low-nutrition foods, how can we give as Christ wants us to give to our church and non-profit organizations that work with those in need? How can we share our time and talents with others if we are feeling stressed and exhausted? Exercise relieves stress and makes our bodies stronger. Eating the right foods helps us feel better, and getting the right amount of rest rejuvenates our bodies. We must take care of ourselves first before we can help others. It is our duty to practice good health habits at home, work, church, and on vacation and pass on those habits to our children and grandchildren.

Our bodies belong to God. Honor God by taking care of your body so that you may do the work in His kingdom. Become that person that Christ wants you to become — a spiritually strong and healthy person ready and able to share your time, talents, and treasures with others.

A VOICE FROM THE PAST
July 2010

Last month my son-in-law called me and very excitedly said, "Listen to this. Your grandmother, Daisy Morey, wrote a paper titled, *Do We Appreciate the Age in Which We Live?* She read it at the Farmers' Institute held in Castalia, Erie County, Ohio, in 1905. Google her name and you will find it."

I did not know that she wrote an article that is now on the internet. I was picturing in my mind what she might have looked like reading her essay before a group of farmers and their families. She was 28 years old at the time and probably very stylishly dressed, a long dress with lace and frills and high button leather shoes. In 1905 my grandmother was a teacher in a one-room school house. This was before she got married. My mother was born five years later.

Daisy was a small woman, less than five feet tall and never weighed more than 100 pounds. Her independent spirit and outspoken manner more than made up for her small stature.

Here are a few excerpts from her essay written more than 100 years ago:

"Now the question to which I would call your attention today is: Do we appreciate these blessings of life and liberty for which our ancestors fought, and bled, and died? Or do we simply take it for granted that this age is the grandest in the world's history without stopping to realize how much sacrifice and privation these blessings cost? Are we utilizing our advantages and opportunities for self-improvement, and are we being benefited by them to the best of our ability?"

Grandma, those are good questions. When you wrote this article, the Civil War was still in people's memories — only 40 years in the past. Since the article was written, this country has fought in World War I and II, Korean Conflict, Vietnam War, Gulf War, and now Iraq and Afghanistan. At the end of May was Memorial Day, Flag Day in June, and now in July we celebrate Independence Day.

Have we truly honored our ancestors for their part in making this country great, or are those days just a day off work for us? Do we appreciate the service and sacrifice our men and women today are making for our country?

"And now let us compare for a while the present age, the one in which we live, with the age just passed, and then let us decide if we really appreciate our wonderful advantages."

Grandma goes on for more than a page, comparing the home of the pioneer with that of the present (1905) family. If we compare our lives today with Grandma's time, just think of the advantages we enjoy. In 1905, automobiles, electricity, and telephones were just coming into fruition. The Wright brothers made their historic first flight in 1903. Inside the home Grandma did not have our modern appliances. And of course,

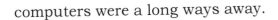

computers were a long ways away.

"By means of the various street car systems, education is brought almost to our very doors. When we consider how the pioneers' children had to walk perhaps miles through drifted snow and brave the dangers of the forests, it is little wonder that their education was neglected, but for us of this age there is no excuse for neglecting education, and the question in my mind is do we fully appreciate our advantages in this life?

"Never before in the history of the United States have schools of all kinds been so numerous as they now are; never have books been so cheap; never have there been so many public libraries, and the day is surely coming when, with the aid of pluck and ambition, the sons and daughters of the poor shall stand on the same educational basis as the wealthier classes."

Yes, Grandma, your future son-in-law was the person you described. With lots of pluck and ambition, he, at the age of eighteen, left his home on a small farm in Southern Ohio to attend college, graduate, and then become an engineer. He never returned to the poverty in which he was raised.

"With the principles and doctrines of Christianity instilled into the minds and hearts of the people by means of the church and Sunday school and other Christian organizations, love for humanity was never taught and practiced so much as at the present time. In almost every city or town, and throughout the counties are the finest of charitable institutions and hospitals where everyone is cared for in sickness regardless of his religion, his wealth, or his social rank. The remarkable surgical accomplishments and wonderful cures that are being affected every day are alone making this age one long to be remembered."

I wish we could honestly make your statements today concerning love for humanity as you did. Wouldn't you be surprised at all of the advancements in medicine today? And just think, Grandma, your great-granddaughter is a doctor, an occupation very few women attained in 1905.

"My friends, before we part today, let us decide that during the coming year, more than ever before in the past, we shall appreciate our blessings and advantages."

Yes, Grandma, your message was not only for your friends and family in 1905, but it is also for us in 2010. Do we truly appreciate our blessings and advantages? God has given us so much that we seem to expect our abundant gifts.

We need to stop, appreciate our blessings, and thank God for them. Everything we have and everything we are comes from God. Let us today, 2010, give thanks to God and return a portion of our blessings by sharing our time, talents, and treasures with others and let your statements concerning love for humanity come true.

The above article can be read in its entirety by googling Daisy Morey, *59th Annual Report of the Ohio State Board of Agriculture*, pages 672-675.

I WALKED WITH GOD!
August 2010

This summer I walked in the forests, meadows, mountains, and on busy city streets. I walked in the headlands overlooking the Pacific Ocean and on the beach of the Atlantic. I walked with friends and family. I walked with God.

I was on an Elderhostel tour of the National Parks in California. I walked with God among the giant Sequoia and Redwood trees. My fellow travelers and I were speechless as we exited the coach. We looked up and all we could say was "Wow!" We were surrounded by trees over a thousand years old and more than 300 feet tall, some as tall as a thirty-five-story skyscraper. The trees formed a living cathedral reaching to the heavens as if they were praising God.

I walked with God in Yosemite where every turn afforded another fantastic view of snow-melted water cascading over gigantic rock faces. This is God's magnificent country. I stood in front of the falls and felt a mist of cold clear water. I walked beside a stream created by the falling water and watched it rush over rocks and boulders ever churning and foaming as it twisted and turned its way down.

I walked with God on Mt. Lassen, a land of contrasts of ice and steam. We could only go a little beyond the Visitor Center as the road was closed due to snow. I stood in front of a bank of snow well over my head.

Yet steam was coming from holes in the mountainside. Boiling, bubbling mud was close by. All of this was a reminder that even though Mt. Lassen hasn't erupted since 1914-1917, it is a volcano. There was beauty in that mountain.

I walked with God along the streets of San Francisco. My friends and I ascended a very steep road to Lombard Street, "the most crooked street in the world." We walked six blocks up from Fisherman's Wharf. All along the way we kept encouraging each other, "Yes, we can make it. We think we can." There are times in our life when we are the encourager and other times we are the recipients of the encouragement. We finally reached the top and the view of the city and bay was fantastic. It was well worth the long climb.

Of course, what goes up must come down. Large hydrangea bushes lined Lombard Street and purplish-red fuchsia flowers were on the walls of the homes.

My walks in San Francisco took me past people begging and sleeping on the sidewalks and city steps. "Why, God have you led me on this path — to open my eyes to despair, suffering, and pain? What do you want me to do? There are so many needing help."

I walked with God to the Cabrillo Lighthouse and saw its beacon ever turning. It was built in 1909 to light the path for sailors and serve as a warning to keep away from the rocky shore. God, you gave us Jesus to be our lighthouse and guide.

I walked with God on the headlands of Mendocino in the early morning. No one was out at that hour but my roommate and me. We walked along a twisting path through tall grasses and wildflowers that overlooked the ocean. We heard the birds greet the new day with their chirps and songs.

The surf pounded against the rocks below in perfect

rhythm. There, oh God, we enjoyed your presence as beauty, peace, and quiet surrounded us with sounds of nature.

Three days after leaving the Pacific Ocean, my daughter and I were walking on the beach of Kiawah Island near Charleston, South Carolina. We saw pelicans dive perpendicularly into the Atlantic to catch their fish. We saw dolphins leap playfully in the sea. We saw the tracks of a giant sea turtle on the sand as it went from the water to the dunes. The beach was beautiful — white, soft, clean sand. In the early morning we saw the sunrise over the beach and water — a beginning of a bright new day. And our footprints from yesterday, completely erased by the incoming tide.

In Virginia, I walked with God as my three-year old grandson took my hand and walked with me in his neighborhood. "What should I say to him, God? What knowledge and wisdom should I impart?"

This summer I walked with God in California, South Carolina, and Virginia. I heard God in many places. God seemed to say, "Enjoy the beauty and sounds of nature, take care of the environment, give thanks and praise, encourage your friends, teach your children, help the less fortunate, and remember to let Jesus be your guide." I walked with God!

"FREELY YOU HAVE RECEIVED, FREELY GIVE" (MATTHEW 10:8)
September 2010

"What makes Mono Lake different from other lakes?" I kept asking my friends on the Elderhostel trip this summer. They made the lake seem so mysterious.

"Just wait," they said, "You will soon find out what is different about Mono Lake."

From Yosemite our coach climbed through the very beautiful snow-covered high Sierra Mountains. As we traveled east and descended the mountains, we looked out in the distance to a lake surrounded by desert. There it was, Mono Lake. The water looked so inviting, so blue. It looked no different from any other lake. But it is different, very different.

Mono Lake is located in the Great Basin in California. Five streams flow into Mono Lake, but no stream flows out. The only way for water to leave the lake is by evaporation, and that leaves the salts behind. It is highly alkaline (pH of 10) and almost three times as salty as the ocean. No fish can live in that water!

Along the water's edge and in the water there are large calcium carbonate towers called tufa. Tufa forms when freshwater springs (calcium ions) mix with the salty lake water (carbonate ions). Some towers have grown to almost thirty feet high. As I looked at those tufa pillars, I thought of Lot's wife looking back on

Sodom and Gomorrah and becoming a pillar of salt. Has Mono Lake turned its back on God and formed pillars of salt in its water?

Two days later we were at Lake Tahoe, a completely different lake. Water flows both in and out of Lake Tahoe. It is a fresh water lake alive with fish. Animals can drink from it. Lake Tahoe is always receiving water from rivers and always giving water to a river, a perfect balance created by God. Mono Lake keeps all the water it receives, it never gives. Mono Lake is brackish and dead.

God has given generously to us. Can we return a portion to Him? Jesus gave His disciples very simple instructions when He sent them out. He said, "Freely you have received, freely give" (Matthew 10:8).

Next month is Stewardship Month. Can we follow Jesus' command? Can we make a commitment to grow in giving, grow in faith, and grow in trust? In thanksgiving to God, let us give a portion of our time, talents, and treasures to others.

"LORD, WHEN DID WE SEE YOU?"
(Matthew 25:37)
October 2010

"For I was hungry and you gave me something to eat, I was thirsty and you gave me something to drink" (Matthew 25:35).

Never before have the food banks in the Valley been stretched so thin. Many people who are unemployed or underemployed are having a difficult time feeding their families. These are our neighbors and friends. Bring your food donations to church on Sunday, October 3, and they will be delivered to Guadalupe Presbyterian Church Food Pantry. Let us do our part so that others will have something to eat.

"I was a stranger and you invited me in" (Matthew 25:35).

The focus for Sunday, October 10, is to invite someone to church. That person might be your colleague from work or a family in your neighborhood. Perhaps, someone is waiting for an invitation from you. Welcome all who come and help make their experience a memorable and joyful one.

"I needed clothes and you clothed me" (Matthew 25:36).

There will be a clothing drive on Sunday, October 17. Bring new or slightly used blankets, socks, and jackets. Yes, it might not seem like autumn yet, but cooler weather is right around the corner. There are less fortunate people in our community who need donations of warm clothes.

"I was sick and you looked after me" (Matthew 25:36).

Haiti was devastated by an earthquake not long ago. They are still in need of our help. On October 24, we will be collecting items for care kits to send to Haiti. Join us in this gift of love.

Lord, when did we see you? We saw you, Lord, when we fed the hungry, invited a stranger, clothed the needy, and helped the sick and downtrodden. Jesus wants us to help others. We grow spiritually as we carry out acts of kindness and generosity.

To help us understand how much God has blessed us and to help us become aware of the needs of others, there will be a soup supper on October 24, Stewardship Sunday. That one bowl of soup will probably be more food than many people in the world eat in a day. Let us be thankful for all that God has given us.

All that we are and all that we have comes from God. We are very richly blessed. Let us share our time, talents, and treasures with others.

ST. FRANCIS OF ASSISI
November 2010

There it was, high on a flat mountain ridge — the most beautiful town with gleaming white stone buildings shining in the sunlight.

Above the city, wisps of cirrus clouds were streaking across the blue sky. I kept staring out the coach window as we were twisting up the mountainside. Along our way, we passed by olive groves, grape vineyards, grain fields, and small villages. We kept climbing higher to Assisi, Italy, birthplace and home of St. Francis.

Upon leaving the coach, my friends and I took an escalator upward among the trees until we reached the top. Inside the city walls, we walked on narrow twisting cobblestone roads and under medieval arches, stopping at a few sights along the way. We were on our way to visit the Basilica of St. Francis.

On the large expanse of lawn in front of the basilica were shrubs in the shape of the Greek letter Tau, capital T, and the letters PAX meaning peace. Francis signed his name with a T, to symbolize faithfulness to the end.

There are two main T-shaped parts to the basilica — upper and lower. The upper level is considered to be the first Gothic church in Italy. The artist Giotto in 1297 to 1300 painted 22 frescoes on the walls depicting scenes from the life of St. Francis. Immediately after St. Francis was canonized in 1228, the lower church was built. Both parts were completed by 1253. The tomb of St. Francis is beneath the lower church. Frescoes also adorn the walls of the lower church.

Francis was born in 1181 or 1182 to wealthy parents. His father was a cloth merchant. As a young man, Francis became a knight, but that did not last long as he was taken prisoner. After a year in jail, he still dreamt of military service. On a military campaign he heard the voice of the Lord saying, "Turn back." In Assisi he felt the need to give away his possessions to the poor. That strained the relationship with his father.

At a small church in ruin just outside the city walls, a voice from the crucifix said, "Go and repair my house which has fallen into ruin."

Francis proceeded to repair that church by selling draperies from his father's home. Francis then renounced his worldly goods and previous lifestyle; thereby he began his life of poverty, giving to the poor, helping the sick, traveling, and preaching from village to village. Francis took the teachings and commands of Jesus very seriously.

Francis is known as the patron saint of animals. There is a legend that he preached to the birds and the birds quietly listened to every word he said, and only when he finished did they chirp and flutter away. In another story, he tamed a wolf that had terrorized a city.

Francis is credited with having set up the first Nativity scene using live animals. He became very ill after receiving stigmata, the wounds of Christ. Francis died in 1226, only 44 years old.

With love and compassion in his heart, St. Francis led a life of following Christ. He gave his time, talents, and treasures to others. He was led by God and inspired by the Bible.

May we also be led by God as we consider our pledges and promises of time, talents, and treasures for the coming year. Let us pray for guidance as to how we can become a part of God's work here at Gilbert Presbyterian Church.

Consider how the church can grow with everyone's support. Let us all come forth with our pledges, our promises to God, with love, joy and thanksgiving in our hearts on Sunday, November 7.

A Simple Prayer of St. Francis:

Lord, make me an instrument of your peace:
  Where there is hatred...let me sow love.
  Where there is injury...pardon.
  Where there is discord...unity.
  Where there is doubt...faith.
  Where there is error...truth.
  Where there is despair...hope.
  Where there is sadness...joy.
  Where there is darkness...light.
Oh Divine Master, grant that I may not so much seek:
  To be consoled...as to console.
  To be understood...as to understand.
  To be loved...as to love.
For:
  It is in giving...that we receive.
  It is in pardoning...that we are pardoned.
  It is in dying...that we are born to eternal life.
Amen.

THE SCROVEGNI CHAPEL
December 2010

Fifteen minutes — that is all. If you could travel back in time, for only fifteen minutes, what part of Jesus' life would you want to see?

Would you want to be there when Jesus was born in the stable or with the shepherds as they followed the star to Bethlehem? Would you want to be there when the Magi came to honor and worship Him; bringing gifts of gold, frankincense, and myrrh?

Perhaps you would want to see Him baptized. Would you want to be present when he spoke to the crowds or healed the sick? What about the last week of His life? Would you want to be there among the crowds waving palm branches, or when He cleansed the temple, or at His trial, or when they crucified Him?

Do you want to look into the empty tomb? Or would you rather have your fifteen minutes spent with the disciples on Pentecost? Perhaps you would want to distribute your fifteen minutes throughout His entire life observing each major event for just a few moments.

This past October, I spent my fifteen minutes with Jesus. Of course I could not physically transport myself back in time to Jesus, but I did experience his presence emotionally and spiritually. I saw His entire life painted in sequence on the walls of the Scrovegni Chapel in Padua, Italy. The forty frescoes in three tiers completely covered the walls from floor to ceiling.

Stars painted on the blue ceiling almost looked like they were twinkling. Giotto painted the Scrovegni Chapel from 1303 to 1305.

One could feel the emotions of the people in the paintings. The frescoes were so realistic that I felt drawn into the picture. In the Nativity scene, Mary appeared sad as she looked into the eyes of her newborn son. Perhaps, Giotto was conveying the feeling that Mary had a premonition of what would happen to her child.

The background of a bright blue sky enhanced the scene of the Magi bringing their gifts. Giotto painted that as a very pleasant and happy event — even the blue-eyed camels were smiling.

Fifteen minutes. That was all — we were ushered out to allow the next group to come in and experience the beauty.

Giotto left a fantastic legacy for many generations. His frescoes in the Scrovegni Chapel have endured for over 700 years. He probably never imagined that his paintings would be enjoyed far into the 21st century.

I wonder if we, too, might not be aware of how we may influence others. Perhaps it is just our smile or the time we take listening to someone that will affect that person forever. Or, maybe helping someone through a problem or difficult time, or sharing a gift is an act that makes a lasting impression.

God has blest us with many gifts and talents, but the greatest gift of all is Jesus Christ. What do we bring to the Christ Child this Christmas? With love and thanksgiving to God in our hearts let us share our time, talents, and treasures with others.

Pass on the love of Christ.

2011

LET THE LITTLE CHILDREN COME TO ME

Then little children were brought to Jesus for him to place his hands on them and pray for them. But the disciples rebuked those who brought them. Jesus said, "Let the little children come to me and do not hinder them, for the kingdom of heaven belongs to such as these." When he placed his hands on them, he went on from there.

Matthew 19:13-14

THE WINTER STORM
February 2011

"Is it possible for me to depart Roanoke, Virginia, tomorrow morning to beat the winter storm coming to the Southeast?"

I was calling U.S. Airways on Sunday, January 9, after a week visiting my daughter and her family in Roanoke. Monday afternoon I was scheduled to fly to Charlotte, North Carolina, followed later by a flight to Phoenix.

The weather report predicted a big storm coming through Georgia and the Carolinas. That was on top of snow they had already received on Saturday. I did not relish the thought of being stuck in Charlotte.

"Can I change my ticket so that I may leave earlier to avoid the snowstorm and not go through Charlotte or Atlanta? I don't care where I might have to go to get to Phoenix, but just get me out of the path of the storm."

The lady at U.S. Airways said, "Yes, you can leave Roanoke at 6:30 in the morning, go to LaGuardia, and then to Phoenix."

"Is the flight to Phoenix from LaGuardia a direct flight?" I asked.

"Yes, it is a direct flight."

"Good, I will take it. And what is the charge for changing a flight?"

"None," she said, "You are changing your flight

because of the weather."

I was feeling very smug and proud of myself for getting an early flight out so that I could avoid the storm. The next morning was cold when my daughter took me to the airport, but as yet no snow. It was not expected in Roanoke until the afternoon. I won! I beat the storm!

It was a wonderful flight — very smooth. As we approached New York, the early morning sun was shining on snow-covered ground. That was the snow left over from their previous storm. All the roads were clear.

I had a couple of hours between flights so I meandered around the concourse to the shops and had a bite to eat. Finally, I wandered over to my gate for my flight to Phoenix, but a sign at the gate made my heart sink.

The sign was repeating: Phoenix/Charlotte, Phoenix/Charlotte... My direct flight to Phoenix was going through Charlotte!

"I don't want to go to Charlotte! That is where the winter storm is headed!" I had assumed my direct flight was non-stop. It wasn't. It was stopping in Charlotte. "Oh, please, dear God, don't let me get stuck in Charlotte. I want to get home tonight." I prayed.

I sat anxiously looking out my window as we were flying into Charlotte. All the neighborhoods were completely white. Streets were obliterated by the snow. It looked beautiful but eerie. There were no vehicles on the roads!

Finally I saw one car on the partially cleared freeway. In the middle of the day, only one vehicle was moving! Monday, and it was still snowing in Charlotte — ever since Sunday evening. The plane was landing in the middle of the winter storm (the storm I had tried so hard to avoid)!

I got off the plane in Charlotte and wandered around near the gate. I noticed on the board that half the flights in and out of Charlotte were cancelled. I prayed, "Please don't let my flight be cancelled. Let it take off safely and continue to Phoenix."

I put my faith in God and in the pilot to get me home. My prayers were answered as the gigantic plane rose ever so smoothly into the air. There was no problem with either landing or taking off in Charlotte. "Thank you, God, for leading us out of the storm."

Isn't that typical of life? We plan and then something happens — a storm. Our plans might be side-tracked, changed, or completely shelved.

Many times we need a "Plan B," but sometimes even "Plan B" goes awry. What to do?

We call on God to help us through the storm. We pray. No matter how cold or dark a day might be, God is always there waiting for our prayer. Day or night, a storm or a clear sunny day, God is always our pilot.

And if our friend or neighbor is experiencing a storm, we listen, comfort, and offer a prayer. Isn't that what Jesus wants us to do — lend a helping hand? The best gift we can give to others is our love and a gift of ourselves — our time, talents, and treasures.

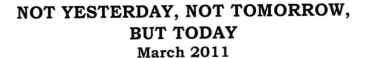

NOT YESTERDAY, NOT TOMORROW, BUT TODAY
March 2011

I enjoy playing the hand bells. Their tone is perfect — so clear and melodious — and never out of pitch.

It is fun to create different sound effects from the same bell. At times we might shake the bell, swing it at our side, strike it on the table, hit it with a mallet, or hold our thumb on the bell. Different techniques of ringing produce a variety of effects.

An ever-constant challenge while playing the bells is keeping our minds completely focused. If we fret over mistakes that we already have made, we are likely to miss our notes. If we are unduly anxious about the score on the next page, again we will probably make mistakes with the immediate measure. When playing bells or any other musical instrument, we must use our minds and hands as one in the present moment with little concern about the past or future. We cannot change what has already been played. We cannot replay the past.

In a similar manner, it does not do us any good to worry about later notes. When we concentrate on playing the immediate measure correctly with proper notes, time, and dynamics, we will harmonize with others and our music will sound beautiful.

Life is the same way. If we live a life filled with "if

only" or "should have," we will lose out on our present moment. Just as we cannot replay a bell, we cannot replay our lives. It is fruitless to be worried about the future.

The future, as we envision it, might not even come about. Yes, we need to plan for the future, but realize that God might have other desires for us. Be ready today, not yesterday or tomorrow but today to hear God's voice speak through prayers, other people, or in the silence of the night.

When our minds are completely focused on the present moment, we will see the beauty of the earth, the sunrise and sunset, and stars and moon in the night sky. We will notice God's wonderful creation.

By living in the present, we can expect to enjoy and pay attention to our family and friends and know when they need us. Not worrying about yesterday or tomorrow allows us to use our talents on this day's challenges. Concentrating on today, we will be able to be creative because we will see what needs to be done.

To live life to the fullest, live in the present moment — not yesterday, not tomorrow, but today.

Pay attention to others, help others, and harmonize with others. Be in tune and help make that beautiful music.

Everything we have is a gift from God. This day, return to God a portion of your time, talents, and treasures for the work in His kingdom.

IRIS — A SYMBOL OF REBIRTH AND RENEWAL
April 2011

It was last November and my friend had given me some bulbs from her garden. She was thinning out her irises. I looked at the lumpy, misshaped balls. There were a few dead leaves sticking out of them. Would those bulbs come to life? They looked dead.

My daughter-in-law, grandson, and I dug holes in my raised garden and carefully placed an iris bulb into each hole. Next, my grandson planted some pumpkin seeds from his Halloween jack-o-lantern. Would any of this grow? Did I have faith?

By February I had noticed thin green leaves pushing out of the ground from the bulbs. Each day they grew taller and taller. From those leaves, stalks began to grow and at the end of the stalks, buds were forming. As time went on, more buds formed on the stalks. Then the first bloom arrived on Monday, March 28.

I very excitedly told my friend that the irises she had given me were blooming. The stalk measured 3 feet tall. That one bloom was very beautiful — purple with gold in the center — wide open, swaying in the breeze on a beautiful day. Other buds will soon open to form flowers. Many of the stalks have 4 or 5 buds each.

My irises have been reborn — once looking dead

but now renewed. Out of a lump called a bulb, they have been resurrected. Now their beauty shines in my back yard.

Springtime is the time for our spiritual renewal. What new beginnings do we anticipate for our lives? How can we renew our faith in Christ? Share with others. Give our time, talents, and treasures to the work of God.

A LETTER TO MY LITTLE GRANDDAUGHTER
May 2011

My Dearest Little Alana,

It was Tuesday, April 19, 2011, and I had just finished my lunch when your daddy phoned me and said, "Come and see your granddaughter. She is here." I heard your first cry in the distance.

You were barely an hour old when I arrived at the hospital. Your mommy was holding you. You were tightly wrapped and snuggly with only your little face and chubby cheeks sticking out of the blanket. Your skin was very soft and delicate, and your hair was dark like your mom's.

You were surrounded by love in that hospital room — your mommy and daddy, big brother, Aidan, two grandmas, grandpa, and an aunt. There we were, all taking turns holding you, rocking you, and examining your perfect little body. Alana Michelle, you were named, after your daddy, Alan Michael.

The day you were born, the palo verde tree in my front yard was completely ablaze with golden color. Spring is here! My aloe plant was also blooming. A hummingbird was flitting among the blossoms gathering nectar. Even my prickly pear cactus was budding.

A few weeks before your birth, my purple irises

opened up and exposed their beautiful golden centers.

Last November a friend of mine gave me some bulbs as she was thinning out her bed of flowers. Each bulb was a misshapen brownish lump waiting for the right conditions of soil, nutrients, and water in order to come to life. In God's time they sprouted green leaves, then a stalk, and finally beautiful iris flowers.

Alana, what a wonderful time to be born — there is new growth everywhere! Buds and flowers are all around us — the beauty of spring.

Alana, we can learn many lessons from the flowers. Just as my bulbs sprouted leaves and grew, you too will grow and mature in God's time. My flowers bend in the wind and turn their blossoms to the sun. Likewise, when we are faced with problems and challenges, we too need to bend and turn our faces to the sun.

Frequently, a little light from God will help us discover solutions to our problems. I have seen poppies in the desert grow and bloom around rocks and crevices.

A rocky path or an obstacle for us can also be an opportunity for growth. Alana, one of my favorite Bible verses is, "Who of you by worrying can add a single hour to his life? And why do you worry about clothes? See how the lilies of the field, grow they do not labor or spin. Yet I tell you, that not even Solomon in all his splendor was dressed like one of these" (Matthew 6:27-29).

Alana, God takes care of the flowers and birds, so He will take care of you. Give your worries and concerns to God. As you grow and mature, take care of the earth. Love and appreciate nature. Look at the beauty all around you and thank God for His creation.

Alana, you were born at a very special time of the year — during Holy Week — between Palm Sunday and Easter. This is the time to reflect on what Christ has done for us. He has given us His all. He has given His life for us.

As you grow, you will learn about Jesus and that Jesus loves you. Learn to lead the life that He wants you to live. Learn to help others and share your time, talents, and treasures.

With lots of love, Grandma

"IT TAKES A VILLAGE TO RAISE A CHILD"
June 2011

As soon as I heard those first few measures of "Pomp and Circumstance," I immediately thought of all the many graduations I had previously attended — first mine then my children's graduations from junior high, high school, community college, university, and medical school. The wonderful memories brought tears to my eyes.

A handsome young man led his fellow classmates down the center aisle and up a few stairs to take their places on the stage. He looked confident and proud in his cap and gown. I wondered what he was thinking. Was he thinking about all his hard work and achievements this past year? Perhaps he was thinking about the friends he had made and the fun he had with them. Or, maybe he was contemplating his next big step. Where would that lead him? I wondered what degree he had earned — bachelors or masters?

No, he was not receiving any degree. That will come later, much later. The young man leading the graduates was my grandson, Nathan Emeott, age 5, graduating from kindergarten at Country Hills Montessori School in Farmington Hills, Michigan.

The kindergarten and preschool classes together sang songs accompanied with hand motions and/ or foot stomping. For one song, the children played musical instruments. Two songs were sung in Spanish. There were fifty children (three classes) on stage performing. They looked so cute.

After their performance, the graduates were called one at a time to shake hands with the director and receive his/her diploma. Yes, they did wear white gowns and mortarboards, complete with white tassels. My daughter and I marveled at how well behaved the children were as they stood on risers on the stage. The teachers were terrific working with the little ones. We said that if we or any other parents were in charge, it would have been complete chaos.

The next day Nathan went to Sunday school while we attended church. In the afternoon we went to Nathan's flag football game. The rules are different for flag football than for regular football.

Of course, there was no tackling and the coaches were allowed on the field during the game. Everyone had a chance to play. Scores were not kept. The importance of the game was learning the different positions, team play, and good sportsmanship. Nathan loves the game. He loves to run.

Yes, Hillary Clinton, you are right, "It takes a village to raise a child." A village comprised of dedicated teachers who work with our children in reading, math, science, history, geography, foreign languages, music, and art is needed.

It takes a village of coaches and scout leaders. And let us not forget our Sunday school teachers and others in our churches.

When children are baptized in the Presbyterian Church, the congregation promises to be a part of the child's spiritual upbringing. Are we living up to our commitment and promise to nurture and guide our children on their Christian path? Are we doing our part in teaching our children to know and love Jesus? Are we teaching them how to pray?

All of us can help children appreciate their many gifts that God has given them and teach them to share a portion of those gifts with others.

Are you setting a good example by praying for guidance and sharing your time, talents, and treasures for God's work at Gilbert Presbyterian Church?

Remember, children learn best by watching others.

THANK YOU, GOD!
July 2011

The breeze felt warm, even though it was only 6 a.m. I knew that it would be a hot day. This would probably be my last long bike ride until the temperature cooled down.

I really enjoy my bike, a 2010 Christmas present to myself. My bike is a pink Hawaiian beach bike with hibiscus flowers painted on the frame and seat. A horn in the shape and colors of a parrot is perched on the handlebar. I named my bike The Pink Panther and of course my parrot is Polly.

The Pink Panther, Polly, and I are off to explore the bike trails around Gilbert. I'm ready to go with helmet on, two water bottles, garage door opener and house keys in my basket. I follow the bike lane down Neely Street and pass a school.

A month ago I saw children playing on the school grounds. Sometimes they would wave to me as I rode by. I catch the bike trail at the end of Neely where the road stops at the railroad tracks.

I feel like I'm in another world when I'm on my bike. It is so relaxing. Because the pace is slower, I notice the trees, flowers, birds, and animals more than when I am driving. The bike trail takes me past horse properties. I see horses and goats, and I hear roosters crowing and birds chirping. I enjoy the trail as it runs along the south side of Freestone Park. The air feels cooler there because of all the grass.

My favorite part of the trail is half-way between Val Vista and Greenfield where a north/south path intersects the east/west path. It is so quiet at that intersection — a half mile in every direction from the major streets. I hear and see only the sights and sounds of nature — no traffic. It is like a country oasis in the middle of a busy city.

The trail is very wide in that area. Its concrete path meanders by a white fence. It is fun to ride up and down the dips in the path. The dips are there for the rain water to drain from the neighborhood streets into the desert. On the other side of the fence are large beautiful homes. I enjoy riding past the homes and noticing their design and landscaping. Each home and yard is different.

When I bike, I see walkers, joggers, other bikers, and sometimes people on horseback. Everyone is friendly. We all greet one another with a big smile, a wave, and a quick hello. There is no road rage on the bike trail.

I stop to drink my water under the shade trees. It is getting hot, so I head for home leaving my country oasis of peace and quiet. I'm back into the city again, crossing the busy streets and hoping that cars will stop for the traffic lights on the trail. I have only been gone for two hours — a most relaxing ride.

When I'm on my bike rides, I feel close to God. I notice the beauty of His creation — the animals, trees, flowers, desert plants and rocks. I feel the warmth of the sun and see the wisps of clouds in the sky. I say thank you, God, for your creation. When a stranger passes me and waves hello, I also think of my friends and family and say thank you to God for all those who have enriched my life — even people I encounter for only a brief moment.

As I pass schools I say thank you, God, for the opportunities to obtain an education. I bike passed a church and say thank you, God, for the freedom we have to attend the church of our choice. I stop, drink water, and say thank you, God, for the fresh, clear, clean water readily available in our homes. My bike ride becomes a prayer of thanksgiving.

God has given us many gifts and treasures. What can we do for Him? How can we ever thank Him?

We can spread the news of His Son, Jesus Christ. We can follow His teachings by loving and serving others. In appreciation for our many blessings, let us share our time, talents, and treasures.

RING...RING...IS ANYONE THERE?
August 2011

What was that I hear — classical music in the background during the morning talk program on the radio? That is not their usual routine. I parked my car at Chandler-Gilbert Community College and sat there for a moment enjoying the music.

I turned off the ignition and held the key in my hand. The music was still playing! That is impossible — the key is in my hand and the motor is turned off. The radio cannot be playing, but it is. Wait! That's not the radio; it's my cell phone.

I did not even recognize the sound of my own cell phone as I rarely turn it on. However, for some reason it was on that morning. I keep telling my friends and family that my cell phone is for my emergencies, not theirs, so my phone is always off.

Do we look upon God the same way as I view my cell phone? Do we only call on God in case of our emergency? "Listen God, I have this big problem and you have to solve it for me. OK? I need your answer now. But God, don't come to me if you want my help. I will not be tuned in."

Is that our attitude? Or, "God, I don't recognize your voice. Are you trying to contact me? There is so much noise in today's world. I cannot hear you." Do we ignore God?

Perhaps God is calling us, calling our name.

Perhaps God is wanting our help and seeking it. Are we able to listen to the voice of God? Can we hear God in the stillness of the night? Can we listen to God speak through the drops of rain and the laughter of children?

Can we see God in the beauty of the sunset, the rainbow, or in the tall mountain peaks? Can we see Him in the flowers in the garden or in the birds flying by? Is God speaking to us through the problems and trials of our fellow man? Are we listening? Can we hear?

Yes, we are here! We must listen. We need to be ever mindful to God's calling. We must be willing to help. All that we are and everything we have comes from God. With thanksgiving in our hearts, let us practice the love of Jesus Christ — the greatest gift from God. Let us be willing to share a portion of our abundance by giving of our time, talents, and treasures to others.

Answer God's call, listen to Him speak, and then allow Him to lead your way.

AN EXPEDITION OF PEACEMAKING
September 2011

My fellow travelers and I hurried to the water's edge and climbed into a keelboat. We were on a Road Scholar Tour (Elderhostel) pretending to be taking off with Lewis and Clark on their voyage from St. Charles, Missouri, to the Pacific Ocean.

However, the boat we were in could not go anywhere. It was tied to the dock. Our boat was a replica of the keelboat that Lewis and Clark used for their travels up the Missouri River in May 1804. It took Lewis and Clark 17 months to complete the voyage from St. Charles to the Pacific Ocean going by boat, horseback, and foot. It took us 17 days to cover the same territory traveling by motor coach.

We were following in the footsteps of Lewis and Clark. The historians on our tour frequently read from their journals. We were reliving the voyage of the Corps of Discovery. We climbed Spirit Mound in the Southeastern corner of South Dakota (Native American tribes have a legend that the mound is inhabited by spirit beings only 18 inches tall).

Lewis and Clark recorded in their journals that they climbed the mound on a very hot day. We did the same, and it too was a hot day. But the view was fantastic, well worth the climb. Pretty little wildflowers grew along our path, but we didn't see any spirit beings.

A few days later, we visited the Knife River Indian

Village in North Dakota. We sat inside large dome-shaped lodges, replicas of those built 200 years ago. We listened to stories of how the lodges were made and heard the melodious tones of a hand-carved flute. This is where Lewis and Clark met Sacagawea and her husband Charbonneau.

On August 8, we climbed Pompey's Pillar in Montana where Clark carved his name on a large rock outcropping. It is the only physical evidence of the expedition that remains today. The Pillar is named after Sacagawea's son. We climbed 200 wooden steps to see his signature. Again, the 360-degree view for miles around was fantastic and well worth the climb.

We also saw the Great Falls of the Missouri River. Actually, there is a series of five falls that the Corps of Discovery had to portage around. The tallest, Great Falls, is almost 100 feet high. We gingerly walked across a swinging bridge in order to get a closer and more wonderful view of the falls.

On August 10 we got our boat ride. The boat was a tour boat, not of Lewis and Clark vintage. We went through a beautiful steep-sided canyon on the Missouri River. As we traveled by water, the canyon walls appeared to open and close across the river — an illusion due to the bend in the river. Lewis and Clark called this the Gates of the Rocky Mountains.

We finally arrived at the headwaters of the Missouri River. After climbing a hill, we were able to overlook the confluence of three rivers that form the great Missouri. The rivers meander around a flat plane before joining to become the Missouri. Lewis and Clark named the rivers after influential men of their time: the Jefferson (President), the Madison (Secretary of State), and the Gallatin (Secretary of the Treasury).

We had it easy traveling through the Bitterroot

Mountains. We even hiked a little way on the Lolo Trail. Lewis and Clark had to fight their way through snow, wind, and cold on horseback and walking. Finally they made it to the Snake River and then the Columbia. It was relatively easy sailing from there, downhill all the way. The Corps of Discovery rejoiced when they finally viewed the Pacific Ocean. We saw a replica of Fort Clatsop, their winter home. We saw the Columbia River empty into the ocean.

The tour group had mixed emotions as we stood on the white sandy beach of the Pacific Ocean. We rejoiced that we had completed our trip, but we were sad knowing that soon we would be leaving the beautiful country and our fellow travelers. Our wonderful tour was over. All we had to do was to catch our plane home. The Corps of Discovery had another year of travels retracing their route home to St. Charles, Missouri.

Over two hundred years ago, Lewis and Clark traveled in the spirit of peace across what was the new American territory of the Louisiana Purchase. At that time it was unfamiliar country inhabited by people whose language they could not speak. They came in peace, trading goods, giving gifts, and presenting the Jefferson Peace Medal to the native peoples.

We too will have the opportunity to plant seeds of peace in foreign lands by giving a peacemaking offering on World Communion Sunday, October 2. This offering is one of four special offerings designated by the Presbyterian Church. Our donations will help promote justice and peace, both locally and abroad.

Here is an opportunity for us to practice stewardship by sharing our gifts with others. We are richly blessed by God. Let us thank Him for our many blessings and bring our peacemaking offering on October 2.

RUN FOR GOD!
October 2011

It was a beautiful autumn day. The weather was perfect. We finally made it through the sizzling hot summer and now we could enjoy the outdoors.

It could have been any day in late October of any year but it wasn't. It was 1964. I had finally completed a particularly long math assignment for one of my courses at Arizona State University. I needed to take a break and go for a walk in the refreshing air. It was so nice outside. I was enjoying my stroll when, on a whim, I took off jogging.

I had jogged only a few steps when a police officer in his patrol car stopped me. "Why are you running? Are you running from someone? May I take you where you will be safe?" I assured him that I was fine. There was no problem; I just felt like jogging. Well, that ended my running career, or so I thought.

Thanksgiving Day 2010 — it was another beautiful autumn day. Thanksgiving dinner would be at my son's home. I was at my house making zucchini bread. According to my children and their spouses, Thanksgiving would not be complete without mom's zucchini bread, our family's favorite.

I decided to go for a walk while the bread was baking. I felt great, everything was right with my world. Then, on a whim I started to jog a few steps. I walked and jogged, walked and jogged all around the block. I kept looking over my shoulder to see if anyone was watching me. As soon as a car came by I stopped jogging and returned to walking. I was just waiting for someone to stop me from running. But this time, no one did.

I told my personal trainer what I had done. "Should I be jogging at my age?"

She was excited. "Yes, you are strong and you faithfully exercise, so you can jog. But no more than one day per week and continue to alternate walking and jogging. Each time, try to jog a little farther. Listen to your body, and if your body says stop, you stop."

At the end of January, I finally was allowed to jog twice a week. Then I really became excited when I jogged a half mile without walking. Before I knew it, I could jog one mile. By July I was jogging 2 ½ miles twice a week on the indoor track at Freestone Recreation Center. I was not fast, but I kept going.

In August I heard that the Susan G. Komen, 5K/Half Marathon would be held November 6 in Scottsdale/Tempe. The runners in the 5K will go around Tempe Town Lake. I asked my trainer, "Do you think I could do a 5K?"

"Yes, definitely go for it." I am now training for the race by jogging three times a week, and increasing the distance each week. On November 6, I will fulfill my promise to run/jog in the 5K and help raise funds for the Susan G. Komen Marathon for the Cure.

Sunday, November 6, is also an important day in the life of Gilbert Presbyterian Church. It is Stewardship Commitment Sunday. We will come forth with our pledge cards promising to share our time, talents, and treasures for the work at GPC. We are truly grateful for God's abundant gifts. And, the greatest gift of all is Jesus Christ.

Pass on the love of Jesus, His teachings, and share with others. Pledge to work in God's kingdom. Remember God uses everyone, even the slow runners. While you prayerfully consider your pledge to GPC, also consider making a promise to help one of our community's organizations that serve the sick, homeless, and needy. What a wonderful way to experience and grow in stewardship. Share with joy your time, talents, and treasures, spread love, and run for God!

Mark the date of Sunday, October 23, on your calendar. Join us for a potluck supper at 5:30 p.m. prior to the Contemporary Service. It will be a Feast of Family Favorites. Share a dish that is a family favorite. I just might bring my zucchini bread.

GOD'S PEOPLE CONNECTING
November 2011

There was not a cloud in the clear blue sky. A gentle breeze was blowing. The oppressive summer heat had finally loosened its grip. It was a perfect autumn afternoon for bike riding. I headed down my favorite bike path, followed the trail from the railroad tracks west of Gilbert Road to Freestone Park, and rode to Val Vista and then Greenfield.

As I was biking, I looked up and saw the electric power lines that crisscross the valley. Some wires were hanging from the top of thick, giant-size poles embedded in the ground. Other wires were hanging from structures that looked like enormous erector sets. I wondered what power station those electric lines were coming from.

We cannot see the electricity flowing through the wires, but we know it is there. We experience electric power by flipping a light switch in our homes or turning on our television, computer, coffee maker, vacuum cleaner or any of our many electronic gadgets. We know when our home electric lines are making a connection with the power station.

Likewise, if we lose connection either by something so simple as an appliance becoming unplugged or from a much greater problem such as a power outage, we immediately know there is a problem. Sometimes during power outages, other lines take up the slack so that we will continue to have power. We are so dependent on electricity that it is difficult to imagine life without it.

In some ways, are we not like an electronic gadget in our home? We depend upon a source of power and that is God. We cannot see His power flowing to us, but we experience His power. It is impossible to imagine life without God. Through God we are all connected one to another. And if someone experiences a loss of power, then we must come together to help that person regain physical and spiritual strength.

All we are and everything we have is a gift from God. He has given us the power and strength to create and use our talents. He has given us time and our treasures. God supplies us with our needs. He has given us the greatest gift of all — Jesus Christ.

Connect to God. Connect to Jesus. Allow Him to be your guide and show you the way. Connect with your friends, family, church, and community. Connect with those who need your help. Remember, GPC also stands for God's People Connecting.

On Sunday, November 6, bring forth your pledge of time, talents, and treasures for 2012; and connect with fellow believers in Christ.

WIN THAT PERSONAL FIRST
December 2011

Up ahead I could see the finish line. I increased my jogging speed. A clock above our heads counted down the minutes and seconds. It said 53 minutes, but from the sidelines people were cheering us on as if we were the first ones in.

I won — not by running faster than anyone else, but by achieving a personal goal of jogging five kilometers around Tempe Town Lake in less than one hour!

Upon crossing the finish line, we all received a well earned bottle of water, a large 5K medal, fruit and other snacks. We congratulated each other. There were a thousand runners, and we all rejoiced in our own personal sense of accomplishment. The weather was perfect. The lake sparkled in the morning sun — a day I will never forget. My first race ever!

When we do something for the first time, we are so enthusiastic and energized. The very thought of accomplishment is exciting. It is an experience we never forget. Yet, at times, doing something for the first time can be scary. Our thoughts can get in our way. We might be afraid to begin or want to quit before we hardly get to the starting line.

A month before my race, I was wondering why I had signed up. What was I thinking? My trainer would not let me quit. Then I hurt my knees during a practice run. I was devastated. I had to take two weeks off from jogging. My trainer said, "Anyone who runs will at some time get hurt. Your knees will be fine by race time. You can do it." She was right.

Before we begin something new, we might be afraid that we aren't good enough. We worry that we can't succeed and that we will make mistakes. The first time trying anything will not be our best — better comes with practice and yes, we will make mistakes. However, we will learn from our efforts.

I well remember my first day teaching at a community college. It was an evening course, College Algebra. The textbooks were not in so neither the students nor I had a book. I made up a wonderful review of beginning algebra for that first class. It was a great lesson until one brave person spoke up and said, "Mrs. Annis, we don't understand a word you are saying."

I forgot the first rule of good teaching practices — find out what the students know before teaching the lesson and don't assume anything. I'm sure my students of thirty years ago have forgotten algebra, but I have not forgotten my lesson. Is it worth it to try something new and out of our comfort zone whether it is jogging or teaching? Definitely yes! We grow with new experiences.

Can you imagine if two thousand years ago Mary had said to the angel, "I am not qualified to give birth to the Son of God. I have never taken care of a baby before, let alone a Savior. Choose someone else to be the mother." I am sure she too had moments of trepidation, asking "Why me, Lord?" But Mary never said no. She did what God asked of her, and Jesus was born.

This coming year, experience the excitement of doing something for the first time. Tackle it enthusiastically.

Let it energize you. You will not be perfect, but you will learn and grow from the experience.

Serve on a committee, teach a Sunday school class, or help the needy and less fortunate. Choose something that is out of your comfort zone. Pray for guidance as to what that experience should be. Allow God to lead you and help you along the way. Serve others as Jesus has taught us.

Give generously as you share with others your time, talents, and treasures. Have a wonderful and enriching experience and win that personal first.

2012

I AM THE GOOD SHEPHERD

I am the good shepherd; I know my sheep and my sheep know me – just as the Father knows me and I know the Father – and I lay down my life for the sheep.

John 10:14-15

JOURNEY INTO 2012
January 2012

I well remember that day 50 years ago when my husband, Roy, and I moved from Ohio to Arizona. It was an exciting time, packing our station wagon with our possessions, carefully studying the road atlas, and making the long trip across the country. Even though it didn't seem like we had that much stuff, the car was overloaded. We even had two pieces of luggage strapped to the top.

The weight and distance was too much for our original four tires. Four times we had to unload our car to get to the spare, change the tire, reload the car, and then look for the nearest town that sold tires. Yes, we do depend upon a good set of wheels to take us many places safely, whether it is across town or across the country.

Think of your life as a wheel — the wheel of life. This year, 2012, we may encounter roadblocks, detours, potholes, as well as hills to climb and descend along a highway on our journey of life.

At times, our life may be very smooth, like a brand-new freeway and other times it can be very rough like an ungraded dirt mountain road. Just as the wheel on a car needs a hub, we too need a hub on our wheel of life. God is our hub.

We wouldn't even think about driving 2,000 miles without consulting a good map. Our map for life is the Bible, along with prayers and devotions. Does your wheel of life need repairs, a patch here or there? The Bible can strengthen you as you run into life's problems. Working through Christ and praying to God, we will find our way. Of course, our family and friends can also help.

How do you know where you are going in 2012, if you don't look back at 2011 and consider where you have been? Analyze your wheel of life. Think of all those parts that make up your wheel — home, family, friends, health, work, recreation, and spiritual life.

Is your wheel of life well balanced? Is any part of your life flat? Do you have a flat tire? Are you spending enough time with your friends and family? Are you taking care of your health, including diet and exercise? Are you giving your time, talents, and treasures to the church? Are you serving others as Christ taught us to love and to serve?

Is there a bulge in your wheel of life? Are you devoting too much time to work? Are you doing too much — loading yourself up with excess baggage? That can cause stress, a blow-out.

You must allow time for recreation — time for yourself. The tires on your car must be balanced, and the same need applies to your wheel of life. A balanced wheel well connected to the hub will give you a smooth ride, even if the road is rough and rocky.

Allow God to be your hub, consult His map, balance your life, and have a wonderful journey in 2012!

WHAT DOES IT REALLY MEAN?
February 2012

The morning sunlight was streaming through my bedroom window. It woke me up. This was my first morning home. I had just returned from my trip to Detroit, Michigan, visiting my daughter and her family right before Christmas.

I missed the sun in Detroit. For the entire week I was there, I never once saw the sun. It was nothing but complete cloud cover, gray skies, and one day of rain. To me it was so depressing without sunshine. I basked in the Arizona sun on December 24 and 25. It was fantastic! I don't think I truly appreciated our wonderful winter weather until I visited my daughter in Detroit in December.

On December 26, I left to visit my other daughter who lives in Virginia. Several days after I arrived, we walked on a trail along the Blue Ridge Parkway near her home. The fallen leaves were so thick they covered our shoes. I picked up a few leaves.

"What are you doing, Mom?" my daughter asked. To her those leaves were so common place, and certainly not worth bringing back to Arizona. But to me they represented the beauty of the Blue Ridge Mountains. I was picturing in my mind the hills alive with color — red, orange, and gold. I miss seeing Virginia in the fall with all its colors.

When I returned home, I gave the dried leaves to

a friend of mine. Her dream is to someday visit the Appalachian Mountains in the fall and see the autumn leaves. She has never been east of the Mississippi River. Even though the leaves I gave her no longer held their beauty, one could still see tinges of red with the brown. She loved my little gift.

Many times we do not truly appreciate what we have, whether it is the sun shining in our bedroom window or the hills ablaze with autumn leaves. When we see things all the time, it becomes ordinary, nothing spectacular.

It is like what Tommy said at the end of the play, Brigadoon, "Why do people have to lose things to find out what they really mean?" Good question, Tommy. Why do we have to leave Arizona in the winter to appreciate our fantastic weather? Do we have to be sick to appreciate good health?

Our friends and family — are we letting them know how much we love them and what they mean to us while they are still with us? Then what about our church? Do we appreciate it as we should?

Let us not say the sad lament of Tommy. Rejoice in beauty around you, tell your friends and family what they mean to you and how much you love them. Look at Gilbert Presbyterian Church with fresh eyes and heart. What do you see? Friendly, caring faces loving God and people doing the work of Christ?

Help us be that beckoning light for everyone. Share your time, talents, and treasures doing what God wants us to do at GPC.

Let us not lose any program here at our church for lack of funds.

What does Gilbert Presbyterian Church mean to you? Express your answer by action.

THE GOOD SHEPHERD
March 2012

I could not believe what I was watching on You Tube. On my computer screen was a video of a little beige bunny herding sheep!

Yes, Champis, the bunny, not only wiggles his nose and hops; but he also herds sheep on a farm in Sweden. He looks very cute as he runs through the field keeping the flock together. If one sheep happens to stray, Champis is right there chasing and guiding it back to the others. According to the owner, Champis was not trained for the job, but rather learned herding skills by watching the sheepdog. Now the dog is resting in the background while Champis is doing his work. Champis is a good shepherd watching his sheep.

When our children were little, we had a collie named Lassie. We did not live on a farm, so we had no sheep for Lassie, but we had four children for her to watch. If one of the children was sick, Lassie was right there at his/her bedside. She would not leave her self-appointed station until the child was up and feeling better. It did not matter who was ill, Lassie was right there. Lassie was a good shepherd, loving and caring for our little "sheep."

In the New Testament Jesus refers to himself as the Good Shepherd. "I am the good shepherd. The good shepherd lays down his life for the sheep" (John 10:11). Jesus watches over us and guides us. If we stray, He brings us back to the fold. If we are sick, He cares for us. He has given His life for us. Jesus is the Good Shepherd, and we are His sheep.

What can we do for Jesus? We can pray for His guidance and follow Him. We can allow Jesus to lead us and help us if we should stray. We grow in faith by trusting Him. We can love and care for others as He has taught us to love. All that we are and everything we have is a gift from God. We can share our gifts of time, talents, and treasures as Jesus has taught us to share. We are the sheep, and Jesus is the Good Shepherd.

MY WALK WITH A BLUE HERON
April 2012

It was a beautiful afternoon...not too hot...just perfect for a walk through the Riparian. The trees and bushes were budding or already in bloom. Spring was in the air. A little rabbit ran across my path. I saw ducks, geese, and egrets in the water.

In the distance I heard the sound of rushing water. Around the bend a little brook meandered over the desert floor and then dropped over some rocks, forming a miniature waterfall not more than a foot high. In the shade of the trees, I stopped, sat on a bench, and drank my water. I was mesmerized by the simplicity, beauty, and music of the little brook tumbling over the rocks.

My afternoon at the Riparian quickly came to a close. On the way back to my car, I walked across the bridge that is over one end of the lake. I looked down at the ducks swimming in the water. Where the bridge made a turn, I looked up and stopped short. Not more than six feet away from me was a beautiful blue heron perched on the railing. He stared at me, and I stared at him.

Neither of us moved. Time seemed to stand still. The blue heron was regal, tall and stately. Finally, he took a step away from me. Then I slowly and ever so quietly took a step toward him. We did this several times. With each step he took, I followed. We both continued to look at one another. Finally, he leaped to the railing on the opposite side and dropped into the water. This time, I did not follow.

I wondered what the blue heron was trying to tell me. Was he saying that this is God's World so enjoy its beauty and take good care of it? Perhaps he was telling me to soar high in the sky, reach for your dreams, flap your wings and try something new. Then when one gets tired from soaring, find peace and rest in the desert with God and drink of the living water.

Perhaps the blue heron was telling me not to worry. If God takes care of him, a blue heron, have faith God will certainly take care of us. When the blue heron stood tall, confident, and with wings outstretched, he reminded me of the cross.

This is spring, the season when everything is alive-- flowers blooming, trees budding, and orange blossoms filling the air with their sweet aroma.

This is spring, the time to celebrate the resurrection of Jesus Christ. Jesus gave his life for us, our greatest gift from God. What can we do for Him? With thanksgiving in our hearts, we can help one another by giving a portion of our gifts of time, talents, and treasures. Let us help create and maintain peace and beauty in the world, our gift to God.

SPIRIT OF GOD
May 2012

I will never forget the picture I held in my hand. A small child about my age was standing on a mountain top, her long blonde hair blowing in the wind. The little girl appeared to be looking at distant mountains and trees. She was surrounded by pretty wildflowers, grass, and rocks. The sky was a beautiful shade of blue with fluffy white clouds.

I received the picture and accompanying story in Sunday school when I was 5 years old. I don't remember the story, but I have never forgotten the picture. For years I kept the picture as I dreamed to be that child on top of a high mountain with my hair blowing in the wind. I loved the wind and mountains, but I grew up in Cleveland, Ohio, with not even a hill for miles around.

Seventeen years later I got my wish and recreated that picture by standing on a mountain top with the wind blowing in my face. For years Roy and I lived in a copper mining town in the mountains of Eastern Arizona. Many times we would go hiking in the mountains and stand on top of a high hill. We were surrounded by wildflowers, cacti, other desert plants, and of course lots of rocks. When we climbed high enough, the wind was always blowing. The scenery at that elevation was fantastic. We could see for miles around.

I love to feel the wind blowing. A gentle breeze pushes me as I bike. I arrive home quickly with little effort. But when I bike against the wind, it is difficult to move forward. A strong wind can cause me to lose balance and even push me over. I cannot move forward. But it is wonderful to pedal with the wind.

I think of the wind as the Spirit of God. Whenever we do what God wants us to do, God will help us accomplish our goals. With prayer, challenges will not seem insurmountable. However, if we go against what God wants us to do, we can encounter so many difficulties that accomplishing anything may be impossible.

Two thousand years ago, a violent wind filled the room where Jesus' disciples were located, and tongues of fire rested on each of them. That was the first Pentecost after Jesus' death and the beginning of the early Christian church. With faith in Jesus Christ, the early Christians were able to spread the Good News throughout the land. Can we too, by faith and the Holy Spirit, love and serve others?

Listen to the wind (the Spirit of God), step out in faith, and do as Jesus wants us to do.

Perhaps that little girl, pictured all alone on a mountain top, represents all the children who need our help. Is she calling out to us?

We will have the opportunity on May 27 to give to the Pentecost offering which helps meet the needs of children, youth, and young adults at risk. Each local congregation chooses where forty percent of that offering is put to use. In a few weeks, we will be announcing what organization will be receiving forty percent of our Pentecost offering. Allow the Spirit of God to blow on you.

THE MOSAIC OF
GILBERT PRESBYTERIAN CHURCH
June 2012

I looked across the room at a large and very beautiful picture. It had a calming effect on me with its muted tones of gray, green, and blue. There were no bright, harsh tones. The black and white parts of the picture also were soft. All the shades blended from one to another. The picture seemed to say, "Come, and I will give you rest." I felt a sense of peace and contentment, a place where I wanted to be.

It is a place where I am! It is a picture of Gilbert Presbyterian Church from Guadalupe Road, photographed by Olan Mills for our directory. I first saw the picture at the Wednesday afternoon Bible Study in the Education Building. It is now in its permanent location hanging in the hallway next to the office.

Come, look at the picture, first from a distance and see how the colors blend together. Experience the calm, and feel the daily stresses of life flowing away from you. Take in its beauty and serenity. Feel its welcoming power.

Now, step closer to the picture and see spots of bright color within the muted tones. Step closer yet and it becomes a mosaic of over 6,000 tiny photographs of everyone in the directory. Each little image is very sharp and clear. Can you find yourself? If your picture was taken by Olan Mills, you are there multiple times. Gilbert Presbyterian Church is made up of everyone. If one tiny photograph were removed from the picture, Gilbert Presbyterian Church would not be complete.

It takes many people blending together with different gifts to share to make a church. It takes the time, talents, and treasures of everyone from the worship leaders, orchestra, choir, and bell members, Sunday school teachers, elders and deacons, to the leaders and members of the committees.

It takes the youth leading us in a Contemporary Service and the young taking part in the Children's Message. It takes many sharing their ideas and experiences in Sunday school and in Bible studies. It takes the Prayer Warriors. Let us not forget all those helping and serving others in our community. Many people take part in more than one activity at Gilbert Presbyterian Church, just like in the picture everyone is there multiple times.

Jesus has taught us to love and serve others. As we share our time, talents, and treasures in the work of our church, we complete the picture of what Gilbert Presbyterian Church is and what it means to us. It is a place to welcome others, a place to experience joy and peace, and a place where we can come to God in prayer.

Come, worship, and become a part of that mosaic called Gilbert Presbyterian Church.

THE ARCTIC CATHEDRAL
July/August 2012

The beautiful Norwegian city of Tromso, known as the Paris of the North, was coming into view. There was land on both sides of our cruise ship. I was looking out the dining room window during breakfast. A tree-covered mountain towered over the city. There were little patches of snow on top of the mountain.

I had to get a closer look. I quickly grabbed my jacket and camera and hurried up the stairs to the upper deck of our ship. In front of me was a very long bridge that was arched in the center. I looked up — would we clear the bridge? I held my breath.

The captain expertly guided the ship directly under the highest point of the bridge with hardly a foot to spare. Then I noticed that one end of the bridge curved toward a beautiful church. The roof of the church came all the way down to the ground and formed many triangles, each one with two equal sides. The roof and the outside walls were one.

On the front wall of the church was a very large cross from the vertex of the triangle down. This church had to be the Arctic Cathedral. Yes, I was north of the Arctic Circle. What a wonderful view — the sun shining, a bridge curving toward the church which became the focal point of the city, and behind the church a mountain with snow.

We docked, disembarked, and took tour buses

around the city. We stopped at the fascinating Polar Museum. Inside were many artifacts from polar expeditions. I wanted to stay longer, but we had to move on. Our next excursion was a tram ride to the top of the mountain. There we had our lunch. It was a beautiful warm day — 66 degrees. The sky was blue with a few clouds. We walked around on top.

What a great view of Tromso! The city was located on a very large island. Directly below us was the Arctic Cathedral, the most distinguishing landmark in the city. Far away on the other side of the water was a high mountain range with snow-covered peaks. It was beautiful to see snow glistening in the sunlight. We were surrounded by snow-topped mountains. As we were contemplating the scenery, someone floated by on a hang glider. He made it look so easy, so graceful, slowly drifting in the wind.

Our next stop was the Arctic Cathedral! It actually is not a cathedral since it is the church of Norway — Lutheran. The church was even more beautiful and unique up close. We entered through doors that were beneath the cross, through the narthex, and into the sanctuary. Exquisite crystal chandeliers hung from the vertices of the triangles. The organ was above and behind the sanctuary and its many organ pipes above that.

In front of the sanctuary was a very large multi-colored glass mosaic window called "The Return of Christ." Christ was reaching down from the heavens to man on earth. It was beautiful. I sat in a pew studying the scene depicted before me. I thought of my friends and family at home. It was Sunday, June 24, 4 p.m., Norwegian time and in Arizona 7 a.m. I wondered what my friends were doing at that hour. Perhaps they were waking up and getting ready for church. I sat there and prayed. I knew that Christ was with me. I felt His presence. In the beauty of the Arctic Cathedral, I was in communion with God.

I did not want to return to the ship by bus, so I walked across the long bridge. The bridge was pedestrian friendly — well protected from the busy traffic. My walk was the climax to a wonderful day in Tromso, my favorite city in Norway.

No matter where we are in the world, God is always with us. He guides us and protects us. I saw His creation in Norway — the lakes, fjords, mountains, glaciers, snow, trees, and wildflowers. I saw many birds, including the comical looking puffins. I saw the wild animals — seals, whales, walruses, and polar bears. I saw pristine beaches of rock and sand. I saw God's world.

What can we do for God? He has given us His creation, our talents, and treasures. His greatest gift of all is Jesus Christ. Let us spread Christ's love at home and wherever we may travel. Let us give a portion of our time, talents, and treasures for the work in His kingdom. Let us take care of His world so that others may enjoy its beauty for years to come.

THANK YOU, GOD, FOR GLAUCOMA
September 2012

"Mom, two years ago when you found out that you have glaucoma, you were very upset. But, glaucoma might have saved your life."

My son, Alan, said that to me as we were on our way home from my ophthalmologist appointment in Tucson. Alan might be correct in his statement. Because of glaucoma, I see my ophthalmologist in Mesa every 3 to 4 months. Because of glaucoma, my ophthalmologist carefully inspects my eyes.

During one of her routine examinations where my eyes were dilated, she discovered an eye tumor in the far lower left corner inside my left eye. She had a very difficult time seeing the tumor and taking a picture of it. She then sent me to Tucson to the top eye cancer specialist in the Southwest.

My eye cancer is a very rare condition. I had absolutely no symptoms that a tumor was growing in my eye. Without glaucoma, would I have made an appointment to see an ophthalmologist and would she have taken the extra time that was needed to discover the tumor--maybe yes, maybe no. Glaucoma might be my blessing in disguise.

I have so much cause to be thankful. On August 15 at St. Joe's Hospital in Tucson, a radioactive plaque was placed on my eyeball. It was removed one week later. I am so thankful that my doctor is the best in his field. His patients are from all over the country and world. I am thankful for his expertise and knowledge. I am thankful for the discoveries made to enable specialists to place radioactive seeds on a disk about the size of a dime. I am thankful for the equipment that my doctor used in order to attach that disk to my eyeball.

The thought of what was done and the knowledge of all the necessary steps leading up to the surgery is just mind boggling. Twenty or thirty years ago all of this would have been impossible.

This is the time for healing, the time for me to be patient. God has given power and knowledge to all the specialists and has guided my surgeon's hand. Now I have to work with God for continued healing in His time, not mine.

After the surgery I could only see out of my right eye. Gradually my vision is returning to my left eye. I have double vision because of the swelling and bruising in my eye. That will gradually heal. I must be patient. Keeping my head still, I have no double vision — right eye is doing all the work. I see double if I move my head from side to side or if there is a big contrast between light and dark.

The other day Karen Gallagher drove me to the grocery store. I did not realize until I was driving a grocery cart that I have very little or no depth perception. I had no idea how far away I was from other shoppers, whether it was a few inches or feet. A little child darted in front of me. I thought I was going to hit him. I missed, but I am not sure how. Turning my head to look at the items was very interesting — everything doubled and danced in front of me. Many times I had to stop and close my eye to get my bearings. I wanted to place a large sign on the front of my grocery cart that said, "Student Driver." Wow, if I can't safely drive a grocery cart, I sure can't drive a car.

That week of radiation made me so exhausted. Even though the radioactive seeds are gone, I am still feeling their effects. Gradually I am getting my strength back, but to me it is a slow process. I must be patient, not do too much, and take my restorative naps. Now I better understand the experiences of others who have had radiation and/or chemotherapy. Only with God's help do we persevere.

I am so thankful for my church, my friends and family, and your concerns and prayers. You have shown me the love of Jesus and the power of prayer. You have been so wonderful. Thank you.

THE ELECTION
October 2012

I am Eloise.

I am six years old.

I live at The Plaza Hotel.

Thus began the little skit I gave while living in Canfield Hall at Ohio State University. I was running for the office of treasurer in my dorm, and I had to present a skit or talk stating why I should be elected.

My skit was a parody of the then-popular book, Eloise, by Kay Thompson. Eloise in the book was a precocious child, always creating mischief at the Plaza Hotel in New York City. It was written as a children's story, but adults (especially college students) really enjoyed the antics of Eloise. I don't remember what I said in the skit, but I'll never forget the reaction of my audience. They loved it and thought it was hilarious.

Many of you might have had similar experiences of running for an office. While in elementary, junior high, or high school maybe it was for student council or class president, secretary, or treasurer. After graduation you might have run for an office in college, a club, or a civic organization.

Perhaps you ran in a local, state, or national election. Basically no matter what the election, from an elementary school student council member to the president of the United States, all candidates must make themselves known to their voting public. They do this by various means — skits, talks, telephone calls, posters, newspaper and magazine articles, letters, and television commercials. Right now we feel we are bombarded by politicians with their promises and negative comments about the other candidates. Soon the election will be over and the ballots will be counted.

Do we have to write a really great speech to get God to know us and vote for us? Do we have to get His attention? No, God already knows us. "Before I formed you in the womb I knew you, before you were born I set you apart;" (Jeremiah 1:5).

Will Jesus cast His ballot for us if we make wonderful promises on how we will create jobs, improve the schools, clean up the environment, stop wars, and of course cut taxes? No, there is no election, Jesus has already chosen us.

"You did not choose me, but I chose you and appointed you to go and bear fruit — fruit that will last" (John 15:16). No election, no voting, no ballots — we are already chosen. We have been appointed to serve others — to share our time, talents, and treasures — and spread the good news of Jesus Christ. We do this in remembrance and because of our love for Christ who died for us.

This month you will receive a ballot to pledge your support of time, talents, and treasures for God's work at Gilbert Presbyterian Church. Prayerfully consider how to mark your ballot and bring forth your pledge on Sunday, November 4.

THIS IS MY PRAYER
November 2012

I sat on my piano bench with hands in my lap and head bowed in silent prayer. I reflected upon what I had done. I had just played a beautiful arrangement of the hymn, "Be Thou My Vision."

The previous day I could only play one hand at a time and now both hands were together. When I was learning that piece, the radiation plaque was in my left eye so I could hardly see. Yet, I was able to read the music and play the piano. Even with my mistakes, the beauty of the piece came out. How ironic that Susan Martinez chose the hymn, "Be Thou My Vision," for me to learn that week. Yes God, you are my vision, because I sure can't see.

Many times as I am practicing I contemplate how I came to take lessons. One Sunday last spring immediately after the church service, I said to Susan how much I truly enjoyed her piano playing. Then I said to her that I would love to take lessons. On the way home from church, I kept wondering why I ever told her that! After all, I'm teaching. I don't have the time to practice.

Of course she e-mailed me and said that we could work something out. Many times in life one door closes only for another door to open. A month or so later, I was diagnosed with a tumor in my eye. With that, my teaching job for the fall semester was canceled, and I gained the opportunity to take piano lessons! Music is my salvation in my recovery. It helps me relax. It is my quiet time for contemplation. It is my prayer of thanksgiving to God. Yes, He is my vision. He is my help in time of need.

My emotions are the same whether I am playing the piano or singing a beautiful anthem. As I sing an anthem I think about the meaning of the words. Religious music to me is as much a prayer as any spoken one. When I hear, sing, or play a beautiful reflective hymn or anthem, I feel close to Christ.

Through music I can pray for peace and healing. Through music I can pray for guidance — how I might best serve Him.

Music is my prayer of thanksgiving — I thank God for all He has given me — friends and family, the beauty of the earth, my time, talents and treasures, and the best gift of all, Jesus Christ. Yes, music is my prayer.

CHRISTMAS MEMORIES
December 2012

I will never forget one Christmas morning a few years ago. My two sons gave me a small rectangular box beautifully wrapped with a bow on top. They said the gift was from them and their two out-of-state sisters. I carefully unwrapped and opened the box. My heart sank.

Inside was a small camera case. I did need a new camera case, but my camera was large. My camera was my mother's from the 1950's. Its lens stuck out from the body of the camera. Even though it was 50 years old, it took excellent pictures. I liked it except for the fact I had to keep changing film. All it needed was a new case, but not one that small. I felt so sorry for my sons. My camera would not fit into the case they had given me.

After a few disappointed moments, my sons presented me with another box of the same small size. Inside Box 2 was a brand new digital camera. Of course, it was the perfect size for the case! What a wonderful surprise!

The very next day I was on the plane with my new camera, sans rolls of film, to visit my daughters.

I have received other memorable Christmas gifts. When I was a child, I asked Santa for a blue stuffed elephant. I don't remember why it had to be blue, but it did. And Santa brought one, just for me. In junior high school I received a lemon-wood bow, arrows, and quiver. I enjoyed archery. That was my sport.

When I was a senior in high school I received the best gift of all — a slide rule! For the same Christmas, my parents gave me two matching blue suitcases. I also received a small white rectangular train case with my initials. It was called a train case because in those days trains were the most common mode of transportation. I had many train rides between my home in Cleveland and Ohio State University in Columbus.

The suitcases and train case were heavy, even when empty, and they were practically indestructible. Several years ago my granddaughter, Desiree, rescued my train case from the dark recesses of my garage. She wanted it as a cosmetic case for college. I gladly gave it to her, and she is proud of it. Her friends all ask her where she got such a neat looking case, and why it has the initials, EMR!

I have many wonderful memories of family traditions. My mother loved Christmas. She especially enjoyed decorating the home and entertaining friends. Every year she led a group of neighborhood children caroling. It was fun for my friends, my brothers, and me. My mother's hot chocolate and cookies tasted ever so good after our evening of caroling in Ohio's cold and snow. It was my mother's service to the community. She was a member of a local women's club and the money collected during the caroling went toward a college scholarship for a high school senior.

Years later my own family established a tradition of attending Christmas Eve service at the Shepherd of the Hills Presbyterian Church in Morenci, Arizona. The sanctuary looked ever so beautiful from the light of the many candles. Friends and neighbors — young and old — gathered that evening to celebrate the birth of Jesus. We held our candles carefully while singing as one big choir the lovely carol, "Silent Night." After the song, we blew out our candles and wished all a very Merry Christmas.

We walked outside into the clear, cold mountain air. The luminarias lit the path to and from the sanctuary door. The stars shone bright in the sky. Yes, it was easy to imagine that they were guiding the way to the Christ Child. Every year our children filled the luminaria sacks with sand and candles and helped decorate the sanctuary. To them it was an honor and privilege to help make the church beautiful for Christmas Eve. What wonderful memories they have!

What memories will we create for our children or grandchildren this Christmas? Is there some object from our past that is no longer useful to us, but just might be cherished by a child or grandchild? Will we create memories of family traditions that include service to God, the church and community?

Will we stop our busy lives for just a little while and think not so much about the gifts we receive, but also the gifts we might bring to the Christ child? God has blessed us with many gifts, but the greatest gift of all is Jesus Christ. In love and appreciation for all we have received, let us share a portion of our time, talents, and treasures. Merry Christmas!

2013

ON THIS ROCK I WILL BUILD MY CHURCH

And I tell you that you are Peter, and on this rock I will build my church, and the gates of Hades will not overcome it.

Matthew 16:18

WE HAVE ALREADY WON THE LOTTERY!
January 2013

Did you buy one or more lottery tickets last month, hoping to win that multi-million-dollar prize? Then, when the numbers were announced, did your heart sink knowing your ticket wasn't drawn?

But wait a minute! You have already won the lottery...not a lottery of money, but a priceless lottery that money can never buy.

I know that in 2012 I won the lottery of modern medicine. At my last check-up with my cardiologist, he said he has known of only one other person who had the same eye tumor as what I had. That was forty-five years ago, and nothing could be done at that time for his friend.

Many types of cancers are now arrested, when years ago they could not be stopped. Think of all the diseases that were prevalent when we or our parents or grandparents were children. Today children do not know what it is like to be sick with measles, mumps, or chickenpox. Polio is a disease of the past, and diphtheria — that is history. Yes, we have won the lottery of modern medicine.

We are surrounded by the beauty of the earth. No amount of money can ever buy the fantastic Arizona sunrises and sunsets. Take a look at God's creation. The moon and numerous stars shine brightly in the night sky. There is beauty in the desert and mountains.

Stand on a high peak and look out in the distance and see the bare outcropping of rock and the tree-covered slopes. Study the beauty of the Arizona rocks, cacti, wildflowers, and little animals that quickly move across the desert. We need only to open our eyes to see the beauty that God has given us. That is a lottery worth far more than money.

Gilbert Presbyterian Church is known as a very friendly, caring, and active church. There are many opportunities for everyone — worship, music groups, mission and evangelism projects, Sunday school classes, and Bible studies to name just a few. Nothing is more important than friends — friends who will pray with you and for you, listen to you, and help you. We have won the lottery for friendship. And should there be a lottery for churches, we have won that one too.

Gifts that God has given us are our winnings. Each one of us, from the youngest to the oldest, has talents to share. Our treasures also come from God. The question is how do we use our gifts. What does God want us to do with our time, talents, and treasures?

In appreciation for all that God has given us, let us share our gifts with others. The greatest gift of all is Jesus Christ. Jesus died for us. He died for our sins. We are saved by grace. Now that is a gift that money can never buy. We have already won the lottery!

WHAT IS LOVE?
February 2013

When I was a child, I loved to swing so high that I imagined my toes were touching the clouds. My dad built the swing for me — long pieces of lumber for the legs and crossbar, a couple of ropes, and finally a wooden seat. Oh, how I loved my swing.

I also loved my mom's made-from-scratch cakes. That was the time before cake mixes. She made seven-minute frosting for her cakes. She took great care in creating little peaks with the frosting while spreading it on the cake. Oh, how I loved her cakes with seven-minute frosting.

In our everyday speech we frequently say that we love an object or love to do something. We might say as I did that we love to swing or love to eat mom's homemade cakes. Or perhaps we say we love to hike in the mountains, love to eat chocolate, love to listen to music, or love to read and travel. But, none of those things can reciprocate our love. They cannot love us back.

Words other than love might generate a more accurate meaning; that is, we enjoy hiking, take great pleasure in traveling, relish chocolate, or have a passion for teaching.

Our friends and family demonstrate their love by helping us, listening to us, and caring for us. We in turn can help them in their time of need. We tell our friends and family how much we love them and what they mean to us. Babies will gaze into their parents' faces to learn who loves and cares for them. We give our babies a smile, and they smile back at us. Babies thrive with love.

We teach our children to share, which is a form of love. Toddlers will share their cookie with mom or dad. Later they learn to share with their friends. Our pets can also express their love for us. Our dog, Lassie, would run to the door, jump for joy, and wag her tail to greet us. Our children loved Lassie, and Lassie showed her love for us.

There is another form of love — the love of a Good Samaritan. You know the story — only the Good Samaritan stopped to render aid, compassion, and care for the stranger in need.

Gilbert Presbyterian Church demonstrates the love of many good Samaritans. At Christmas time the narthex was filled with gifts bought and wrapped with love. More recently, warm blankets and jackets have been donated to those in need. We personally do not know the ones we are helping. The recipients of our gifts are strangers to us; likewise, we are strangers to them. But we do know that they are our brothers and sisters in Christ who need our help.

Further, the deacons have packed bags of snacks and hygiene items to be given to the homeless. Many at GPC have experienced the expression of thanks as a bag is handed out to the one in need. When we help others, we know we are spreading the love of Christ.

God has given us many gifts — time, talents, treasures, and the gift of love. Because God loves us, He gave us his Son, Jesus Christ. Jesus taught us to love and serve others with joy in our hearts. He gave His life for us.

This Valentine's Day, spread the gift of love to your friends and family. Do something special for your loved ones, but also help a stranger. Lend a hand. Help someone in need. Perhaps all that is needed is a smile and a helping hand. Be a Good Samaritan.

ONE DAY IN THE LIFE OF A DOCTOR
March 2013

It was a busy day at the clinic. Patients were coming in with the flu, sore throats, and other infections. Some patients needed check-ups and prescriptions refilled, and others needed a referral to see a specialist. There was only one female physician on the staff, and she was always busy. Her patients loved her; likewise, she enjoyed caring for her patients. On that busy day she was running late.

The doctor looked at her watch. It was time for her to be at the elementary school to see the principal. She couldn't leave yet — one more patient to see. She called the school and asked if she should come on a different day. The principal said, "Don't reschedule. Come when you can. I will wait for you."

Finally, the doctor was able to leave her office. As she was driving to the school, she was thinking about what she needed to do — see the principal, pick up her two sons from the after-school program, stop at the grocery store, then head home to make dinner. And, of course, she would make sure her boys did their homework.

The school was located at the intersection of a side road and a very busy city street with three lanes in both directions. The fire department was directly across the street from the school. The school was set back away from the intersection. A drive for school traffic circled the building. Behind the school were softball and soccer fields and a fenced-in playground. The after-school program was located in a room that exited to the playground. In the distance were the beautiful Blue Ridge Mountains of Western Virginia.

The doctor arrived at the school and met with the principal. They left together, walking down the hallway toward the front door. At that moment, a car crashed into the school no more than thirty feet in front of them. The doctor ran, opened the passenger door, turned off the ignition and unbuckled the seat belt. The driver, alone in the car, was a lady in her fifties. She was slumped over the steering wheel, moaning. The doctor quickly looked for identification. She spoke to her, calling her name, Kathy.

Kathy's pulse got weaker and weaker. Her moans became barely audible. Then Kathy's heart stopped and she stopped breathing. She had died. The doctor quickly dragged Kathy out of the car, laid her on the ground, and immediately started CPR.

Meanwhile the principal called 9-1-1 on her cell phone, and the paramedics arrived with their life-saving equipment. Three times the paramedics had to shock Kathy's heart. Finally, it started beating again. As soon as she was stabilized, the ambulance transported her to the hospital. Later the doctor heard that Kathy was making a complete recovery.

If the doctor had been on time to see the principal, she would not have been at the school when Kathy had her medical crisis. The doctor would have been at the grocery store with her sons. The principal would have been on her way home. The staff of the after-school program would not have heard the crash because they were in the rear of the building. If Kathy had lost consciousness a few minutes earlier, she would have been on the busy highway. Or, in a potentially worst-case scenario, if Kathy had lost consciousness a few minutes later, her grandchildren would have been in the car with her and she would have been driving on the busy street.

The timing of her medical crisis was absolutely perfect. The crash occurred off the busy highway, directly in front of a doctor, and paramedics were stationed across the street. Was this a well-scripted television show or a DVD exhorting the value of knowing CPR? No, this really happened two weeks ago in Roanoke, Virginia. This was told to me by the doctor, my daughter Karen.

I shudder to think of what could have happened in the above story. Everything took place so precisely that it was unbelievable. It was a miracle. Truly, God was protecting Kathy. How else can one explain the precision of events? God made sure that Kathy had instantaneous medical help. Instead of Kathy's family planning a memorial service, they are celebrating that she is alive.

God has given all of us talents to share. My daughter's talent is the knowledge of medicine and the ability to react quickly to emergency situations. That is her calling. The paramedics also have a gift of medical knowledge and the love for helping others. Working together they were able to save Kathy.

All of us have talents to share. Although our talents might not be expressed in quite the dramatic way as the above story, they are just as important. When we serve food to the homeless, we certainly are giving them a better day.

When God calls us to help others, can we quickly respond and say, "Here I am Lord?" We must be ready. My daughter and the paramedics certainly were.

The greatest gift God has given us is His Son, Jesus Christ. This month, let us think of the love and teachings of Jesus and contemplate the events that lead to the cross. As we get closer to Easter, let us reflect upon the Last Supper, His disciples denying Him, Jesus in the garden to pray, and the cross. He died for us, for our sins. But, He is not dead. He is risen!

Easter is a time for joy. Come to the cross, celebrate life and celebrate our risen, Lord. Happy Easter!

WHAT IS IN YOUR BUCKET?
April 2013

Several weeks ago, Ed Blake from our church, gave me an empty five-gallon bucket. It is white, inside and out, with a lid. It had held a plastic coating used in repairing the church roof.

At first I thought I would use the bucket for water when I mop the kitchen and bathroom floors. But, maybe not, because it is large enough that if I filled it with water, it would be very heavy. The other day I placed a large plastic bag inside the bucket. I did a little garage cleanup, and the trash went right into the bag in the bucket. That was handy.

I think my bucket would be good to hold small gardening tools for working in the yard. Another thought: I remember all the bats, balls, and rackets my kids had when they were growing up. At that time I could have easily used a large bucket like Ed gave me. In fact, I could now put the balls my grandkids play with in my bucket.

My children and grandchildren love Legos. The new bucket could be used as a Lego container since it has a lid. If not for Legos, then maybe I could fill it with other toys such as blocks, cars, trucks or wooden trains and track that are so popular with pre-school children.

I think it would be fun if I placed toys and surprises into my bucket. My grandchildren could reach down into my bucket and uncover something new and exciting each time they visit me. And if I was into knitting, my bucket could hold yarn, needles, and even have room for the project. Wow, I never thought a five-gallon bucket could be used in so many ways!

Our minds are like a bucket. God places all of our interests, abilities, and talents into our minds (our buckets) at birth. Into some buckets, He places the ability to teach, and in others, the ability to build or heal. He gives some people an interest in math and science and to others an interest in English and foreign languages.

God might place a talent for music or art into some buckets; whereas, others receive a talent for growing vegetables and flowers. Each of us receives many gifts from God. And each person receives a unique set of gifts. Our talents are what make us who we are.

As we grow, learn, and mature we use our talents from our buckets. Perhaps we discover we are interested in engineering, business, music, or health. We develop those talents according to what we believe we are most interested in and have the most ability to perform. That becomes our occupation.

We may also use our talents for volunteer work. Perhaps years later something happens. Maybe we become bored with our job — it no longer holds our interest. Perhaps we are laid off or maybe our physical body will no longer allow us to continue our work. We may retire, or we just would like to expand our horizons and pursue additional talents.

Now comes the exciting part. God placed many talents in our buckets, some of which we never pursued. Be like a child who digs for a hidden toy from a bucket. Reach into your bucket and uncover that hidden talent. It is there ready to be discovered.

God gave you not one talent, but many.

God wants us to share our talents with others. As we share, our gifts become stronger. A teacher becomes better with teaching, a musician improves with practice and playing for others, and a craftsman becomes more skilled with each project.

Every time you use your talents, give thanks to God for your wonderful gifts. What is in your bucket? Reach in, discover your talents, and share as Jesus has taught us to share and care for others!

WELCOME TO ARIZONA
June 2013

"Well boys, welcome to Arizona. What do you want to see?" I asked my two grandsons, ages 6 and 8, as soon as they arrived at my home on Monday, April 1. This was their first trip west. They were on spring break from school in Virginia.

In unison they immediately shouted, "The Lego store."

"Don't you want to see the Grand Canyon, Kartchner Caverns, cacti, javelina, bighorn sheep, and cowboys? You can see Lego stores anywhere, but you can only see the Grand Canyon in Arizona." The boys got to see all of the above and much, much more including the Lego Store at Chandler Mall.

Right after lunch we drove toward Williams, stopping first at Montezuma Castle. The stop made a nice break in our long car ride. It was great walking along the path looking at the desert plants and rocks, and the bubbling creek. We marveled at Montezuma Castle. How did the Sinagua farmers in the 1100's ever build their five-story, 20-room dwelling recessed in a cliff 100 feet above the valley floor without the use of modern equipment? How did they ever climb to their home carrying water and other necessities along the way? My grandson, Matthew, was impressed with seeing the pueblo dwellings of the Southwest — he had been studying them in school.

The next morning we saw a Wild West Show at the hotel before boarding the train to the Grand Canyon. My grandsons got to see cowboys. Aaron turned 6 on the day of our train ride. The cowboys and a cowgirl sang Happy Birthday to him on the train. That was his thrill of the day.

It was fascinating to watch the landscape changing from scrub brush to tall pines as we chugged along to the canyon. The day was perfect for walking. In fact, one of the most beautiful scenes I have ever experienced at the Grand Canyon occurred as we were ready to leave. The sun's rays were shining down through the clouds creating fantastic shadows across the canyon walls. That was God's creation in all of its magnificent glory. What a beautiful ending to a wonderful day.

On Wednesday we drove to Tucson, stopping at the Desert Sonora Museum. The boys got to see all the different exhibits of the museum from the rocks and desert plants to the many animals. Yes, they saw the javelinas, bighorn sheep, snakes, scorpions and many other desert critters. After I had explained to them that a saguaro has to be at least 50 years old to grow an arm, they kept asking me the age of each cactus. The evening in Tucson was beautiful. From our hotel balcony we could look across the road and see saguaros covering the nearby hillside.

The next day we toured Kartchner Caverns, an underground cathedral made by God. Kartchner Caverns is a living cave — its stalactites and stalagmites grow ever so slowly with each tiny drop of water. After the caverns' visit, we were off to Tombstone and more cowboys and even a Marshall. The boys loved testing their reading skills on the tombstones in Boot Hill Cemetery.

On that first week of April, Arizona was at its

prettiest — desert plants beginning to bloom, perfect weather, and the sky with just the right number of clouds to produce delightful shadows. It was clear enough to see for miles around.

God created beauty in the earth from the deepest canyon to the highest mountain, from the sun during the day to the moon and stars at night. Each little creature that roams the earth is part of God's handiwork. This is God's gift to us. But with this gift there is responsibility. God has made us the stewards of the land. He has given us the responsibility to care for the environment — the plants, animals, earth, and sky.

How are we doing? Are we preserving and protecting God's work for future generations to come? Stop and marvel at God's world and enjoy the beauty, but be a good steward.

A DAY OF REST
July 2013

"By the seventh day God had finished the work he had been doing; so on the seventh day he rested from all his work. And God blessed the seventh day and made it holy, because on it he rested from all the work of creating that he had done" (Genesis 2:2-3).

If God rested on the seventh day, why can't we? And do we keep it holy? In the adult Sunday school class, taught by Susan Lucas, we have been watching a very interesting DVD series called "24/6" featuring Matthew Sleeth, MD. That is right, it is 24/6 not 24/7.

Today many of us are plugged into our work 24 hours a day, 7 days per week. What has happened to that seventh day — a day of rest and relaxation — a day to think of God?

One Sunday after watching our DVD, Susan asked us where we would like to go that would be restful and relaxing. My immediate response was that I would take a walk in the woods beside a river.

Later, I tried to think of where I had taken a walk like that — was it on one of my trips? Perhaps, but the image that came to mind was one from my childhood. I was raised in Lakewood, Ohio, a suburb of Cleveland. Our home was on a corner of a busy street. No quiet there, but less than two miles away from our house was the entrance to the most wonderful park, Rocky River Reservation.

The river is aptly named; it is very rocky and shallow. It meanders around south of Cleveland and then heads north forming the boundary of two suburbs, Lakewood and the city of Rocky River. Finally, the river empties into Lake Erie.

The park, known as Cleveland's "emerald necklace," is quite extensive. Rocky River is in a V-shaped valley, 150 feet below the ground level of Cleveland and its surrounding suburbs. In some places the valley is quite wide, and in other places it's narrow. A road follows the river, crossing it in several places. The crossings were just that — concrete drives through the river bed rather than bridges. When the river was high, crossings were closed.

As a child, I loved Rocky River Reservation. Sundays after church and my mother's delicious chicken dinner, we frequently took a drive through the park. There was so much to do. My dad would park the car and we would walk through the woods and then along the babbling river. We skipped rocks across the river, or at least tried skipping them.

We marveled at the beauty of the place — the river, trees, rocks, shale and sandstone cliffs, and ledges. Yes, we even gazed upward at the beautiful High-Level Bridge connecting Lakewood to the city of Rocky River. My dad, the engineer, took many pictures of that bridge. If it was spring, we kids looked for the budding wildflowers along the trail and river.

In the summer we felt the cool breezes blowing through the trees. In the autumn we loved our walks among all the beautiful colored leaves — gold, red, yellow and brown. The winter was beautiful too with the ice and snow. My brothers and I loved to go sledding on the hills. Any time of year Rocky River Reservation was a place to find quiet away from the frenzy of Cleveland.

Rocky River Reservation was our place close to home for our day of rest and relaxation. It was the time to think of God and His creation. Looking back, I can understand why my parents needed and enjoyed that time to take walks among the trees and beside the water. It helped them relax and feel refreshed for the new week.

The Sabbath day is our gift from God. Cherish that gift as much as if it were a special talent or treasure that He has given you. Be a good steward of your gift of rest. How can we help others if we ourselves are not refreshed? How can we effectively use our talents when we are tired and exhausted?

Take the seventh day off — God did. Relax and look around you at His handiwork of creation. If your work does not permit you to take Sunday off, choose another day as your special Sabbath day of rest. On the seventh day, worship Him, honor Him, and thank Him for all He has done for you!

EMBRACE THE UNEXPECTED
August 2013

"Quick, Mom. Now's your chance. Get into the jeep." My daughter, Karen, beeped her horn to let her husband, Barry, know that I would be getting into his jeep. He was directly in front of us. We were stopped at a traffic light.

I just made it and got my seat belt buckled before the light turned green. We were on our way from their home in Kennett Square, Pennsylvania, to the Winterthur Museum and Garden in Delaware. Barry thought it would be best to take two vehicles in case the boys got restless in the museum. That way he could take them home early if need be.

Instead of driving the twenty-minute direct route along the busy highway to the museum, Barry took the back roads. This doubled our time to get there, but it was well worth it. That was the best ride, bouncing along in a red, noisy 1979 jeep. We practically flew up in the air when we hit a rut in the road, and the back roads provided many potholes.

I wasn't the only one enjoying the ride. My grandsons loved that jeep. Barry had removed the front doors so the wind blew though the vehicle. Aaron kept saying, "Hang on Grandma," with each bounce. I guess he didn't want to lose his grandma out the open door.

We meandered around the countryside and saw beautiful farms of corn and cattle. Along the way, we saw many original stone houses several hundred years old. The grass and trees were very green, not at all like Arizona. Flowers were growing beside the road. We even drove through a covered bridge! Oh, how I loved that! It was so unexpected. That bridge brought back memories of years ago riding with my father in Southern Ohio purposely looking for and driving through covered bridges.

Winterthur was once the home of Henry Francis DuPont (1880-1969) and is now a decorative arts and Americana museum. There are 175 period-room displays and about 85,000 objects. We took the tram ride around the estate grounds, briefly stopping at the many gardens.

We got off at the Enchanted Woods, a fairy-tale garden for children. My grandsons loved running around the garden to the fourteen stations of fun and imagination. At one stop, there was a Fairy Ring with cool mist coming up from the ground creating an illusion of a child disappearing from view. Aaron and Matthew loved climbing into a large pretend bird's nest and then looking down on us from their perch. They enjoyed the Tulip Tree House and Faerie Cottage where grandma bumped her head forgetting to duck walking through the doorway. They looked for the troll under the bridge. All of us had so much fun in the Enchanted Forest as we did not know what to expect around each bend in the path.

After a tour of the museum, I went back with the boys in the jeep. The clouds rolled in and we felt a few sprinkles of rain coming in the open jeep. I did not care. What a wonderful day! I felt young and silly, wind blowing, bouncing along in a jeep over the countryside and through the covered bridge. I loved it — a totally unexpected experience, from the jeep ride to the Enchanted Woods!

We need to savor those unexpected moments. We need opportunities to laugh and act like a child. We need to delight in spontaneity and try something we have never done before.

It is now August, and activities are beginning again at GPC. Seek out and try something new and different this year. Sign up for a committee you have never served on, or if music is your forte, join the choir. Attend a Sunday school class, Bible study, or teach a class, serve as a greeter, usher, or lay reader, or help serve food to the less fortunate.

Embrace the unexpected and love it. Be like a child — explore, create, wonder, and imagine. Share your time and talents with others, and you will receive unexpected joys. What unexpected moments will you cherish and embrace this year?

THE FIVE ACTIONS OF GRATITUDE
September 2013

Six of us, Pastor Terry Palmer, Mike and Karen Gallagher, Rocky Mackey, Grace Mossman, and I attended the stewardship conference, "Nurturing Generous Hearts," sponsored by the Synod of the Southwest. The event was held in Phoenix from Thursday, August 22, through Saturday, August 24. During the three days we heard three dynamic speakers during the plenary sessions and we also attended four workshops. I found the information presented very interesting and thought provoking.

One of the workshops I attended was "The Stewardship of Gratitude for Congregations," presented by Dr. Ed Brenegar. The speaker focused on 1 Thessalonians 5:16-18, "Be joyful always; pray continually; give thanks in all circumstances, for this is God's will for you in Christ Jesus." What a simple command for stewardship — be joyful, pray, and give thanks. With gratitude in our hearts and generosity in our actions, we respond to God's love and Christ's love for us.

According to Dr. Brenegar, there are five actions of gratitude. The first is to say thanks. Say thank you every day to God in your prayers. Say thank you to those who have made a difference in your life, work, and faith. Write a short note in appreciation for the contributions they have made. Dr. Brenegar said not to use e-mail or tweets for your thank you notes, but rather write a simple, sincere thank you note and mail it the old-fashioned way.

The second action of gratitude is to give back. Give back by serving others, your community and church. In appreciation for the difference that they made in your life, work, and faith, give back to others. Along with this second action of gratitude is the third one that says to make people feel welcome. Practice the hospitality of openness and opportunity so that people feel comfortable making a difference. Encourage people to serve others, their church and community.

The fourth action of gratitude is to honor others. Honor people for their participation and contributions of faith and stewardship. Finally, Dr. Brenegar's fifth action of gratitude is to create goodness in response to God's call to faith and stewardship.

These five actions of gratitude are all very simple and complete. Say thanks, give back, make welcome, honor others, and create goodness that is our response to God's love and Christ's love for us.

MY PATH TO TITHING
October 2013

Do I presently tithe to the church? Yes. Have I always tithed to the church? No.

When we were raising our four children, Roy and I felt that we could not tithe. We wanted to give more to our church, but there were always expenses in raising a family. Each of our children attended the college of his/her choice. In those years our budget was strained, even with me teaching. For several years we had three kids in college at the same time. Our children all were able to obtain their desired degree by working, receiving scholarships, obtaining student loans, and getting some money from us. Roy retired the same month our youngest child graduated from college. Finally, our part of college expenses was over.

When Roy retired, we moved to Gilbert and joined Gilbert Presbyterian Church (GPC). At that time our giving was approximately 5 percent of our income. The thought of tithing was scary. Could we give 10% to the church and still have enough money for living expenses on Roy's retirement and my part-time teaching position?

About that time our younger son, Alan, said to us that when he gives money to a non-profit organization, he also becomes involved by contributing his time and talents. That way he will learn firsthand how the organization is spending their funds. Yes, Alan, I firmly believe in your statement. I am active at GPC, and I do know how the money is spent.

Roy passed away during the summer of 2003. For six weeks my income was zero. I did not teach during the summer, so for those months I had no income in my name. And until Roy's death certificate was accepted by the state, I could not receive his retirement benefits. I was tithing to the church — ten percent of zero was zero! In the middle of September my tithing joke was over. I was back to teaching, and at the same time I received his retirement incomes. I thought about tithing, but wondered if I could afford to do so. I was now a widow. All monetary decisions were mine and mine alone, a new and daunting experience. I was still at the 5% level of giving to the church.

During the Fall 2004 Stewardship Campaign, the Stewardship Committee encouraged everyone to increase their offerings by one percent more than the percent given the previous year. Of course since I was on the Stewardship Committee, I did so. I was now at the 6% level. Perhaps every year I could raise my pledge by one percent until I was tithing.

I knew the church needed money — money for salaries for Pastor Terry and other staff members. The church must pay for utilities, office supplies, the Christian education program, music, mission and evangelism programs, and the pledge to the Presbytery. Also, we need to keep our church in good working order, dealing with normal maintenance and repair issues. A growing and dynamic church has many expenses.

Finally, several years ago, I made the leap to tithing. I came forward with my pledge to tithe. I dropped my pledge in the basket, but then wondered what I had done. Each year I was raising my pledge by one percent, and that did not bother me. But now, somehow, the word "tithe" scared me. Could I afford to tithe? At that time I was writing a check every week to the church. However, my retirement incomes were automatically deposited on the first day of the month. If I should tithe, would I have enough money left over at the end of each month to write a check to the church?

Then I made an important decision. God will get my first fruits, not my leftovers. The first check I write each month is my monthly tithe to GPC. My priority is first to God and my church. When He is first in my heart, mind, and wallet, everything else will fall into place.

And why shouldn't He be first? Everything we have and everything we are comes from God. We give in gratitude and love because God has so richly blessed us. And He gave us the best gift of all, His son, Jesus Christ. Let us not forget the monetary benefit of giving. As Jesus said, "Give to Caesar what is Caesar's, and to God what is God's" (Matthew 22:21). Every year in April when we add up what is "Caesar's," we can deduct what we have given to God.

This year the Stewardship Committee would like to encourage everyone to give one percent more of his/her income over last year. That is, only $1 more for every $100 income. Think of all God's work Gilbert Presbyterian Church could do with one percent more from everyone.

Prayerfully consider your pledge to God and Jesus Christ through our church — a pledge of your time, talents, and treasures. Come forward with love and thanksgiving in your hearts with your pledge on Commitment Sunday, November 3.

WHAT IS A CHURCH?
November 2013

When you hear or see the word "church," what do you think of?

Do you think about Gilbert Presbyterian Church as seen from Guadalupe Road with its light-colored exterior walls and roof line that points toward heaven? Or, do you think of the sanctuary with the stain-glass circular window and beautifully carved Celtic cross?

Perhaps in your mind you see the church of your childhood. What did it look like? Was it large or small? Or do you imagine a two hundred year-old church on the east coast with a tall spire reaching toward heaven? Perhaps you see a church located in a small town, nestled in a valley surrounded by rolling hills. Or, does the word "church" convey to you the large cathedrals of Europe with their tall inner columns, stained-glass windows, and murals on the walls? What is a church to you?

Do we need a building in order to hold worship services? Of course not! Think of our "son-rise" services early Easter morning. They are a very meaningful worship service held outdoors.

When we lived in Morenci, a copper mining town in Eastern Arizona, one Sunday every summer the congregation in our Presbyterian church carpooled to the nearby mountains. Our church services were held outside, followed by a potluck luncheon. We were surrounded by tall trees that pointed toward heaven. The woods were our cathedral on those Sundays. We might not need a building for one worship service, but we certainly need a building for the many services and activities conducted during the year.

When I was seven years old, I remember taking a family vacation trip to Virginia. We stopped at Natural Bridge. We sat on wooden benches and faced the beautiful arched bridge that was completely made by God. I remember a minister giving a sermon on the creation story from the Bible. Sitting there listening to the sermon and hearing the babbling brook, birds, and crickets made a lasting impression upon me, one that I have never forgotten.

But, something was missing at Natural Bridge, Virginia. Yes, it was a church service, but was it really a church? No, it was not a church. There was a component missing — the bonding of the people. To have a church, there must be four components — the building, worship, and people connecting. And, at the center of this triangle of building, worship, and people is the fourth component, Jesus Christ, the cornerstone of the church.

A church is a community of believers.

Is Gilbert Presbyterian Church a church? Most definitely! We have the building, worship, and people connecting in love and prayer with Jesus Christ as our center.

Have you seen the latest document, "Who Are We?" produced by a session-approved task force? The report describes who we are, our history, an overview of our community, and our congregation. It describes how we glorify God in worship, how we plant seeds of faith within our church and community, and how we cultivate disciples through our committees. It describes our gifts of time, talents, and treasures and our opportunities and challenges.

Read this document. We are a caring, friendly church and have many talents and skills that are used for the glory of God. We are truly blessed by God!

OUR GIFTS OF TIME AND TALENTS
December 2013

Have you seen the scroll on the inside of the sanctuary door? This scroll is a compilation of all the small scrolls that were placed in the basket along with your pledge card on Pledge Dedication Sunday. On the small scroll you wrote your promise to God about how you will use your gifts of time and talents in the coming year.

Read over the scroll. It shows a diversity of the many talents and gifts we have and wish to share. A number of people listed music as their gift. Yes, our congregation is blessed with many willing to share in the chancel choir, bell choir, orchestra, children's choir, and children's bells. Some of you share your musical talents by performing solos whether it is singing or playing musical instruments. Also mentioned was acting in plays and skits. It has been fun to watch the youth grow in their talents of music and/or acting throughout the years.

Your gift of supporting the church was mentioned many times. Several said they pledged to do their best by helping where needed. This help might be as a greeter, usher, lay reader or helping with the youth and teaching Sunday school. Several mentioned helping maintain the buildings in good condition by repairing or replacing things as needed. One pledged to take a more active part in the activities of the church. And some pledged to be faithful in their financial gifts and offerings.

Some people pledged to take an active part in mission work. Also evangelism, including reaching out to others and inviting people to church, was mentioned several times. One person listed the making of prayer shawls, and others mentioned the activities of Presbyterian Women.

Many pledged to take an active role in spiritual activities including praying for one another, encouraging others, supporting one's faith journeys, sharing faith with others, and reading the Bible. One person pledged to be a more dedicated Christian. Another person said, "I will greet everyone with a joyful smile to show God's joy within me!" Amen to that!

For those of you who perhaps forgot to make a pledge of your time and talents to God and the church, I urge you to do so. Think about what your response might be. God has given us many gifts, including the finest gift of all, Jesus Christ.

This month we are celebrating the birth of Jesus. What is your gift of time and talents that you are bringing to the Christ Child for this coming year? Please join me in a challenge to periodically refer back to the promises we have made on our scroll.

During the year, look to see how well you are doing. Are you growing in faith and stewardship by sharing your time, talents, and treasures with others? With love, joy, and thanksgiving in our hearts, let us fulfill our pledge to God and GPC!

2014

BUT GOD SAID TO HIM, YOU FOOL!

And he told them this parable: "The ground of a certain rich man produced a good crop. He thought to himself, 'What should I do? I have no place to store my crops.' Then he said, 'This is what I'll do. I will tear down my barns and build bigger ones, and there I will store all my grain and goods. And I'll say to myself, 'You have plenty of good things laid up for many years. Take life easy; eat, drink, and be merry.'" But God said to him, "You fool! This very night your life will be demanded from you. Then who will get what you have prepared for yourself? This is how it will be with anyone who stores up things for himself, but is not rich toward God."

Luke 12:16-21

HAPPY NEW YEAR!
January 2014

I woke to the aroma of coffee wafting through the house. Oh, how I loved the smell of freshly brewed coffee. My parents were eating their breakfast. We all had slept in that morning as we stayed up late welcoming in the New Year.

Every year from the time I was ten until I graduated from college and left home, our family had spent New Year's Eve with our next-door neighbors, the Fosters. We alternated years — one year we celebrated at our house and the next year at theirs. They had one child, Marilyn, two years older than I. My older brother Cal and I played many games with Marilyn. Our favorites were Parcheesi, Monopoly, and Authors.

I laid there in bed, not wanting to get up, and thinking about last night and the fun we had. Mrs. Foster made very yummy desserts. Our families had whistles and other noise makers to welcome in the New Year. Cal usually played his latest piano piece, a Beethoven sonata or a Chopin waltz. Mrs. Foster was a pianist herself — she played for our church. In fact she was my first piano teacher.

Later when I was in high school, we watched on our grainy black and white TV the New Year's Eve special featuring Guy Lombardo's band and the dropping of the ball in New York City. Enough reminiscing of last night — the celebration is over. I must get up. There is work to be done.

Our family's tradition was to put away the Christmas decorations on New Year's Day, something I continue to do as an adult today. We kids would carefully take the ornaments off the tree, wrap them in tissue paper, and place them in a box. In those days they were made of glass. Next, we would take off the paper chain that we kids had made for the tree. Then, off came the tinsel, and finally the lights.

Even as careful as we were in removing the lights, it seemed like the strands somehow got tangled while stored. For six years or so, my dad purchased a living tree. If the ground was not frozen, he would be outside digging a hole for our Christmas tree. We had a row of Christmas trees across our backyard.

After the tree was removed from our living room, we swept up the fallen needles and moved any furniture back to where it belonged. The Rose Bowl Parade was first televised when I was in high school. It was fun watching the parade and marveling at all the sunshine in California. We wished we could be there instead of Cleveland, Ohio, where the sun rarely shone in winter.

Many of you may also have a tradition of taking down your Christmas decorations on New Year's Day or perhaps a few days before or after. No matter the precise day, it always entails carefully packing the decorations away for another year and getting the house back in order.

The New Year signifies a fresh start, new hopes and dreams.

What about our lives? Do we need to put our lives back in order? Do we need to make a fresh start and forgive someone? What are our dreams for the coming year? What are our dreams for GPC for the coming year? Have you made resolutions — resolutions concerning family and friends, your spiritual life, health and fitness, and finances? Do your resolutions include learning something new, helping others, and getting more organized?

Think about your plans and goals for 2014. Say thank you to God for giving you gifts of time, talents, and treasures that may be used for the work in His kingdom. Let Jesus lead you as you explore how you might use your gifts in 2014. Have a wonderful new year!

AN ACT OF TRUE LOVE
February 2014

Have you seen the Walt Disney computer-animated movie, *Frozen*? It is based on Hans Christian Andersen's fairy tale, "The Snow Queen." The high mountain scenery is fantastic. A small village is nestled right at the foot of the mountain on the edge of the fjord. This is Norway, and even a family of trolls plays a part in the story.

Briefly, this movie is about two princesses growing up in the kingdom of Arendelle. The older sister, Elsa, has special powers of making anything turn to ice and snow just by the touch of her finger. On the day of her coronation, she gets into an argument with her sister, Anna.

Elsa flees, and in doing so, turns the kingdom into eternal winter. Anna, accompanied by a mountain man, his pet reindeer, and an animated snowman, sets off on her search for Elsa. They have many adventures along the way, but they do find Elsa in a self-made ice palace high in the mountains.

When they meet, Elsa accidentally strikes Anna in the chest, causing her heart to become frozen. The trolls declare that only an act of true love can thaw her; otherwise, she will remain frozen forever.

At the right moment, Anna is able to throw herself between her sister and an assailant. However, she immediately becomes a solid block of ice. Anna's decision to sacrifice herself to save her sister was an act of true love. As Elsa grieves for her sister, Anna begins to thaw. Elsa then realizes that love is the key to controlling her icy powers. The snow melts and flowers once again bloom in the kingdom. "Frozen" is a beautiful fairy tale of sacrificial love.

Jesus said, "Greater love has no one than this, that he lay down his life for his friends" (John 15:13). Jesus sacrificed his life for us. He died for us and our sins. Most of us will not have to die for someone, but we can practice generous love by listening, caring, and encouraging others.

With love and thanksgiving in our hearts, let us share as Jesus taught us to share our time, talents, and treasures. Practice the love that will melt a frozen heart!

ANGEL'S STORY
March 2014

After I returned from my two-week trip to the Holy Land, my brother, Cal, asked me what I appreciated most when I arrived home. Immediately I said, "My freedom." Throughout my daily life here in the United States, I have not given a thought to issues related to my freedom. But when I visited Israel, I became acutely aware of how fortunate we are to live in a country such as ours. We are truly blessed.

There were 22 of us from the Synod of the Southwest touring the Holy Land. In Bethlehem, we met Angel, a 28-year-old Palestinian Christian. After she obtained her Bachelor's degree from a college in Bethlehem, she wanted to attend the University of Wisconsin for her Master's program. She needed a visa to come to the states. That does not sound like a difficult problem, but in Bethlehem it is, since the city is in the West Bank.

Palestine, or the West Bank, is not a country. It has been under Israeli military occupation since 1967. Angel needed to obtain her visa from the U. S. Embassy which is located in Jerusalem, Israel. However, since she is a young adult Palestinian, she is not allowed to enter Israel. Many times she asked permission from the military but was denied.

After many prayers, Angel finally was contacted one evening at 10:30 p.m. She was told she could cross into Israel between 8 and 10 a.m. the next day. She had to be back in Bethlehem by 10 a.m. or risk serving time in jail.

Yes, Angel did obtain her visa and make it back across the border in time. Then her next challenge was finding a way to get to America. Angel knew she could not go to the airport in Tel Aviv since it is in Israel, so she flew from Jordan. She did not risk coming home for a visit during her time in America. Instead, she waited until she received her Master's degree before flying home through Jordan.

Angel took us on a tour of the library at Dar Al Kalima University in Bethlehem. Think of any American college or university library — a large building, centrally located on campus, filled to capacity with volumes of books and magazines. By contrast, the library at Dar Al Kalima consisted of one room no bigger than our sanctuary at Gilbert Presbyterian Church. The shelves were only one-fourth to one-third filled with books. I probably have more books in my home than that library had in Bethlehem.

We were told that if they order books, they are stopped at the checkpoint. The books might possibly be delivered to the library in a year or two, if they are lucky. If a book is ordered by a Palestinian, the person receiving the book is taken in for questioning by the military as to why the book was ordered and who sent it. Books sometimes can be smuggled in the luggage of a visitor from another country. If we had only known, I believe every one of us on our Holy Land tour would have smuggled in a book or two in our suitcases.

I asked about the internet and E-books. The Israeli government censors the internet into the West Bank. However, Palestinians are writing and publishing books. I cannot imagine a life without books.

A concrete wall built by the Israeli government divides Israel and the West Bank. We saw it. It is ugly, 30 or more feet high. There are only a few checkpoints. Many Palestinians cannot cross into Israel. The wall has shut off roads and divided neighborhoods. The wall has kept people from their jobs, churches, doctors, and hospitals.

We visited the Tent of Nations, a peace project and dream of the Palestinian Christian, Bishara Nassar. International and local groups come together on the farmland in the tree-planting program and summer work and study camps. Olive, grape, and almond trees are grown. Just two days before we arrived, the road to the Tent of Nations was completely blocked by two rows of gigantic boulders taller than any man. Of course, our bus could not get through so we carefully squeezed around the barrier one person at a time, and then climbed the hill to the farm.

We also heard the story of Elias Chacour, Archbishop of Galilee of the Melkite Greek Catholic Church. He has written books of his peacemaking experiences and building schools in Palestine. To build a school requires a building permit which he continuously was denied. He went ahead anyway and built the schools without a permit. There is always a chance a building without a permit will be destroyed, but so far his buildings remain standing.

Elias Chacour asked us to tell our friends and family what we heard and saw in the West Bank upon our return home. All of the Palestinian Christians said, "Pray for us." Yes, we must pray for our brothers and sisters in Christ. Let us also pray for the Israeli and Palestinian leaders that they may achieve a peace that will grant justice and freedom for all.

I WALKED WHERE JESUS WALKED
April 2014

Twenty-two of us from the Synod of the Southwest toured the Holy Land in February. We followed the life of Jesus from his birth in Bethlehem, baptism in the Jordan River, his ministry along the shores of the Sea of Galilee, and finally his last days in Jerusalem. We walked the paths, climbed the stone steps, and sailed on Galilee as He had done 2,000 years ago.

I have seen many pictures of the Holy Land, but pictures are not the same as being there. I was not expecting so many mountains. All of the cities and towns are built on hills. I was surprised at the number of rocks and boulders everywhere, all the same off-white color. The rocky ground was terraced into fields to grow the crops. Rock walls divided the plots.

The rock has become their building material. Looking at any city from a distance, all the buildings appear to be constructed from the same light-colored rock. Whether it was an office building, store, or home, they had the same angular, boxy shape. There were no buildings completely made of wood. The ever-present rock was Jerusalem limestone. David would have had no problem at all finding the perfect rock for his sling shot, based on what we saw there.

On our first full day in the Holy Land, the bus took us to a hillside overlooking the outskirts of Bethlehem. This was Shepherds' Field, a beautiful park with well-manicured bushes and other plants, mostly succulents. A church was built over the site where the angel appeared to the shepherds. Some of the murals inside the church depicted the shepherds caring for their sheep. Another mural showed the birth of Jesus. There was also a fountain with sculptures of a shepherd and his sheep in front of the church.

It was very peaceful that day, not many people other than us. It was easy to envision shepherds tending their flocks on that hill and an angel appearing to them announcing the birth of our Savior.

The next day we visited the Church of the Nativity and Manger Square. We had to stoop to get inside the church as the doorway was made low for defense purposes at the time of the Crusades. It is one of the oldest churches in the world, built over 1,600 years ago. About 200 years later the Church of the Nativity was built utilizing parts of the original church.

The church is directly over the cave where Jesus was born. There are numerous caves in the surrounding hills of Bethlehem, and in Biblical times the farm animals were kept inside these caves. Yes, it is believed that Jesus was born in a cave.

We waited in a long line going down some very steep steps to see a giant silver star set in the floor over the spot where Jesus was born. We also saw the manger where He laid.

Our visit to Nazareth included a walk around a small recreated Biblical village. On the hillside, shepherds were tending their sheep. In one building a carpenter was working, and in another a woman was making blankets of wool. We were told that carpentry in Biblical times did not mean the same as it does today. Carpentry meant making thatch roofs and working with stone. A carpenter was really a stonecutter. The

Holy Land did not have enough trees to have houses built of wood in Biblical times — the same holds true today.

There are two different places along the Jordan River that are said to be the site of Jesus' baptism. It is up to the visitor to decide which is correct. The first one we visited is where the Sea of Galilee flows into the Jordan River. This is a very beautiful and fertile part of lower Galilee with olives, grapes, fruits, and vegetables grown on the rolling hills. The baptismal site itself is lush with vegetation. We sat on benches overlooking the water contemplating Jesus' baptism.

At the end of our trip we visited the other baptismal site. There the Jordan River meanders through the desert of sand and rock. Only when we arrived at the banks of the river did we see vegetation of any kind. We watched a group of people all dressed in white gowns being baptized by getting dunked in the water. They actually were in Israel while we were across the river in Jordan.

One of my favorite activities was the boat ride on the Sea of Galilee. It was a dark, cold, and windy evening when we arrived at Ein Gev Kibbutz along the Sea of Galilee. That night I looked out our hotel window and saw the wind whip the water into white caps. As I was drifting to sleep, I wondered if Jesus would calm the sea for our boat ride the next morning. He most certainly did!

The day was beautiful with clear blue skies and water as smooth as glass. From the middle of the lake we could see churches along the shore. Later we visited the Church of Multiplication, built on the site of the Miracle of the Loaves and Fishes, Chapel of the Primacy of Peter, and the Church of the Beatitudes. It was easy to imagine Jesus calling his disciples as they were tending their nets along the shore — or seeing them fishing from a boat — or speaking to people on the hill overlooking the Sea of Galilee.

On the northern shore of the Sea of Galilee is the ancient city of Capernaum. Jesus conducted his ministry there, and it was home to Peter and other disciples. It is now an archeological site. We were able to walk among the tall Roman columns in what was once the synagogue.

Our journey also took us to Jerusalem. Our hotel, St. Mark's Lutheran Guesthouse, was located within the walls of the Old City of Jerusalem, but our bus was not allowed to enter. Many of the streets in the Old City are very narrow alleyways with the old stone buildings either against each other or just a few feet across from one another. I am very glad we had a guide. I definitely would have gotten lost in the maze of those alleys.

I counted 84 stone steps from the Jaffa Gate where the bus left us off to our hotel. The 84 steps were not all at once, but rather spread out — we took two or three steps up and then walked 10 to 20 feet to a few more steps. The Old City of Jerusalem is not at all handicapped accessible. It is built on a hill with many uneven stone steps and inclines.

As is true with any large city, we encountered masses of people every place we went, many of whom were visitors like us. If the crowds 2,000 years ago were like they are today, I can completely understand why Jesus wanted to be alone and pray. However, today the Garden of Gethsemane is not a quiet place.

Our bus left us off on top of the Mount of Olives and we walked down a steep road to the Garden of Gethsemane. The olive trees are very old with gnarled trunks, perhaps even 2,000 years old. We looked across the Kidron Valley and saw the Old City Walls and the Temple Mount with its brilliant golden Dome of the Rock.

We were met by the bus at the bottom of the Mount of Olives and we rode across the Kidron Valley to Caiaphas' House where Jesus was imprisoned. We walked down the steep steps into the dungeon. That was very sobering.

A few days later, we took a walking tour around the Old City of Jerusalem. We stopped to pray at the Wailing Wall. We went to the Temple Mount, but of course were not allowed inside the Dome of the Rock. We stopped and went inside St. Anne's Church, located at the place where Mary's parents are said to have lived. The sanctuary ceiling is dome shaped so the acoustics are fantastic. We sang several hymns, while inside, and yes we did sound great.

Beside the church is the Pool of Bethesda where Jesus healed the paralyzed man. We walked the Via Dolorosa, the fourteen Stations of the Cross. That path took us up and down stone steps through the narrow streets of Old Jerusalem. The last five stations are located inside the Church of the Holy Sepulcher. There the line slowly snaked around to the places where He was laid on the cross, crucified, and buried.

To me, the trip to the Holy Land made the Bible come alive. Now when I read a passage, I can say I was there. I can visualize what the cities and countryside might have looked like 2,000 years ago. Like Jesus, I too wanted to get away from the crowds. I felt the closest to Christ on Shepherds' Field, boating on the Sea of Galilee, and beside the Jordan River. Yes, I walked the paths, climbed the stone steps, and sailed the sea as Jesus had done long ago. It was truly a wonderful, unforgettable adventure!

IS THIS THE VOICE OF GOD?
May 2014

I have often wondered about the voice of God. What does it sound like? How do we know when He is speaking to us? Are we sure it is actually God's voice we hear? At times I feel like Samuel who believes it is Eli who is calling. Three times the Lord calls Samuel before Eli finally tells the boy to listen because it is God who is speaking.

Does God have a deep, booming voice like the roll of thunder during a summer monsoon storm? Or is God's voice gentle and mild like a babbling brook or the quiet rustling of the leaves? I once had a boss who always spoke very softly whenever he had something important to say. We staff members had to stop and listen very carefully to hear him. Is God like that? Are we missing out on what God is saying because we are not listening? Or, are we not attuned to His voice? Can God get our attention above the noise of the 21st century?

Does God speak to us through our friends and family? I would say definitely yes. Does he speak to us through our dreams — perhaps? When we have a gut feeling to do something, is that God speaking to us? Quite possibly. Does God speak to us through His beautiful creations — sunsets, mountains, lakes, rivers, flowers, and the stars and moon in the night sky? To me, that too is yes.

Does God speak to us through His little creatures? Perhaps. A few weeks ago, I was feeling rather discouraged when practicing my piano. Nothing was sounding quite right. I just could not get my fingers to cooperate. I took a short break and opened my front door because it was so nice outside. When I went back to practicing, I heard a bird in my palo verde tree chirp ever so beautifully. It seemed like the faster I played, the faster he sung. Was he singing to my beat or was I playing to his? He did not stop until I stopped.

The next day I did not hear him at first. He was not in my tree. Then, as I began playing the piano, I heard through my open door a flutter of wings and his beautiful song. I don't think he has missed coming by on a single afternoon in this past month. He is always in my tree singing as I play. Was he sent by God to encourage me? Is that little bird the voice of God?

Stop and listen carefully as God may be speaking to you. Listen to what He has to say. Is God encouraging you or perhaps telling you what to do? Seek His help and guidance. Hear Him speak through prayer, worship, and devotion. Listen and become attuned to the many different voices of God.

THE LIBERTY BELL
July 2014

It was warm that afternoon as we stood in line at the Liberty Bell Center in Philadelphia. I was on a Road Scholar tour. My fellow travelers and I looked for shade (what little there was).

While waiting to enter the building, we looked at panels explaining that on this site was the slave quarters owned by President George Washington. How ironic to learn that over 200 years ago slave quarters existed where the Liberty Bell, a symbol of freedom, now hangs!

Before construction of the Liberty Bell Center in 2001, archeologists uncovered the footprint of the President's home used by George Washington and John Adams from 1790 to 1800.

It was now our group's turn to enter the long glass and steel building. Inside were exhibits and panels highlighting the history of the Liberty Bell. There were even X-ray pictures of the bell showing the extent of the crack. Another panel showed a picture of Nelson Mandela next to the Liberty Bell and a quote by him, "The Liberty Bell is a very significant symbol for the entire democratic world."

Walking a little farther, we saw the Liberty Bell hanging from its yoke in front of floor-to-ceiling windows. Looking through the windows, we saw Independence Hall across the street. What a fantastic message of freedom, the Liberty Bell and Independence Hall!

I was quite surprised at the size of the bell, as I expected a much larger bell. At first I thought maybe it looked small because it was hanging in a very spacious building. But no, it is not that large. True, it weighs 2,080 pounds, but considering the circumference of its lip, which is 12 feet, it is not a large bell. A 12-foot circumference makes the diameter at the bottom of the bell 3 feet 10 inches. The length of its clapper is 3 feet 2 inches. To me, the symbolism portrayed by the bell is far greater than its size.

American history happened here in Philadelphia. Of course we think of Benjamin Franklin entering Philadelphia as a young man with a big loaf of bread tucked under his arm or flying his kite and discovering static electricity. But Ben Franklin isn't all there is to Philadelphia.

After looking at the Liberty Bell, we went across the street to Independence Hall. There in the Assembly Room, both the Declaration of Independence and Constitution were written and signed. Can you imagine listening to the Declaration of Independence read to the public in 1776? How exciting!

It must have been a thrill to think of breaking away from England, but signers surely also felt fear regarding what lay ahead. The signers of the Declaration of Independence were now traitors!

We also saw the Betsy Ross House and Christ Church where President George Washington worshiped when in Philadelphia. On another day, we went to the National Constitution Center. The tour began by listening to "Freedom Rising," a theatrical production narrated by an actor tracing our history of freedom.

The theater was a complete circle. From our

seats we looked up and as the actor was speaking, we saw pictures showing the important historical happenings and people of our country. Afterwards, we walked around and experienced interactive exhibits highlighting the history of the Constitution. I could have easily stayed longer in the National Constitution Center.

What does liberty and freedom mean to us in the 21st century? Do we thank God that we live in a country such as ours? Do we appreciate all that our ancestors have done for us — fighting and dying for us? Do we say thank you to our military servicemen and women? Do we appreciate our liberty and freedom? That is, to name a few — the freedom to choose where we worship, freedom of speech, our liberty to vote for our representatives and the freedom to obtain an education.

There are many people in the world whose governments deny them their liberties and freedom. To paraphrase President John F. Kennedy, what are we doing for our country so that our children and grandchildren can continue to enjoy liberty and freedom?

Let us not forget the words inscribed and cast on the Liberty Bell — "Proclaim liberty throughout all the land unto all the inhabitants thereof" (Leviticus 25:10).

A SPIRITUAL LEGACY
August 2014

The conductor raises his baton. As soon as the orchestra plays the first few notes, the entire audience stands. This tradition began in 1742, when the King of England rose upon hearing the first note. Everyone knows this triumphant piece even before the choir sings out, "Hallelujah." Yes, this is the Hallelujah Chorus, just one part of George Frederic Handel's Messiah.

When Handel completed the Hallelujah Chorus, he said, "I think I saw all Heaven before me, and the great God Himself."

Handel composed the Messiah in only 24 days. When we listen to the Messiah, we experience Handel's profound belief in God. For over 200 years, this composition has influenced generations of listeners. Every musician in the orchestra and every singer in the choir performing the Messiah pass on Handel's wonderful spiritual legacy to us.

Johann Sebastian Bach was also very religious. When Bach began composing, he would write at the top of the page, "Help me, Jesus" and when he finished, "To God alone, the glory." Franz Schubert, when writing letters, thanked God for his talents. Felix Mendelssohn on his manuscripts wrote, "Let it succeed, God!" We learn of the spiritual beliefs of great composers by their musical compositions and their comments and prayers to God. That is their legacy to us.

The book, <u>Spiritual Lives of the Great Composers</u>, by Patrick Kavanaugh, is very fascinating. It contains biographical sketches of twenty famous composers with emphasis on their religious beliefs. All of the above examples are from this book. On page 205 of his book, Kavanaugh poses an interesting question: "If a biographer should someday research my life, what tangible verifications of my faith would be evident?"

Most of us do not have the expertise to compose music. We are not Handel, Bach, Beethoven, or Mozart. Yet, we can leave a legacy of our faith to our children and grandchildren. My grandmother gave me her Bible, King James, marked with her comments and favorite passages. I, in turn, passed on her Bible to my daughter. My daughter never met her great grandmother, but she knows her favorite Biblical passages, her beliefs and faith. By passing on her Bible, my grandmother left a spiritual legacy to my daughter.

Back to Patrick Kavanaugh's question, what proof of our faith are we leaving our children and grandchildren? Do we freely talk to them about our faith? Do we write about our faith? Do we leave little messages of our faith on our letters, e-mails, or text messages? Do we write in our Bible, marking our favorite passages so that they will be discovered and read by our great-grandchildren?

Pass on your beliefs in God and Christ and leave a spiritual legacy to your loved ones, now and in the future.

A 21st CENTURY PARABLE OF THE FOOLISH HOMEOWNER
September 2014

My two grandchildren, ages 3 and 5, excitedly raced up the stairs. They wanted to show me their prospective bedrooms. My son, Alan, and his wife, Suzy, had picked me up one Sunday afternoon a few weeks ago to show me a model home they were considering buying. It was located in the southern part of Gilbert in a neighborhood with a walking trail, children's play areas, and a nearby elementary school. The home and neighborhood looked ideal for my son and his family.

While there, I walked through a smaller model home which would be perfect for me. I could live near Alan, Suzy, and my grandkids. I liked the house. It was a little larger than my present home. The extra space would be great when my daughters and their families come to visit me, and the closets were very spacious. I had a lot to think about. Do I want to move?

I did not realize how far south we were until we started back to my house. We went straight up Val Vista and finally turned west on Guadalupe Road. Almost a half hour later we passed Gilbert Presbyterian Church. As many times as I am at church, do I want to drive that distance? Absolutely not! My present home is in an ideal location — only one mile from church.

I looked over my house. What is wrong with it that I would even consider moving to a larger one? Eighteen years ago my house was perfect. Now it, especially the closets, is too small. Did they shrink in the hot Arizona sun? Of course not.

I have accumulated too much stuff. I laughed to myself. Am I the 21st century version of the parable of "The Rich Fool?" Jesus spoke of the farmer who had so much grain he decided to tear down his present barn and build a bigger one so he could store all his crops. Am I the foolish homeowner who wants to build a bigger home to store my stuff? And the bigger home would be located farther from church. "No," I said to myself, "don't act like a fool!"

Instead of needing a larger house, I need less stuff. I must be a good steward and donate any items that I no longer use such as clothes, jackets, or blankets to GPC West or the Goodwill. I must pass on any books I no longer need to the Friends of the Library. Evangelism Committee is considering another "Weigh to Fundraise" event. That will be a good time to get rid of unneeded items.

And all those notes, lesson plans, and tests left over from my teaching. I certainly don't need those. They can go in the blue recycling bin.

It is important for all of us to take control of our belongings before they control us. No, I am not a rich fool!

PAY IT FORWARD AND PLANT A TREE
October 2014

A few years after my husband Roy and I moved into our new home in Gilbert, we spotted orange trees that were on sale in Walmart. Roy loved oranges, so we purchased two little trees. They were not much more than twigs with a few leaves. He dug two holes in the corner of our backyard. They were so small that I wasn't sure they would ever produce oranges.

Roy, on the other hand, knew they would bear fruit. He planted the trees, watered them, talked to and about them, and prayed for them. He could almost taste their juicy fruit. Roy proudly showed our granddaughter, Desi, his orange trees. The first few years the trees did not produce any fruit, as they were still very small. But when Desi was about eight years old, she and Roy were finally able to pick an orange and eat it.

Several years later, our grandson, Davy, was born. He was only an infant when Roy carried him outside telling him about the trees. The following year Davy toddled along with his sister and grandpa to pick oranges from the trees. Roy was so very proud of his two grandkids and his two trees.

It takes time — God's time — for a tree to mature, produce wonderful shade, and bear fruit. And many times the person planting the tree is paying it forward for the next generation to enjoy the tree and reap its harvest. Roy planted the orange trees and lovingly cared for them. The trees have grown considerably since that day when Roy helped Davy at age 2 pick oranges from his trees. Every year since then, I imagine that Roy has been looking down from heaven and smiling as he watches six more little grandchildren picking and eating sweet, juicy oranges from his trees.

Jesus has already paid it forward for us to reap the harvest. In John 15:5, Jesus said, "I am the vine; you are the branches. If a man remains in me and I in him, he will bear much fruit; apart from me you can do nothing." What fruit will we bear? How shall we respond to God's love?

We have received many gifts — gifts of time, talents, and treasures. How can we pay it forward and share our gifts with others? October is Stewardship month. Before the end of the month, you will be receiving a letter along with a pledge card. Prayerfully consider your pledge to God and Jesus Christ through our church — a pledge of your time, talents, and treasures. Then on Sunday November 2, come forward and present your pledge with love and thanksgiving in your heart.

SIGHTS AND SOUNDS OF AUTUMN
November 2014

The early morning air was dry and crisp as I walked in the neighborhood. I knew by the feel in the air the monsoon rains of summer were now over. Yes, no more oppressing heat! I love the cool days of autumn — my favorite season.

On my walk I saw the Arizona trees — palo verde, mesquite, and palm — but visualized in my mind the oak, elm, and maple trees of my childhood. There I was back in time, skipping off to school. The tall trees lined the walk, their branches reaching out like giant umbrellas. I loved the autumn trees with their full array of colors — gold, yellow, orange, red, and browns. The dry leaves that had already fallen now crackled beneath my feet. What a neat sound! I stopped to admire a leaf or two or perhaps gathered a few pretty ones to give to my teacher. In the next block, squirrels were scampering about gathering nuts for the winter ahead.

As a child, I loved autumn — a time when my family would take a Sunday afternoon drive to the orchard to buy fresh apples and cider. In those days, that was real apple cider — cloudy in color, the type that would ferment in a few days. I loved Thanksgiving — family and friends together, surrounded by mounds of food. I loved the smell of freshly baked pumpkin pies, homemade bread, and turkey just coming out of the oven. There was nothing better than fall with the anticipation of Christmas around the corner.

My favorite time of year is still autumn — a time to reflect what God has given us — bountiful harvest, friends and family, beautiful countryside, and brightly colored leaves. It is a time to look forward to Christmas, the celebration of God's greatest gift to us — the birth of the Christ Child.

Yes, autumn is a time for gratitude and giving thanks to God. It is a time to make a promise to God to give back to Him a portion of that with which He has so richly blessed us. Everything we have and everything we are comes from God.

Just as it takes many different trees ablaze in color to create a beautiful autumn scene, so does it take all of us to create a wonderful growing church that is welcoming to everyone. This month make a pledge to God through the church to share a portion of your time, talents, and treasures.

On Dedication Sunday, November 2, come forward with your pledge with thanksgiving, joy, and love in your hearts.

"I WAS SICK AND YOU
LOOKED AFTER ME" (Matthew 25:36)
December 2014

This month we celebrate the birth of Jesus, born a little more than 2,000 years ago in a manger. He taught us to care for others and help those who are sick and lonely.

Jesus was not afraid to touch and heal the sick of His day, and that included people with skin diseases such as leprosy. Those who had leprosy were ostracized in their community. Everyone shunned them. No one loved or touched them. They were forced to fend for themselves and live in caves away from everyone. Leprosy was a very contagious disease.

In the 19th century, people's reactions to those with leprosy were no different from the reactions lepers received during Biblical days. There was no medical cure for the disease; therefore, to keep the disease from spreading, the solution was to isolate people with leprosy. At that time, leprosy was rapidly spreading among native Hawaiians.

King Kamehameha V in 1865 signed the "Act to Prevent the Spread of Leprosy." It essentially forced anyone into exile who had symptoms of the disease. The Kalaupapa Peninsula on Molokai Island was chosen to become the leper colony for Hawaii. It was thought to be an ideal location for isolation as 1,600-foot-high cliffs separated the peninsula from the rest of the island. And, of course, the ocean surrounded the other three sides.

In January 1866, twelve people were the first to be exiled on Kalaupapa. Through the years, hundreds more followed. In 1873 a Catholic Priest, Father Damien, chose to minister to the people of Kalaupapa. He devoted his life to them by building a church, teaching, preaching, and caring for them.

Father Damien brought about many changes to the colony. While he was there, 44 orphan children were under his care. Unfortunately, the priest's dedication came with a price. In 1885, Father Damien was diagnosed with leprosy, and fifteen years later he passed away.

On my recent Road Scholar trip to Hawaii, I felt quite honored to visit Kalaupapa. Kalaupapa is very beautiful with its towering cliffs, green fields, forest, and the blue ocean lapping on its shore. But there is sadness too, thinking of the people who were forced to live there for the remainder of their lives.

Families were torn apart because of the disease. Children were forced to leave their parents (the youngest child was only 3 years old). Parents were forced to leave their children.

Our group visited the church that Father Damien built. We saw the quarters where visitors remained on one side of a glass partition while those with leprosy remained on the other. They could not touch one another.

We ate our picnic lunch in a beautiful forested area overlooking the ocean. I looked up at the cliffs and thought that there was no way anyone could escape Kalaupapa. Yes, now there is a trail to the top so one can take a mule ride or hike it. But in the time when it was a leper colony, the only way in or out was by boat. We were transported to and from the area in a nine-passenger propeller plane. It was the shortest plane ride I have ever had — 10 minutes. The pilot had to make four trips to get everyone in our group to Kalaupapa.

In 1941 a medical cure for leprosy was discovered, but it wasn't until 1969 that Hawaii's isolation laws were abolished. Yes, people still can get leprosy, but with medication it is not the disease that was once so feared.

There are still a few people with leprosy who are living in Kalaupapa. Today they are not required to reside there, but they choose to stay because it is their home. Now they are free to go "topside" whenever they desire. Our bus driver in Kalaupapa told us a story about a visitor to Kalaupapa some time ago. The visitor asked a patient, "What would you like me to tell about Kalaupapa when I return home." The patient said, "Tell the people topside that our church is so very important to us." There once were three churches actively involved in Kalaupapa — Catholic, Protestant, and Mormon.

Today, people are still ostracized in their communities, perhaps not for leprosy but for other reasons. A few years ago it was AIDS and now Ebola. Sometimes people are shunned just because they look or act different from the so-called norm. Perhaps they are mentally ill, homeless or, for other reasons, they are ignored.

We must remember that God created all of us. Jesus wants us to love and care for others and help those who are sick and lonely. Our church is our salvation and so very important to everyone.

2015

OUR FATHER IN HEAVEN

Our Father in Heaven, hallowed be your name, your kingdom come, your will be done, on earth as it is in heaven.

Give us today our daily bread. Forgive us our debts, as we also have forgiven our debtors. And lead us not into temptation, but deliver us from the evil one.

Matthew 6: 9-13

A LITTLE PRAYER
January 2015

As I was driving to Target to do some Christmas shopping, I thought about the little boy, age 2, I chose from our Angel tree. What did he look like? I immediately pictured a cute little boy with sparkling brown eyes, dark tousled hair, big wide grin, and infectious smile. What did he like to do? Probably like most 2-year-olds he was always on the go, running (as walking was too slow for him).

He would be curious and stop to investigate things like a bug on the walk. Then he would look up to his parents or caregiver wondering why. He might have a funny little laugh. And after a full day's activities, he would instantly fall asleep, looking ever so peaceful — just like a little angel.

I thought of my own grandsons when they were 2 and what they liked to play with. There was no problem choosing toys for my little angel. I had fun that day knowing that perhaps what I chose might be the only toys he would receive for Christmas.

I thought about my little angel as I was driving home. I prayed for him. I prayed that he is attending Sunday school and learning about Jesus. I prayed that he will always have an inquisitive nature and do well in school. Then I prayed that he will rise above the poverty he is presently living in and will not be influenced by drugs and other problems of society.

I prayed that somehow he will obtain an education, whether in college or in a skilled trade. My prayer was full of dreams for my little angel.

Later I thought why not, during 2015, silently pray for the recipients of all our Mission projects? Why not say a little prayer every time we drop off food or clothes in the narthex? Pray for that person receiving our gifts. Why not say a little prayer when we serve meals or make sandwiches for the shelters or donate our time and treasures to any of the other charitable agencies we help? Why not say a little silent prayer for the recipient of our homeless kits?

Our prayers do not have to be spoken aloud — only God needs to know our prayers and thoughts. Even though I do not know my little angel and he does not know me, that anonymity will not stop me from praying for him!

Note: Each recipient of gifts from GPC members is represented by a Christmas tree decoration in the shape of an angel that carries information about the anonymous child — hence, the label "Christmas Angel."

LEARNING TO LOVE
February 2015

The baby cries. The parents stop whatever they are doing and care for their infant. The needs of their child take precedence over whatever the parents might be doing. That is love.

The baby grows, and the parents take their little one to church, making sure the child learns about Jesus in Sunday school. That is love.

The child enters school, and throughout the years he enrolls in activities such as sports and music. The parents attend his games and concerts. That is love.

The parents give the child responsibilities according to his age. The parents encourage the child to share with others. That is love.

Now the child is a teenager. They teach the child to become a responsible adult and, along with that, how to drive. The parents pray for their child's safety. That is love.

The family participates in the church's mission programs by buying gifts for someone on the Christmas Angel Tree, serving meals in the shelters, making food boxes, and handing out homeless kits. That is love.

The years quickly go by. Now the child is an adult with a family of his own and remembers what his parents did for him, so he passes on their love to his children. The parents, now older and retired, continue to serve in their church as long as they are able. That is love.

Soon the roles of parent and child become reversed and the child is now the one who is concerned with the health and welfare of the parents. That is love — a full circle of love.

Love is demonstrated in many ways, but it always requires some form of action. Love is not passive. We cannot say we love someone and then do nothing. That is not love. We express love by doing for others — our families, friends, and even those we do not know. We care and love our children because we want them to grow intellectually and spiritually and succeed in life. We give them unconditional love. We are kind and help our friends because we love and appreciate them.

We do charitable acts for strangers who are less fortunate than we are because we remember Christ's teachings. We feel good that perhaps our gift will bring some measure of comfort to those with many needs and challenges.

God is love. God gave us many gifts — the beauty of the universe, our time, talents, and treasures. But the best gift of all — God gave us His son, Jesus Christ. Because of God's love for us, we pass on that love by serving and helping others.

GOOD STEWARDSHIP — STAY WELL
March 2015

My friend and I were slowly walking from our class to our dorm at Ohio State University. That was a long time ago, spring 1958. I will never forget her. She kept telling me to walk on ahead because she was so slow. I said no that I wanted to walk with her. She was a delightful person. We did enjoy each other's company. But, there she was trudging across campus with a heavy brace on her leg. She had polio as a child. It left her crippled.

I remember one day in my senior year of high school my classmates and I stood in a long line that snaked around the gym floor. We were getting vaccinated against polio. We and our parents were thrilled. Now we would not get that dreaded disease. I well remember, on the front page of our newspaper, pictures of children completely enclosed (except for their heads) by monstrous breathing machines called iron lungs. Those were the years everyone feared polio. My parents did not take my brothers and me to the county fair or to the beach because of polio. We avoided crowds; however, sometimes that was difficult since we lived in a suburb of Cleveland, Ohio.

Thankfully, through the diligence and prayers of our parents, we three kids did not get polio; but we did get measles, mumps, and chickenpox. I remember my mother saying that I was very sick because I was only two at the time. My older brother was in 1st grade when he came home from school sharing his germs with me, one disease at a time. Actually, I was glad I had the diseases early because later, when I entered school, I was not absent like my classmates with measles, mumps, and chickenpox.

I have my older brother, Cal, to thank for sharing his childhood diseases with me, and my younger brother, Gil, to thank for rubella. One day when Gil was in 3rd grade and I was in 11th grade, he came home from school sick with rubella. At that time our mother was a substitute teacher in the same high school I attended. She called the high school and said that she could not sub as Gil had rubella.

The principal said, "We need you more than Eloise. Tell her she has to stay home to take care of her brother." That was a first for me — where the principal told me I had to stay home! So guess who got rubella during finals week and had to take her finals during summer school? Actually, I was glad I had rubella. It is a mild disease, but it is very dangerous for an unborn child should the mother get sick while pregnant. That was always the first question my obstetricians asked me — if I ever had rubella. Gladly, I said, "Yes."

The other day my daughter said to me, "Mom, the problem today is that the only people who remember measles, mumps, chickenpox, rubella, and polio are the older generation. People are becoming complacent." And thankfully no one today remembers small pox or diphtheria which has been eradicated by vaccines.

Share your time, talents, and treasures with others, but not your germs. Keeping ourselves well is a form of stewardship. How can we help others if we have to stay home because we or our families are sick? Staying well is not only maintaining the good health habits of eating right, exercising, sleeping well and washing hands thoroughly with soap and warm water; it is also getting vaccinated against communicable diseases.

There are some people who cannot be immunized; for example, infants and toddlers, those for whom the vaccines do not take, and those with medical issues such as receiving chemotherapy. It is good stewardship for those of us who are able to receive the vaccines to get immunized and thus contribute to "herd immunity" for others. This is an important way we can be good stewards by helping protect our neighbor.

SHARING
April 2015

Last year in a souvenir shop in Tabgha, Israel, I carefully looked over all of the souvenir plates, bowls, cups, and platters and wondered which one to buy. They all were glazed ceramic of the same motif, a mosaic pattern of two fish and five loaves of bread in a basket. Their colors were beautiful, predominately blue with yellow, orange, and a red basket and fish. I finally chose a shallow bowl seven inches in diameter, small enough to fit into my suitcase. That becomes my bread dish when my family comes over for dinner. What an appropriate souvenir of my vacation in the Holy Land!

The bread dish sits on my kitchen table at all times to remind me of the miracle that Jesus performed in the feeding of the 5,000.

A little boy gave Jesus his lunch of two small fish and five loaves of bread. Jesus blessed the bread and fish, and miraculously, 5,000 men along with women and children were fed that day. Jesus multiplied a small amount into enough food for everyone. This story is to remind us that whatever small amount we offer to God (even if we do not believe it is enough), He can turn it into all that is needed.

An excellent example of God's turning our small offerings into a large amount is the church-wide special offering — One Great Hour of Sharing. This program began in 1949 in response to the devastation from World War II. Today more than 100 countries, including United States and Canada, are benefited by One Great Hour of Sharing. The offerings Presbyterians worldwide give to this program amount to $8 million annually. And this money provides for disaster relief, food, clean water, educational opportunities, and many other resources to people in need all over the world.

Share a portion of your treasures to One Great Hour of Sharing on Easter Sunday, April 5, and let God work miracles. Please use the special envelopes in the pews or designate on your check the amount for One Great Hour of Sharing.

Not only can we share our treasures worldwide, but we can also give our time to people right here in Maricopa County. The hours we spend serving meals in shelters, making food boxes, and handing out Homeless Person Assistance Kits mean so much to the recipient. We may not be aware of the outcome of our efforts, but what is important is that God can turn our efforts into miracles!

Our talents are shared with all at Gilbert Presbyterian Church. The beautiful banners hanging in our sanctuary, Sunday school teachers, musicians, greeters, and everyone with a warm welcoming smile are just a few examples of sharing our talents with others. And let's not forget those who make quilts, prayer shawls, and those visiting the sick in hospitals. We are very blessed to have so many talented people willing to share their gifts here at GPC!

We can also share ideas. A few years ago I mentioned to a friend of mine who is not a member of GPC our Homeless Person Assistance Kits. She was so impressed by what we do that she wanted a list of suggested items for the kits. Every Thanksgiving since then she makes enough kits to give to her family and friends who gather at her home for dinner. Each adult receives instructions to give a kit to a homeless person. That is now her family tradition — a tradition of sharing with those in need.

Share a portion of your time, talents, treasures, and ideas and allow God to work miracles in turning your small offerings into something great and wonderful. That will mean so much to the recipient of your love and care!

EXPLORING MY HERITAGE
May 2015

I love thinking about my ancestors — where they came from, when they arrived in America, who they were, and what they did. My interest first developed during a summer family vacation to New England when I was 14 years old. The American history I had just learned in 8th grade came alive as we explored Concord Bridge, the Old North Church, Paul Revere's home, Faneuil Hall, Bunker Hill plus many other sites in and around Boston.

Mother said her ancestors and mine came from England and settled in Rhode Island and Connecticut. They fought in the Revolutionary War. After the war they moved west to Northern Ohio.

When our children were young, my husband, Roy, and I took them on a wonderful vacation trip by car all the way from Arizona to Ohio. We wanted to show our children the place of our birth and where we were raised. They learned about our heritage, growing up in Ohio.

We visited the Ohio State University campus where Roy and I first met. We drove to Roy's hometown, Beach City. We explained to our children that Beach City was named because of all the sand deposited there by the glaciers millions of years ago. We also visited Lakewood, a suburb of Cleveland, my hometown. We spent a day with my best friend from high school.

Her children and mine played together on a beach along Lake Erie. We visited museums and parks in the Cleveland area. And, of course, we stayed several days with my dad who at that time was still in Ohio.

I knew about my mother's heritage, but I wasn't familiar with my father's background. I knew that his last name, Robinson, is Scots-Irish. The Robinson family lived in Southern Ohio at the time of the Civil War. But how and when they arrived in Ohio, we did not know.

That mystery was partially solved when our youngest daughter, Karen, moved from Arizona to attend college in Roanoke, Virginia. Upon graduating, she continued living and working in Roanoke. A few years ago, Karen found out that my father's ancestors lived in the Roanoke Valley before moving to Southern Ohio. Unbeknown to Karen at the time, she chose a college just a few miles from the birthplace of her ancestors.

During the summer of 2006, I had a wonderful trip to England and Scotland. I thoroughly enjoyed Scotland with its highlands and heather. One day our tour bus was traveling along Loch Ness, just as the sun was setting. That was beautiful. Perhaps on my trip to Scotland I might have passed through the area where my ancestors had lived.

While in Edinburgh, I attended a Sunday morning worship service at St. Giles' Cathedral, the Mother Church of Presbyterianism. Toward the back of the church was a larger-than-life statue of John Knox, pastor of St. Giles' from 1559 to 1572, at the time of the Protestant Reformation. That is my church's heritage and mine too.

While in Scotland I purchased a toy stuffed sheep to remind me of my trip. I named him Patches because he has a brown diamond-shaped patch on each side of his body. Yes, he sleeps with me on my bed.

In February 2014, I visited the Holy Land, the land of Jesus, the birthplace of Christianity, our heritage. Our tour took us to important sites in the life of Jesus beginning in Bethlehem, then to the Jordan River and the Sea of Galilee, and finally to Jerusalem. While in Israel, I bought a stuffed camel that I named Gali. Gali and Patches are both on my bed.

When I look at Gali, I remember my trip to the Holy Land. I remember standing by the Sea of Galilee at the Church of the Primacy. In a small park next to the church is a sculpture of Jesus saying to Peter, "Feed my sheep" (John 21:17). Then I look over at my little sheep, Patches, and say, "Yes Jesus, I will feed your lambs, I will care for your sheep, and I will share my time, talents, and treasures with those needing my help and love."

REMEMBERING OUR JOURNEYS IN FAITH
June/July 2015

In Pastor Terry's letter to the congregation dated May 14, he said, "Through this sabbatical we can all remember who we are..." Yes, Terry, we are all children of God, ever growing and ever learning in our faith journey. Our journey in faith is a life-long process made up of many unique experiences bringing us closer to Jesus and God.

Some people can identify a single day in their lives when they started to believe. Others, like me, were born in a church-going family so we felt like we always believed. But there are times we have all wondered where God is and why our prayers are going unanswered.

There are occasions when we remember experiences that are sometimes mundane and other times challenging where our faith takes a leap forward. Certainly, in the midst of doubts and disappointments, our faith can grow.

Baptism of a youth or adult is a very memorable event, especially for the person being baptized. I do not remember my baptism because I was an infant, but I remember by parents telling me about it. My dad held me while mom came down from the choir loft, and together they made their promise to God to raise me to know and love Jesus Christ. Likewise, the congregation also made a promise to assist in my spiritual upbringing.

It was a thrill when my children were baptized. My faith grew ever more when I heard my children give those same promises to God at the baptism of their children — my grandchildren.

By the time we are adults we have received communion a number of times during our lives. Sometimes one special communion stands out as being quite memorable. Perhaps that is our first communion — I remember my first communion.

At that time my parents belonged to the Methodist Church. I was about four years old when my parents and I walked down the center aisle of the sanctuary and partook of the elements placed before us as we knelt at the railing. Of course, I was too young to understand the meaning, but I remember the occasion with fondness.

As an adult, my most memorable communion was in Scotland at St. Giles' Cathedral, the Mother Church of Presbyterianism. We went forward, formed a large circle and passed the elements around. Since it was summer, I knew the church was filled with visitors from many different countries. To me, that was the meaning of worldwide communion.

Even in sickness and death of our loved ones, our faith can grow. I was only 21 years old when my mother became very ill with cancer. Why God why? I would question. But even in her death, my faith leaped forward. I was present and watched as she lifted herself into a sitting position with arms outstretched. Her sparkling blue eyes were focused on something that I could not see. All I saw was a wall, but she saw something more. I believe at that moment she saw Christ and entered heaven. Watching that scene transpire was one of the most profound experiences I have ever had.

Today we are forever bombarded with world and local tragedies in the newspaper, television, and on the internet. There is no escape. I will never forget the day I first joined the choir at Morenci Presbyterian Church in Morenci, Arizona. It was Wednesday evening, October 17, 1989.

My family and I were home watching the news on television of the Loma Prieta Earthquake as it was occurring in the San Francisco Bay Area. I soon felt overwhelmed, listening to the tragedy. I had to escape. I told my family I had to go to church and join the choir. I find solace and peace in church. In music I feel close to God. That evening after choir practice, we prayed for the people of California.

I find God in the beauty of the earth — sunrises, sunsets, rainbows, and the moon and stars in the sky. I love the mountains and valleys, rocks, trees, and flowers. When I practice piano, there is a little bird that comes chirping to my open door. His song is in time with my music. Perhaps God is speaking to me in the chirps of a little bird.

I remember who I am — I'm a child of God, ever growing in faith and ever learning what Jesus, God, and the church mean to me. This summer as Pastor Terry and Jan are away on their fantastic journey, can we share with one another our unique experiences in our faith journeys? Let us all remember who we are.

REJOICE AND BE GLAD
August 2015

I looked out the front windshield of my daughter's truck. The sky was dark with heavy rain clouds. Then I noticed one very black ominous-looking cloud dipping down into a funnel shape. It was not yet touching the ground, but later I learned that tornadoes were in the area.

My grandsons, ages 8 and 10, were at Lego Camp at the YMCA near their home in Kennett Square, Pennsylvania. My daughter, Karen, and I had just finished exercising in the Fitness Center there at the "Y." I was waiting for her in the parking lot while she got the boys. The three of them made it to the truck just as it was starting to rain. At first there were only a few sprinkles, but it quickly turned into a deluge.

We had an adventurous ride home with the wind and driving rain. This is Pennsylvania where large trees line the highways, and their branches arch across the roads like tunnels. I love the trees: they are so beautiful. But this was a storm, and in the wind these overhanging branches can be very dangerous. Limbs, twigs, and leaves were falling all around us, and one branch even hit the truck. Karen dodged the debris.

At one intersection, we had to turn around as trees had fallen and blocked the entire road. Fortunately, my daughter's neighborhood did not sustain as much damage as others. She drove into her driveway, stopped the truck, and clicked the garage door opener. Nothing happened — there was no electricity. The power lines on her street are buried underground, but for the lines to get to her neighborhood from the power station, they pass over and through areas from one old pole to another. And even before the storm, some of those poles were not standing perfectly perpendicular to the ground.

Karen and her family live several miles from the center of town. Even though her neighborhood was built in the past twenty years, it is not connected to the city water system. Everyone on that street had the best tasting well water. It might have been wonderful water, but without electricity to operate the pump, the water remained deep underground.

That was 6 pm Tuesday evening. The next day there was still no power; but fortunately, the YMCA had electricity so we returned there to exercise at the Fitness Center and take a wonderful shower afterwards. The boys went off to Lego Camp and swimming.

Thursday morning we woke up, flipped the light switch, and there was light. We rejoiced with shouts of gladness. We have power! We have water! Even their big chocolate lab caught our excitement.

Many people in the world do not have running water or electricity in their homes. They might have to walk for miles to get clean water. But in this country, we expect good clean water when we turn on the faucet. We expect light when we flip the switch. Only during a storm when the power goes out do we truly become aware of how much we depend upon electricity.

Rejoice, be glad and be thankful for all those things that make our lives easier and more comfortable. Be glad we live in America where power and water are so commonplace that we assume they are always available.

Water and electricity are not the only things we sometimes take for granted. Do we tell our family and friends often enough how much we love them? Do we always thank them when they do something for us, no matter how small?

Are we thanking God for the many gifts he has given us? Do we rejoice in the beauty of the earth, the sunrises and sunsets, the night sky with the moon and stars? Rejoice and be glad that God has given us time, talents, and treasures to be shared with others. Rejoice that God is with us and that he gave his only son, Jesus Christ.

Be glad for your many blessings and express your love for Christ by sharing your gifts and talents.

BUILD A BRIDGE
INTO THE FUTURE — RENEW
September 2015

A year ago I was looking at new homes with my son, Alan, and his wife, Suzy. They selected one that fit their family needs. I too dreamt of a new home in the same development where Alan was locating; but no, it was in the southernmost part of Gilbert. His new home was too far away from church to even think about moving.

At that moment, I knew the only problem with my present home was that over the years I had collected too much stuff. I needed to revitalize my home, get rid of the clutter, and renew the home that I once loved. That was my goal.

Alan and Suzy also took me to a furniture store to see what they were buying for their children's bedrooms. My two grandkids, ages 6 and 4, were excited. Aidan ran to show me the bunk bed he would be getting. Alana took my hand to show me a very pretty white princess bed for her.

In one aisle over from the children's furniture were bedroom sets for adults. I looked and found a wonderful bed with a headboard, but no footboard. That is what I had always wanted. Then I asked Alan and Suzy if they would like my bedroom set for the guest room in their new home. Immediately, they said yes. Perfect, then I will buy new furniture for my bedroom. My bedroom thus became the first part of my renewal project for my home.

I made a list of what I had to do before I could order my new bedroom furniture. My list kept getting longer. A few weeks ago, Alan (along with Suzy's dad and brother) moved my bedroom set to their guest room. With my bedroom empty, it was the perfect time to completely remove everything from my closet.

I made three piles of my stuff—keep, toss, and donate. Next I thoroughly scrubbed the closet—shelves, walls, and baseboards. Presently, I am placing my good stuff (things to keep) back in the closet in an organized manner. Next on my list are cleaning my bedroom, including windows and blinds, and having the walls painted and carpet shampooed. Only then will I order my new furniture.

To keep me from procrastinating, I posted my goal and timeline where I can easily see it. A sketched floor plan helps me visualize the way I want my bedroom. Right now, my renewal project is a work in progress. I call it "moving in place."

On Saturday, August 22, we at Gilbert Presbyterian Church participated in an excellent workshop conducted by Reverend Brad Munroe. We are building a bridge to the future of GPC. What are our plans and what are our goals? What is our role in our community? What has Christ called us to do? How should each one of us respond? What time, talents, and treasures can we bring to the renewal of GPC?

Think about your answers to the above questions for those can become a springboard to our discussion at the next workshop in October. What do you believe God is leading us to do? Come, share your thoughts and ideas.

REMEMBER, REJOICE, AND RENEW
October 2015

Yes, I am still at it. I am still going through my stuff that once was in my closet. Over a month ago I emptied the contents of my closet onto my bedroom floor, and from there I have been sorting it into three piles—keep, donate, and toss.

In the past several weeks, each item I have picked up has brought back fond memories. I found my children's handmade Mother's Day cards, some scout badges, and a Christmas Sunday school program when my youngest children were the little angels and my oldest a king.

Clothes that no longer fit went into the "donate" pile. Among the chaos were items I definitely wanted to keep such as my cap and gown from my graduation at ASU. I even found my parents' bachelor degrees from Heidelberg College in Tiffin, Ohio. Their degrees are written in Latin on parchment paper. Only their names are in English.

Each item I touched brought back wonderful and happy memories of what my family and I were doing at that time. Maybe that is why it is taking me so long to sort through everything. Other items that I had once saved were relegated to the "toss" pile. The thirty-year-old newspaper clippings are dirty and dusty. Their condition made me want to immediately toss them. Why did I ever save them?

I should be finished sorting in another week and then comes washing the blinds, windows, and walls. Finally, my bedroom walls will be painted and the carpet cleaned. I will rejoice when all is finished, and I can order new furniture. Each day is bringing me closer to reclaiming my bedroom from the clutter and chaos that once held it captive. My renewal project will be complete, at least for one room in my home.

Look over your rooms, closets, and garage. Are you like me — have you saved far too much stuff? Perhaps you have an item you no longer use and wonder why you ever kept it. Donate! Do you have any clothes you no longer wear? Donate!

On Saturday, October 24, we will have a Weigh to Fundraise event at GPC. Bring the household items you no longer use. Your donated items can help those who are less fortunate. Also, we will receive funds from Weigh to Fundraise based on the total weight of our donations.

Remember the good times you had with that item, and rejoice that someone might find it useful and wonderful. You too can renew and refresh your home and get clutter under control.

Our theme for the Stewardship 2015 Fall Campaign is Remember, Rejoice, and Renew. Remember what God has done for you. Rejoice in all that God has given you: your friends and family, your time and treasures to help those in need, your talents to share, and the most wonderful gift of all, Jesus Christ.

Let us all remember the love of Christ, rejoice in our friends, and renew our spirit in our faith journey.

A FITBIT FOR STEWARDSHIP?
November 2015

This past May I joined the Fitbit craze. A Fitbit is a personal fitness tracker. Mine is purple and is worn on my wrist like a watch. It tracks my steps, heart rate, distance traveled, floors climbed, and calories burned. By pressing a little button on the side of my Fitbit, I can see the totals in real time. It can also track my sleep if I should wear it during the night. My son set up my Fitbit so that I can get daily, weekly, and monthly totals and bar graphs of each of the categories on my computer.

The Fitbit comes with a default goal of 10,000 steps per day. When that goal is reached, the Fitbit vibrates and the screen flashes 10,000 and shows a happy face. What a cute little way to be encouraged by a fitness tracker. The Fitbit is like a game — how soon will it buzz me or how many days in a row can I make my goal? It becomes a motivator to move more throughout the day. One time after working a long time on my computer, I looked down at my Fitbit and said to myself, "That is the same number of steps I had several hours ago."

I immediately got up and went outside for a walk. Another time I wanted to watch TV, but I was 800 steps short of my daily goal. What to do? Easy, during the commercials I walked back and forth from the living room to the kitchen. It was surprising how few commercials it took to achieve my goal. By the end of the day, though, I feel like Cinderella. That's because at the stroke of midnight, all my wonderful hard-earned totals for the day are stored, and the screen of my Fitbit shows zero. Each day is a new beginning in exercising with a Fitbit.

What if we had a Fitbit for stewardship? Every smile or hug we give to someone would be like a step. Our magical Stewardship Fitbit would track the time we spend helping others. It would track the talents we use and the treasures we share. We might serve at a shelter, hand out H-pacs to the homeless, make quilts for veterans, teach Sunday school, buy a gift for an angel on the Christmas tree, or be an usher.

Just as there are many different ways to exercise our bodies, there are many different ways to share our time and talents with others. All types of helping others would count on our magical Stewardship Fitbit.

We could also track our stewardship of the environment. Are we mindful of the amount of water we use or do we pick up empty soda cans and water bottles on our daily walks? We could set our own personal goals for stewardship. And when we achieve a personal goal, our magical Stewardship Fitbit would buzz us and say, "Job well done." Just like a fitness tracker, our stewardship tracker would store all hard-earned totals for the day and then reset to zero. The next day would be a new and exciting beginning to sharing our time, talents, and treasures with others.

On Sunday, November 1, many of you came forward with your pledge of a monetary gift to God's Work through Gilbert Presbyterian Church. Now prayerfully consider your pledge to God of your time and talents. What goals would you enter in your magical Stewardship tracker?

A THANK YOU NOTE TO GOD
December 2015

How many thank you notes do you write per year? Yes, I mean actually write by hand, place in an envelope, address, stamp, and send by mail. I do not mean a thank you by phone, e-mail or text messaging. So, how many do you write per year — 5, 10, 15, 20 or more? Many of us probably only write a few thank you notes during the entire year.

I recently finished an interesting little book, <u>A Simple Act of Gratitude, How Learning to Say Thank You Changed My Life</u>, by John Kralik. One year John Kralik had a goal of writing a thank you note every single day. Yes, that is right, 365 thank you notes. Actually, it took him fifteen months to accomplish his goal of 365 thank you notes. To me that is very impressive. In his book he wrote about his experiences and how in that one year his life turned around from concerns and problems in personal life and work to friendships, love, and peace of mind. He attributes that to the writing of his thank you notes.

I wonder if we would get the same results as John Kralik if we were to write a thank you note every day of the year. Perhaps we need to try his little experiment. Christmas is coming. Undoubtedly, you will give some gifts and likewise receive gifts from others. What a wonderful opportunity to begin this experiment as soon as you receive that first Christmas gift.

Immediately write a thank you. That was easy, so try some other thank you notes where the gift is a gift of service, time or love. Is there someone that means a lot to you? Surprise that person with a note. Write notes to your children or grandchildren, make their day a happy one. Maybe a clerk in a store or a waiter or waitress in a restaurant helped you. Write that person a note about your appreciation for their hard work and time spent with you. That would certainly make their day. I doubt they receive very many notes.

Your thank you note doesn't have to be long — just a few lines written simply, sincerely, and appreciatively.

Can we expand this activity to writing a thank you note to God every day? Each day, try writing down what God has done for you. Let every day be a different thought. Perhaps one day thank Him for the beautiful sunrise, sunset or the beauty of the earth. Another day, thank God for your family and friends — people who mean so much to you. Or thank Him for a child that made you laugh. Thank Him for showing you that someone needs your time and help.

Thank God for your talents and treasures, and then ask Him how you can best use the gifts He has given you. A thank you note to God would be like a morning or evening prayer or devotion. It would be your special time with God. Write in a diary and keep each entry short and meaningful. At the end of the week, read over your thoughts and prayers.

I wonder if we would become more appreciative and positive people if we did that every day in 2016. Would we become more aware of the needs of others? Would we become the people that Jesus wants us to become?

This is something to think about as we approach Christmas and the New Year.

2016

HOW CAN I REPAY THE LORD?

How can I repay the Lord for all His goodness to me?

Psalm 116:12

THE FIRST STEP
January 2016

Are you making any New Year's resolutions for 2016? Do you have any goals you desire to achieve?

One year ago I made quite an extensive list of goals I wanted to accomplish during each month in 2015. My dream was to de-clutter every room in my home and have it all finished before 2016. I designated February as the month for my bedroom.

Looking back, I completely underestimated the time it would take. I kept procrastinating with my bedroom until August 1st when I gave my son and daughter-in-law my bedroom furniture for the guest room in their new home. I had to do something. Finally, I took that first step. I removed the contents of my closet and started to go through my stuff — tossing, keeping, or donating. It took me three months to finally achieve my goal for my bedroom. My new bedroom furniture was delivered on Halloween day.

This is the nicest looking bedroom I have ever had. Everything is so well organized and easy to find. It was well worth all the hard work. Now I am encouraged to de-clutter the rest of my home. My computer room is next on the agenda.

Whatever we set out to achieve, we must take that first step. Last year I was dreaming what my bedroom would look like, but my dreams and desires did not make it happen. I could believe I could do it, but until

I took that first step, nothing was going to happen.

Have you made a New Year's resolution to exercise more? Literally take that first step. What about your diet? Are there areas you want to improve? Take that first step. Start now with the first step of turning off the TV. What about your family and friends? Are you making any goals of spending more time with your loved ones? Take that first step and become involved. Play with your child or grandchildren.

Are you making any goals as I did last year of de-cluttering your home? Begin with one box or one drawer. You will become encouraged as the junk disappears and chaos turns to order. I know that that is true. Do you want to learn a new skill? Remember it takes time, patience, and hard work, but take that first step. It is very rewarding to learn something new.

What about your faith and your church? Are you making a resolution to attend church, Sunday school, or Bible study regularly? Do you have a goal of serving those who are less fortunate? Are there any committees that interest you? Take that first step.

Think of a small child taking his/her first step in learning to walk. The child falters and falls down, but immediately is back up on his/her feet and trying again. Soon the child is up and running.

We are the same when we make a resolution. At first our goal might seem so daunting that we give up before we even try. Be like a child — get up and try your goal again. Break it down into parts, take that first step, and you will succeed. Just think — a year from now, you will be able to look back and say to yourself, "Look what I have accomplished."

Good luck with your New Year's resolutions. You can do it, one step at a time.

WHY ME, LORD, WHY ME?
February 2016

Have you ever felt frustrated or perhaps even angry with God? Have you ever been tempted to ask God questions such as these, "Why have you allowed my loved one to get sick, to have an accident, or to die?" Then out of despair have you felt like saying, "Why me Lord, why me?"

These questions do not have answers. That is life. It seems like whenever we have everything under control, stuff happens. We are human — we will get sick, accidents will happen, and yes, our loved ones will die.

It is fruitless to ask God why. That leads to inaction and discouragement on our part. Instead, let us ask for strength in faith, guidance, and direction to lead us through our difficulties. Ask God for acceptance of the situation or a new path to take. Perhaps that new path will be the next exciting chapter in your life. And that new chapter might lead to positive action.

Open your heart and mind and allow God to speak to you. Listen to what He is telling you. Even in our darkest moments, God is always teaching us and showing us the hope and love of His son, Jesus Christ.

My mother was always a very positive person, strong in faith. Even in her darkest moments of cancer she never became discouraged or felt sorry for herself. My mother and I had a wonderful conversation the night before she died. She was asking me my plans for the future, my college classes next semester, graduation, and then a wedding in June. She said nothing about her pain and suffering.

The next day, December 17, 1960, I was with my mother as she lifted her weak body to a sitting position with arms outstretched. Her beautiful blue eyes sparkled as if she was looking at something wonderful. I could not see what she saw. But at that moment, I knew my mother entered heaven. I will never forget that evening. God was with me and through my mother, God was teaching me about love, faith, and heaven. What a wonderful lesson for a 21-year-old.

In 1980, I was diagnosed with a very rare medical condition where my thymus and thyroid glands grew into my chest. It was benign. At that time we lived in Morenci, a small mining community in Eastern Arizona. I had to have open-chest surgery at Good Samaritan Hospital in Phoenix.

After surgery I was in a very large ICU room with six patients, nurses, and multiple machines humming. I woke up frightened, scared, and could not get comfortable. I wanted my husband, Roy, but the nurses had told him to get some rest as he had been with me all night.

A lady came into the room, and asked if I needed anything. She was black. The head nurse immediately said, "No, she only needs to relax and allow the medication to take effect." The lady then came over to me, and I whispered, "Take my hand." We silently held hands together black and white. The entire room became very quiet except for the hum of the machines. No one spoke, no one moved, time seemed to stand still. I felt the love, strength, and power of Christ through her hands. The last I saw of her, she was quickly leaving the room with tears in her eyes.

I relaxed, fell asleep, and the next I knew Roy and our pastor were looking down on me. I did not know who my angel was, but she was there when I needed her most. Through her, God was showing me and teaching me about love that can take place between two strangers.

One Sunday after church in April 2012, I said to Susan Martinez that I really enjoyed the piece she just finished playing, and I would like to take lessons from her. All the way home I thought, why did I ever tell her that? I can't take piano lessons. I don't have time to practice. I teach and have papers to grade. I was hoping that Susan would forget what I said, but she hadn't. Two weeks later she was telling me we could work something out.

A few days later, my eye doctor discovered a small tumor in the corner of my left eye and sent me to Tucson for radiation treatment. The treatment caused cataracts and double vision. Well, I couldn't teach or grade papers with double vision, but I certainly could take piano lessons. My music became my spiritual escape and my salvation while going through the treatments and surgeries. I know God is with me when I hear the birds sing with my music. God is showing me that I am not defined only as a math teacher, but I also have new paths to explore and more gifts to share.

Even in our deepest problems and turmoil, God is always with us, guiding us, and teaching us.

Listen to Him. Perhaps He is telling you to take a different path, one that is not that familiar. Be of strong faith and look for the positive side to life's challenges. Allow the power and love of Jesus Christ to shine in and through your heart to others. Share your gifts that God has given you.

MY SIX CROSSES
ALL A MESSAGE OF STEWARDSHIP
AND LOVE
March 2016

The cross — the cross of Jesus — is a symbol of His suffering and shame. The cross — also a symbol of compassion, humility, faith, and joy. What meaning do we place on the cross? Are there any messages of stewardship and love?

I have six cross pendants. Each cross gives me a different message. Each one tells a different story — a story of stewardship and love.

My first cross is from a small Scottish shop in Williamsburg, Virginia. It is a Celtic cross — like the one in front of our sanctuary. A circle surrounds the center. This cross reminds me of my Presbyterian heritage. I think of John Knox in Scotland and other reformation leaders of the sixteenth century giving of themselves, their time and talents to the beginnings of the Presbyterian Church. When I wear this cross, I think of my gifts that I might bring to the church — my gifts of time, talents, and treasures.

I purchased my second cross from the Native Americans in Canyon de Chelly. It is a very simple cross, but it's painted in an array of colors — blue, red, green, gold, and purple. It reminds me of the Arizona desert, colored rocks, and bright blue sky. The red and gold remind me of the brilliant wildflowers that make our desert come alive. This is the cross that represents our beautiful earth, God's creation. And the colors in my cross — they could be a rainbow in the sky — are a symbol of God's promise to us. What is our promise to God? We promise to take care of His creation because we are the stewards of His land.

My brother gave me my third cross. It is simple — box shaped, an outlined cross. This cross speaks to me of the love of my family and friends. This is the cross to remind me to slow down and help those I love, listen to their problems, care for them when they need my assistance, and share with them sorrows and joy. Stewardship begins with our family and friends.

My fourth cross is from Limoges, France. It is porcelain and shaped like a Greek cross. Each end of the four equal arms is painted gold. This cross reminds me that stewardship is praying for and caring for people throughout the world. I think of third-world countries where innocent children are starving, people are sick and dying from diseases hardly known in America, and where senseless wars and hostilities are commonplace. This is my worldly cross, it reminds me to help and pray for those who are on missionary journeys far away.

I received my fifth cross on my Walk to Emmaus. This is the cross that reminds me that Jesus walks with me wherever I may go and in whatever I may do. Jesus is always with me. With this cross, I think of Philippians 4:13: "I can do all things through Him who strengthens me." This cross tells me to stop and thank God for everything I have received from Him and especially for the gift of His son, Jesus Christ.

I purchased my sixth cross from a shop in Bethlehem on my journey to the Holy Land. It is a gold Jerusalem cross composed of one large cross surrounded by four tiny crosses. It can be worn in its closed position or spread open to better reveal the four little crosses. When I look at the large cross, I think of Jesus born in Bethlehem and ultimately dying on the cross. Also, when I open it and see the four little crosses, I think of how Jesus' word and love has spread to the four corners of the earth.

My six crosses — each one representing a different story but at the same time, each one communicating the same message of stewardship and love.

I AM NOT MY EYE
April 2016

You know me. You know who I am. I am someone who loves music, the mountains, sunsets and sunrises, flowers, and the birds that sing when I play my piano. You know I love my family and friends. I love God and Jesus Christ. You know that I am not defined as that lady whose eye looks a little funny because it was removed due to a fast-growing tumor. You know me because we are friends.

You have been wonderful — your prayers, concerns, and on-going offers to give me a ride. You have been patient with me should I accidentally bump into you because I cannot see you on my left side. You know that I am not my eye, for I am much more than that.

I wonder, though — what about people we do not know? Are we as caring, kind, thoughtful, and concerned for their welfare as we are for our friends? What about those who might look a little different from us, such as the homeless or those who are mentally and/or physically challenged? Are we defining them by their challenges without really knowing them?

We at Gilbert Presbyterian Church are wonderful at participating in our mission projects, but can we do a little more? When we serve meals in a shelter, can we say more than just a polite hello? If allowed the opportunity, do we actually sit down and listen to and converse with the people we are serving? When we give out an H-PAK to someone alongside the road, do we wish that person well and silently say a prayer for them as we drive away?

Are we patient with the elderly who may take longer purchasing items in a store? Are we patient when speaking to a person whose native tongue is not English? And can we refrain from negatively classifying people because of their nationality or ethnic background?

Several years ago I was on a tour of the Holy Land. The majority of our time was spent in the West Bank. We met people whose basic desires were similar to ours. They were not terrorists. All they wanted was peace and a safe place to live and work. They wanted good schools for their children and the ability to freely travel from place to place within their country. Isn't that what people all over the world desire? And yet, today there seems to be much fear and hatred reported in the news against certain ethnic groups and nationalities.

Let us strive to look beyond people's physical features, their attire, and their nationality and get to know them for who they are. Respect them as you would respect your friends. Do as you know Jesus would like you to do — spread love, kindness, and thoughtfulness to your fellow man, no matter what the circumstances.

Remember that Jesus served the poor, forgotten, and marginalized during His ministry. He loved those who others feared or looked down upon. Let us also serve others!

LET YOUR LIGHT SHINE
May 2016

It was fascinating to watch John mix the oil colors on his palette and then paint with precise little strokes on a piece of white plastic acrylic. I have never seen a brush with such a sharp tip as his. The object he was painting was not very large so he positioned it under a magnifying glass. And that object — well, it became my new eye!

John was my ocularist; that is, he makes prosthetic eyes.

Every few strokes, John would pop the eye into my socket and then compare it with my good eye or he would hold the artificial eye up against my face. For two and a half hours he basically painted, compared, and at times scraped off a little paint. He was not satisfied until the artificial eye matched his standards of perfection.

John used very fine red silk thread to represent blood vessels. I asked him what eye color is the most difficult to paint. He said, "The one I am presently working on." I took that to mean every eye is unique and has its own challenges. Then I asked what he does if the iris is really dark — is that easier to paint? "No," he said, "Even the darkest eye has color."

The doctor can see many shades of color; whereas, I cannot. For my eye, he used about six different colors and, at times, mixed two or more together. Even the white part of my eye did not remain a pure white. It also received color — a tinge of yellow. He told me that he does not paint the artificial eye to look exactly like the good eye because the left and right sides of our bodies are not mirror images. He paints an eye to look like living tissue.

I asked John if he was a painter first before he became an ocularist. He said, "Yes, and my favorite medium was oils." But, he told me, that it has been awhile since he has painted a picture. Then I asked him what made him decide to make artificial eyes.

It turns out that he became an ocularist because of his little sister. She lost an eye in an accident when she was just a baby. For thirteen years she had to wear a patch over her eye, because no one was able to make an eye that fit properly. Can you imagine what it must have been like for a child growing up with a patch over her eye? Most likely she was teased by her fellow classmates. Looking different must have hurt her self-esteem and self-confidence. I can only imagine she wanted to hide from people.

John is enough older than his sister to be aware, while growing up, of her many challenges. So, John became an ocularist to help others who have lost an eye by accident or disease. What a wonderful story. God gave John artistic talent. Through his sister, he saw a way to use his gift from God. And yes, he has made prosthetic eyes for his sister and they do fit.

God has given each of us many talents. Some people are given the gifts of art, music, teaching, serving, praying, or an infectious smile and warm heart (to name a few). What is your talent? Gifts from God are not to be jealously guarded, but rather they should be shared with others.

Perhaps, like John, we can see a need through

other people's challenges. Our God-given talent just might be a solution to someone's problem. Remember that Jesus said, "In the same way, let your light shine before men, that they may see your good deeds and praise your Father in heaven" (Matthew 5:16).

Thank God for your many talents and pray for guidance as to how you can use your talents. Let your light so shine by sharing your gifts and talents with others.

SPRING INTO SUMMER AND GROW!
July 2016

My son, Dave, called out, "Mom, you're right! The birds do chirp when you play the piano. They start when you start and stop when you stop. You have trained the birds to sing with your music."

"No, Dave, they have trained me. When I hear them chirping at my door, then I play the piano."

I love spring, when I can open the front door and enjoy the cool breeze and hear the birds sing. I miss my winged chorus during the summer. It is too hot to keep the door open.

I enjoy watching spring flowers break through the ground and subsequently open into beautiful, colorful blossoms. I was in Michigan about ten years ago during the last week in April. At that time, the weather was perfect — sunny days. Everywhere tulips were in bloom. I saw thousands of tulips in all different colors. It was beautiful.

I think of the resurrection when I see tulips. Tulip bulbs look dead, like a glob of nothing. However, the bulb gradually changes when it is planted in the ground and gets the right amount of sun and rain. It sprouts, grows, and finally develops into a beautiful flower.

I was in Michigan again this year at the end of April. However, the weather was disappointing. It was cold and rainy. The tulips had not yet broken through the ground; but, I did see one daffodil. The trees were beautiful in their full white blossoms. I certainly enjoyed seeing a family of geese and their little goslings waddling across the road. Spring is a season of change — birth, growth and rebirth.

In spring I think of graduations. Before we know it, a child is no longer that ever-questioning kindergartner, but in what seems like no time at all, he/she is a high school graduate with dreams and plans of his/her own. As soon as we congratulate the new graduates on their fine achievements, we are quickly asking about their goals. Will they be attending college, working, or perhaps joining the military? Spring is the time for dreams.

For graduates, summer is a time for change. Perhaps they are leaving home for a place miles away with new responsibilities and decisions to consider and make on their own. Inevitably, change brings growth to the new graduates.

What about the rest of us whose graduation is only a memory? We can still think of spring and summer as the time for change and growth. Did you make any New Year's Resolutions in January? If so, are you like most people who abandon their resolutions by February? Get them out, dust them off and determine if the resolutions or goals you made in January are worth resurrecting. If not, consider new goals — things that interest you and that are attainable. Remember, a flower takes time to grow and bloom. A child is 17 or 18 years old before he/she graduates from high school. Likewise, achieving anything worthwhile takes time. You might find it useful to break up your goal in little incremental pieces — then it is not so daunting.

This summer, pray that God will lead you to something new and exciting — then act upon it.

Do you have goals for your spiritual life; that is, your prayer life, church attendance, Bible study, and service to others? What about your health and fitness goals? Do you want to learn something new? Think about registering for a class at a community college in August. Did you play an instrument in high school? Dust it off, practice your skills during the summer and join the GPC orchestra in the fall.

Finally, don't forget your family and friends. Make some new plans with them. God gave every one of us different gifts. Just as it takes many flowers to make a beautiful garden, it takes all of us using our God-given gifts of time, talents, and treasures to make a vibrant church and community. Spring into something new this summer and grow!

WHAT IS OUR RESPONSE?
August 2016

Last month I was sitting in my doctor's office anxiously waiting for the results of my bone biopsy. Would the doctor give me good news or bad? I was glad I was not alone. My daughter-in-law, Suzy, was waiting with me. My mind kept thinking about all the medical procedures I recently had — CT and PET scans and MRI's of my brain and lower spine.

Since those scans were inconclusive as to an area of concern on my lower back, I had to have a bone biopsy. I knew the doctor was looking for any evidence of cancer in my body. After all, my eye cancer was a melanoma which could spread and be deadly. But if it had spread, I was ready to fight, with God's help.

We did not have to wait long. My doctor came into the room and immediately said, "Which do you want to hear first — the good news or the good news?" I believe my mouth flew open, but I could not speak. My oncologist went on to say that there were no cancer cells in the area of concern in my lower spine. Most likely the problem is arthritis.

The second good news was that he spoke to my eye surgeon who said that my cancer was completely contained within the eye; therefore, there was no chance for the cancer to spread. I was overwhelmed with the news. I was shaking more leaving the doctor's office than going in. I was glad that Suzy was driving.

Perhaps you too have received a similar report from your doctor — test results came back negative; i.e., no sign of cancer or some other dreaded disease. Perhaps you did have cancer and, after treatment, it is now in remission or even cured. What do we do with good news like that? What is our response?

Then there are accidents waiting to happen. How many times do we drive our cars and narrowly miss being involved in an accident because someone runs a red light, drives too fast, is distracted by kids in the back seat, answers a cell phone or sends a text while driving? Somehow we quickly respond by slamming on our brakes and/or swerving. We survive yet another day driving on the busy freeways and city streets.

Even walking across a busy intersection like Guadalupe and Gilbert Roads can be dangerous. When the danger is gone and we arrive home safely, what is our response?

Do we, after receiving good news from a doctor or narrowly missing being involved in an accident, forget about the event and forget about thanking our Creator for the gift of life? God has richly blessed us with the beauty and riches of the earth, our health, our family and friends, our time, talents, and treasures. Most of all, He has blessed us with his son, Jesus Christ. How should we acknowledge our many blessings — with our prayers of thanksgiving!

After our prayers of thankfulness, then what is our next response? In appreciation for all our gifts from God (especially our gift of life), let us do as Jesus has taught us to do — to love and share our gifts of our time, talents, and treasures with others.

WHAT IS OUR LEGACY?
WHO WILL TELL OUR STORY?
September 2016

"Mom, are you sure you want to see 'Hamilton'? The music is hip-hop, rap. You like classical."

"Yes, Karen, I know," I said to my daughter. "I want to see Hamilton — that's history. But will you be able to get tickets?"

A few days later, Karen called again to say, "I got tickets for the matinee on Saturday, August 6, at the Richard Rodgers Theatre on Broadway in New York City!" My daughter and her family live near Philadelphia, a two-hour drive from New York City.

During the above phone conversation, Karen told me the musical was based on the book, <u>Alexander Hamilton</u>, by Ron Chernow. With that, I knew I had to read the book before I saw the musical. I'm glad I did. All I could remember about Hamilton from my school days was that he is pictured on the $10 bill, was the first Secretary of the Treasury under President George Washington, and was killed in a duel with Aaron Burr.

However, Alexander Hamilton left us with a far greater legacy than that. I did not realize he was such a prolific writer. During the Revolutionary War, he worked alongside General George Washington as his aide. Many of Washington's letters and papers were written by Hamilton, including Washington's Farewell

Address. Hamilton also wrote extensively in favor of the Revolutionary War, he was one of the signers of the United States Constitution, and he did everything he could to see that the Constitution was implemented by writing essays called "The Federalist."

Perhaps Hamilton is best known as founder of our nation's banking system. Alexander Hamilton left us a tremendous legacy, even though he had a humble and difficult childhood — born in the West Indies of parents who were not legally married and orphaned at the age of 12.

The musical opens with monologues of those who lived and worked with Alexander Hamilton, including George Washington, Aaron Burr, Thomas Jefferson, James Madison, a good friend John Laurens, and his wife Eliza Hamilton. What a grand introduction to the life of Alexander Hamilton. The musical was wonderful. I thoroughly enjoyed it. It moved quickly to the beat of rap. All costumes and stage settings were of the Revolutionary War time period.

Yes, Karen, I loved the dancing, songs, and the beat. I can enjoy other music genres beside classical. During dinner we discussed our favorite character. I liked King George. His lines were funny, but yet true to history. Of course no one really knows what King George said at the beginning and end of the Revolutionary War, but Lin-Manuel Miranda wrote wonderful imaginative dialogues for King George. Lin was the creator of the hip-hop musical, "Hamilton." He wrote the music and lyrics.

The musical, "Hamilton," ends on a very touching note. As in the beginning of the musical, people who knew Hamilton came forward telling of his legacy to the beat of the song, "Who Lives, Who Dies, Who Tells Your Story?" Finally Eliza Hamilton, his wife who survived him by 50 years, comes forward telling of her legacy — raising funds for the Washington Monument, speaking against slavery, and establishing the first private orphanage in New York City. Then she comes forward with Hamilton to the edge of the stage facing the audience and repeats the words, "Who lives, who dies, who tells your story?"

Yes, who tells our story? What is our legacy? Do we write memoirs, our thoughts and feelings about what we hold so dear to our hearts? Do we make something that can be handed down to our children, grandchildren, and great-grandchildren?

When I was born, my grandmother, Mae Robinson, made a quilt for me using leftover scraps of material from dresses she made her daughters. She intended the quilt would be for my crib, but instead it fits perfectly on my queen-size bed. That is her legacy to me. I can tell her story.

What is our legacy to our church and community? Will we be remembered when we share with others and give gifts of our time, talents, and treasures? Who will tell our story? What is our legacy?

A FAITH ODYSSEY
October 2016

"Mom, would you like to go with me to the grand opening ceremony of the OdySea Aquarium on Saturday, September 3?" my son Dave asked.

I said, "Sure, I would love to go with you." Dave had received free passes for that opening day from a friend of his who is in charge of marketing at the venue.

Both Dave and I felt that the aquarium was aptly named. An odyssey is defined as a journey, and in this case a journey through many different waters — fresh water rivers and lakes, saltwater oceans, swamps, bayous, and coral reefs. There were over 500 exhibits containing all kinds of fish including little jellyfish and crabs and the big sharks. Yes, we even found Nemo and Dory.

We also saw otters, penguins, and turtles. The 3D movie was good too. I enjoyed riding down a long escalator into an underwater tank. Fish were swimming above us and on both sides of us. That was fun. To me the highlight of the morning was entering an auditorium built on a large rotating floor. It was like a merry-go-round except we had very comfortable seats. We slowly moved from one exhibit to another, stopping in front of each to view the fish, turtles, or sharks. I had never experienced that at an aquarium. Yes, we had a lot of fun that day on an odyssey at the OdySea Aquarium.

A fish – this is the symbol for Christ and Christianity. If a Christian, long ago in the days of persecution, met a stranger along the road, the Christian would draw an arc in the dirt. If the stranger drew the second arc to complete the drawing of a fish, both would know they were Christians and were therefore safe. One arc drawn in the dirt would have no meaning to a pagan. These early Christians traveled from place to place spreading their faith. They were on a faith journey, a faith odyssey. The fish became their symbol to identify themselves and their places of worship.

We too, at Gilbert Presbyterian Church, will be on a faith odyssey on Sunday, October 9. Between services, each committee will have a booth in the courtyard with an overview of their committee and responsibilities, along with their dreams for 2017. Please come and take that faith journey from booth to booth. This is a celebration of where we have been and where we want to go.

Are you interested in the mission of the church? Stop by the Mission Committee's booth and explore their projects. What about the Education, Evangelism, or Worship committees? Have you wondered what plans they have for 2017? Further on, you might be interested in the work of the Buildings and Grounds, Finance, or Stewardship committees. Stop by their booths and hear what they have to say. Explore all the committees' displays, ask questions, and be informed as to their plans for 2017. Should any committee interest you, discuss it with the chair of that committee to learn how you might give your time and talents. Travel on an odyssey of faith at Gilbert Presbyterian Church on Sunday, October 9th.

October is Stewardship month. Toward the end of the month, you will be receiving a letter and a pledge card. Prayerfully consider your pledge to God and Jesus Christ through our church — a pledge of your time, talents, and treasures. Then on Sunday, November 6, come forward and present your pledge with love and thanksgiving in your heart. Rejoice in all that God has given you, and look forward to that journey of faith in 2017. Where will your faith odyssey take you?

HOW CAN I REPAY THE LORD FOR ALL HIS GOODNESS TO ME?
(Psalm 116:12)
November 2016

The weather was beautiful that day — sunshine, perfect temperature, and a little breeze blowing. Sunday, October 9, was a wonderful day for our Faith Odyssey, a journey with God and our friends at Gilbert Presbyterian Church.

Were you there enjoying the fellowship with one another and becoming reacquainted with the ministry and mission of our committees and other groups at GPC? Did you walk around the patio and talk with the committee members concerning their visions and new ventures for 2017? And did you receive and read the tri-fold brochure that was mailed to you prior to that Sunday?

Yes, we have read, we have talked about the dreams of Gilbert Presbyterian Church, and now is the time for our response. How can we serve in these new ventures for next year? The worship committee always needs ushers, liturgists, and communion servers. It takes no particular talent to be an usher except to have a welcoming smile and a warm hello for all entering our sanctuary on Sunday morning.

Do you have a talent in music and time for practice? Then you are needed. The Education committee said that they want updated storage and support for materials and costs for special events. That sounds like they need us to share a little of our money with them. The Evangelism Committee would like family-centered events. Those are always fun, but it takes people to organize, plan, and lead those events. And that can take our time, talent, and also treasure.

The new ventures for the Mission Committee include Feed My Starving Children and serving more meals at the Justa Center. We can help in one or both of these activities by giving our time on an occasional evening helping and serving people with far more challenges than we can ever imagine. The Youth Council would like to recruit new adult youth leaders. Is it your passion to work with our youth? They need you.

Building and Grounds has a big wish list and almost all the items on the list require our treasure. One item on their list is resurfacing and striping the parking lot. That project is expensive; however, the parking lot is noticed first by visitors to our church. Our buildings are showing their age and are in need of maintenance and repair. The foundation of the Education building needs to be leveled, and the air conditioners require regular maintenance as well as periodic replacement. Painting the buildings requires our time and talent.

What is your response to our journey into 2017? Some of the dreams and new ventures only require a minimal amount of our time. Others require our talents. Almost all require our treasure.

We at Gilbert Presbyterian Church have been wonderful coming through with money for special needs, items that are mentioned and are highly visible. I well remember several years ago when our roof leaked in the narthex and pails were set out to catch the rainwater. After the rain stopped, the pails were again set out, but this time to collect checks, dollars, and coins for roof repair. That generated a wonderful response from everyone. But for our everyday needs such as paying the electric bill, water, landscaper, office supplies, staff, and mission pledge, we at times have fallen short.

On Sunday, October 23, we looked over the proposed budget and approved the pastor's terms of call. That part was easy. Now comes the difficult part — we must follow through with our promises to move forward and allow our dreams and new ventures to happen in 2017. This will require everyone's prayers, faith, and support.

Everything we have is a gift from God — our time, our friends and family, our unique talents, the beauty of the earth, our treasures, our health and life, and the best gift of all, Jesus Christ. In appreciation of what God has given us and His love for us, let us share a portion of our time, talents, and treasures to the work of His kingdom at Gilbert Presbyterian Church.

You soon will be receiving in the mail a pledge card for 2017. Please prayerfully consider your response as you fill it out. With love and thanksgiving in your heart, not only consider your gift of a monetary pledge but also a gift of your time and talents. Perhaps this year you will be able to increase your pledge to help make the dreams of Gilbert Presbyterian Church come true. Then on Sunday, November 6, come forward with your pledge to God through our church. Together with God's help and guidance, let this be an exciting odyssey of faith into 2017. Thank you.

"LET PEACE BEGIN WITH ME"
December 2016

My brother, Cal, called a few days before the presidential election and said, "You must turn on TV and watch CNN. Donald Trump will soon be speaking."

I replied, "I have already mailed in my ballot. At this point I am not interested in what either candidate is saying. I am sick of it, and I can't wait for this election to be over. No, Cal, I am NOT turning on TV. I have had it. Enough is enough!"

The ballots were barely counted when demonstrators in many cities began to march. People now were talking against Donald Trump's choice of advisors. The election was over, but division in our country was not. Everyone seemed to have very strong opinions, highly polarized. Will the hatred ever stop? Will our country ever heal?

Christmas is coming, but where is the peace? I thought about the shepherds of long ago tending their sheep on that hill overlooking Bethlehem. What a beautiful idyllic scene. They looked up and saw a star — what beauty, what wonder! The star guided them to the Christ child, lying in the manger. That is peace. Oh, God, the birth of your Son, Jesus Christ, conjures up wonderful visions of peace, but where is that peace today? Can we ever attain peace? Then I thought of the beautiful song frequently sung at Christmas time, "Let There Be Peace on Earth."

Let there be peace on earth
And let it begin with me;
Let there be peace on earth,
The peace that was meant to be...

Yes, that is it — that is the answer: Let peace begin with me. When I think of peace, I think of no fighting, discord, or hatred; but rather that peace consists of harmony, love, joy, hope, contentment, compassion, and understanding. I believe that God wants us to live in harmony, love, and understanding with one another.

How can we attain that peace that God wants us to have? It begins with each one of us showing our love and understanding to one another.

With God as our Father
Brothers all are we,
Let me walk with my brother
In perfect harmony.

God is our creator. He created each one of us. God created us to be wonderfully diverse with many different gifts, talents, thoughts, and feelings so that we might share with one another. We must listen in order to understand each other. We are all brothers and sisters in Christ, so let us walk together in peace and harmony.

Let peace begin with me,
Let this be the moment now;
With every step I take,
Let this be my solemn vow

To take each moment and live each moment
In peace eternally.
Let there be peace on earth
And let it begin with me.

A vow is a promise to God. Let us promise God that for as long as we might live, we will think, act, and promote peace each and every day. Let us make a commitment to lead a life filled with love, joy, compassion, and understanding. Yes, let peace begin with me!

"Let There Be Peace on Earth," song written by Jill Jackson Miller and Sy Miller, 1955.

2017

THE LORD IS MY SHEPHERD

The Lord is my shepherd, I shall not be in want. He makes me lie down in green pastures, he leads me beside quiet waters, he restores my soul. He guides me in paths of righteousness for his name's sake. Even though I walk through the shadow of death, I will fear no evil, for you are with me; your rod and staff, they comfort me.

You prepare a table before me in the presence of mine enemies. You anoint my head with oil; my cup overflows. Surely goodness and love will follow me all the days of my life, and I will dwell in the house of the Lord forever.

Psalm 23

LISTEN TO THE VOICE OF GOD
January 2017

My daughter, Ann, sent me a card a few days before Christmas. On it was a picture of a dove with the words above the dove saying, "Creating Peace This Holiday Season." Inside the card was the message, "In your honor, I'm helping to create peace this holiday season." In my honor, Ann had contributed to an international organization promoting peace by working to end injustice, inequality, discrimination, and unequal access to food and water. I was deeply touched by her gift in my name. My thought was that she had responded to my December article in *The Crossroads* on peace.

I immediately called her to thank her for the gift and to tell her I was overwhelmed by her thoughtfulness from reading my article. Her immediate response was, "What article are you talking about Mom? I never saw the December Crossroads." She went on to explain that peace was one of several areas that people can contribute to in that organization. Ann said, "Mom, as soon as I saw that I could choose peace, I knew that one was for you."

Why did Ann feel so strongly that peace was me? Of course, she is my daughter — was that it? Or, was it purely coincidental for her to choose peace and my article was on peace? Was she responding to some higher force or power and that power, of course, was

God? I'm inclined to think that God was in charge. When I have a strong feeling about something, I believe it is God speaking to me.

How does God speak to you? Do you at times get a strong feeling, such as what Ann had, that there was something you just had to do? That could be God speaking. Or are you more likely to hear God's voice in the stillness of the night or perhaps in a beautiful sunrise or sunset? Perhaps God is speaking to you through the voices of others — your friends or family. Then too, you might hear God's voice in the beautiful rhythm and flow of music or poetry. When God is speaking, are we listening?

Was Ann listening to God when she contributed in my name to peace? I believe she was. What about you? Is there something that God wants you to do in 2017? Are you listening to His voice? Perhaps you hear a small persistent voice saying come help serve meals to those in need or pack food boxes or fill bags of food for starving children. Is God calling you to clean out your drawers and closets and donate gently used items?

What about your spiritual life? Do you hear a voice advising you to come to church and participate in worship, Sunday school, and Bible study as well as pray and read your Bible and devotions? What about your family, friends, and neighbors — are they receiving your love and care, that love exhibited by Jesus Christ?

This is 2017, a new year, a new beginning. Listen for God's voice. Listen to what He might be saying. Listen and pray for His guidance and care.

HIDDEN ANGELS
February 2017

The date was February 20, 1962. Everyone in the country was glued to a television set watching the Mercury Astronaut John Glenn take off into space. He was cleared to make seven trips around the earth; however, his voyage was cut short. The heat shield on his spaceship came loose at the end of the second revolution and he had to return to earth after three orbits.

Would he be safe as he came back through the atmosphere with a loose, much-needed heat shield? Mission Control made a decision that after the retrorockets were fired, John Glenn would keep the rocket pack attached to his spaceship instead of jettisoning it. Hopefully, that would keep the heat shield in place.

There were a few minutes of communication blackout as the spaceship decelerated, left its orbit, and approached the earth. At that point, no one knew for certain if John Glenn would make it home safely. I do remember watching on live television the tension in Mission Control. The room was filled with white, male engineers all in silence waiting for communications to return. Then all at once, cheers — John Glenn safely splashed down in the Atlantic Ocean — the first American astronaut to circle the earth!

A few days prior to that eventful day, John Glenn

had said, "Get the girl to check the numbers. If she says the numbers are good, I'm ready to go."

What girl and why check the numbers? Don't computers do the math? Well, in 1962, John Glenn did not trust computers. He trusted humans who did all the calculations by hand, using slide rules and adding machines. At the time, these people were called "computers," a person who computes. And "the girl" he was referring to was Katherine Johnson, a brilliant mathematician who was black.

Katherine Johnson was not the only female "computer" working at Langley Memorial Aeronautical Laboratory in Hampton, Virginia. During World War II, many women were hired to do the necessary calculations for the engineers. At Langley, there was a building off to one side away from the other buildings called "West Computing." A large room was filled with human computers, all female and black. In Virginia at the time, workers were required to be segregated; so the white computers worked elsewhere.

Katherine began working at "West Computing" and later she was transferred to the Flight Research Division where she worked at the time of John Glenn's eventful voyage.

I had never heard of Katherine Johnson. I did not know who she was until I saw the movie, "Hidden Figures." I do not recall any news in 1962 that said anything about a black woman doing the mathematical computations for John Glenn's historic flight. Yes, she was hidden from view and not shown on television cheering with the engineers. John Glenn did not know who she was — he called her "the girl," and yet he depended upon her and trusted her calculations. She was indeed a hidden figure.

Are there any hidden figures at Gilbert Presbyterian

Church? Of course there are, but they're not doing difficult calculus equations by hand to send astronauts into space. Our hidden figures are hidden angels, volunteers working behind the scenes, without recognition, and unknown by many.

Before each service on Sunday morning we see the children lighting the candles, but who fills the candles with oil? The sanctuary is neat and orderly, but who straightens the hymnals and bibles, puts the giving envelopes in place in the pews, and picks up any paper trash? Who prepares the pre-service slides for the computer? We see the ushers passing the offering plates, but who counts the money and takes it to the bank? We see the communion servers, and we know who they are, but who is behind the scenes baking or buying the bread, filling the cups, cutting the bread, and cleaning up afterwards?

At Christmas time we see many gifts around the Christmas tree for GPC West, but how do they get there? Who gets the ushers, greeters, and lay readers? It takes someone to call. Who knits the prayer shawls? Who provides the flowers when no one has signed up? For that matter, who gets the flowers from the florist? Who takes the church towels and communion cloths home to wash and iron? Then who locks and unlocks the doors, sweeps the patio, and changes the light bulbs? These are just a few tasks done by our hidden angels at Gilbert Presbyterian Church.

Serving our church and helping others is a wonderful example of stewardship of time and talents. Many of the tasks done by our hidden angels require very little talent and mostly just a little time. Would you like to become a hidden angel? If any of these tasks or others not mentioned interest you, Carole Blake could lead you to the committee or person in charge of that task.

We thank all of our hidden angels who work behind the scenes, unknown by many but known by God.

Information about John Glenn and Katherine Johnson was obtained from the movie and book, <u>Hidden Figures</u>, Margot Lee Shetterly, Harper Collins Publishers, 2016.

ARE WE LISTENING?
March 2017

"Stop complaining, hip. I am ignoring you because I want to complete my goal." I was talking to myself as I was walking as fast as possible around the track at Freestone Recreation Center. My right hip began to hurt on my 30th lap, but I had six more laps to go. I wanted to walk 36 laps in less than 47 minutes. Yes, I made it — 36 laps in 46 minutes 55 seconds!

The next morning my hip was hurting. I could hardly walk. I was limping. I thought after a few days' rest my hip should be fine; but it did not improve, so I finally saw my doctor.

Fortunately, the x-ray showed no fractures. My doctor said it was gluteal tendonitis and hip flexor strain. I have specific hip exercises to do, limit my walking and allow the hip to rest. Looking back on that day in January, I should have listened to my hip and stopped walking as soon as it began to hurt. If I had only listened to my body, I might have either recovered faster or perhaps had no injury at all.

Do we at times have the same attitude with our family and friends as I did with my hip? We sometimes say to our children, "Not now, I'm busy." And what about our friends? How many times do we say to them, "Sorry, later, gotta run." I'm sure all of you have seen in a restaurant someone texting or checking e-mails instead of conversing with the person in front of them. Do we really need to communicate with our electronics so often that we are missing out on human interactions? Are we really listening to our family and friends?

Do we ignore our neighbors? How do we know if someone might need our help unless we listen? When we stop and listen, we become acquainted with that person. We learn of their thoughts, feelings, and desires. There are times when we ourselves might need someone to talk to, someone who will listen to our concerns. If people would only listen to each other, there would be less misunderstanding in the world.

If we truly listen to another person's viewpoint, we will be able to discuss our similarities and differences. Perhaps your differences are not so great after all. Not only do we need to listen to one another in our conversations, but it becomes very important if we are singing in a choir or playing an instrument in a band or orchestra. We must listen to one another.

Do we listen to God? Can we hear God in the midst of all the noise of modern society? Go to a quiet place and listen to the voice of God. To me, God is in His creation in the woods, desert, hills, rivers, lakes, sunsets, sunrises, rainbows, trees, flowers, and all the creatures of the earth. God is in our family and friends. God's voice is in the music of the birds, the bubbling streams and waterfalls, and the music we play and sing. God's voice is in the Bible. Listen to the prophets of old and to Jesus telling his stories. Listen to God.

Pause from your busy life and listen to your family, friends, and neighbors. Truly listen to your body so that it won't let you down. And, listen to God's voice — His voice is everywhere!

A FAMILY REUNION
April 2017

Have you ever attended a family reunion? For some families it is an annual event; whereas, other families' get-together of grandparents, parents, aunts, uncles, and cousins occurs only at a wedding or funeral of a family member. Invariably someone will say, "Let's get together again for a real family reunion instead of a funeral." Then the years somehow fly by without any family get-together.

On my father's side I don't remember the extended family coming together except at the funerals of my grandparents. My mother's side was different. Every summer my parents would drive to Sandusky, Ohio, to the Morey family reunion. That was a happy time for me. My cousin, Nancy, was the same age as I. When we were 11 years and older, after the reunion, I would get to stay with her for a week or she would come home with me for a week. That was a wonderful time for both of us because her home was on some of the original farmland settled by the Morey's in the 1800's, and I lived in a suburb of Cleveland.

I especially remember one summer when I was visiting Nancy and we found a large circular tub with a hole in the bottom. We corked the hole and both of us climbed into the tub and floated down a creek behind her home. We kept turning around in the water and getting stuck on the rocks. We also got wet because the cork kept popping out, but we sure had fun that day going nowhere.

Family reunions sometimes get interesting when one branch of the family moves to a different area of the country. This was true with my husband's family. When Roy's father was a young man, he moved from North Carolina to Ohio. That made for two branches of the Annis family — those in the north, Ohio, and those in the south. When my daughter, Karen, was a freshman in college in Virginia, her uncle from Ohio picked her up on his way down to the Annis reunion in North Carolina. She had a very good and interesting time at the reunion meeting many relatives for the first time.

One elderly matriarch asked Karen if she was a southerner or a northerner. Before she could even answer, someone said, "Of course, she is a southerner, she is from Arizona." A little later Karen listened to some of the elders in the family talking about those Yankees who burned their grandparents' farms during the Civil War on Sherman's March to the Sea. Fortunately, Karen did not tell them that my great-grandfather, John Robinson, served for the Union under General Sherman on the March to the Sea.

For a few days this coming summer, my immediate family of four children, their spouses, and eight grandchildren will be at Karen's home in Kennett Square, Pennsylvania. Not since Roy passed away have all my children been together in one place at one time. Then we only had two grandchildren — now there are eight. Karen has a wonderful home for a reunion — it is large and is located on the edge of a forest preserve. The forest trails are easily accessible, just down the hill, behind her home. What a great place for the grandkids to run and play. Her big friendly chocolate lab, Thumper, will accompany the kids wherever they go.

Then too, Kennett Square is close to historic places of interest — Philadelphia, Baltimore, Washington D.C., Valley Forge, and Gettysburg. Each family is planning trips to see some of the sights either before or after our reunion.

We have had many e-mails, text messages, and phone calls back and forth for this family get-together. First, we had to decide upon a date. That was not easy considering my grandchildren's school schedules are so different. Then of course my adult children and their spouses have to plan their time off from work. Right now the plans are that I will be with Alan and his family before the reunion, and with Ann and her family afterwards. Can you imagine the plans that Karen and her husband have to make to host us all? I am really looking forward to our family reunion this summer.

For my part, my planning will come when it gets closer to the time to leave. I will be thinking about what to pack, stopping my newspaper, holding my mail, and who will watch my house. Then there is one more item I cannot forget. I must remember my offering to Gilbert Presbyterian Church. Even if I am not present, GPC still needs to pay their bills — electric, telephone, water, and salaries plus babysitter, landscaper and other bills. Before I leave I could write one check for all the Sundays I will be absent. I know some of our members prefer to write one check to cover the entire summer whether they are present or not. That is a good idea since the church's income is usually down during the summer. Another possibility is to pay one month ahead and stay ahead for the rest of the year. I like that idea because my yearly pledge would be completely paid by November. And with eight grandkids, that would certainly help my Christmas expenses. That is something for me to think about as to what is best for my budget — pay a month ahead now and keep ahead or write a check just before I leave for the time I will be gone.

Begin planning now for a wonderful summer, whether you stay here, attend a family reunion, or go on an exciting trip to new destinations. If you stay in the Phoenix area, visit some of the fantastic museums and other places of interest in the valley. Remember they are cool on our hot summer days. Plan ahead, plan now, and have a fun summer.

May God be with you, whatever you choose to do and wherever you may go!

ONE SMALL STONE
May 2017

I walked to the front of the sanctuary, and on the communion table was a container of water filled with pretty little stones. Our facilitator, Rev. Deanne Hodgson, told us to choose a stone, look it over, feel it, and think about what it is telling us. I, along with other women at Gilbert Presbyterian Church, was on a retreat one Saturday morning in March.

I quickly looked over the stones in the water and was instantly drawn to a very pretty, smooth, and creamy white oblong stone. The small stone was a little over an inch long. It reminded me of Jesus — pure, white, and without a blemish. But the reverse side was not perfect. It had streaks, dots, of brown and orange. The reverse side is not Jesus, but instead it is like us with all our blemishes, problems, and sins.

Last week when I was having the inside of my home repainted, I encountered some unexpected problems. The painters discovered the wall behind my washer was damp, not from the washer, but from tiny leaks in the water pipes within the wall. I held my little stone and looked at the side with all the streaks and squiggles. Yes, that certainly was my day with lots of problems and concerns. Then I turned my stone over, and that side represented Jesus. I literally had turned over my problems (along with all my stress) to Jesus.

My small stone reminds me of all the happy times

my husband and I had hiking in the mountains of Eastern Arizona. We were out in God's creation — the hills, valleys, desert plants, trees, flowers, and rocks — collecting small rocks that we could carry and admire.

We found many beautiful agates of different colors. There were copper rocks (azurite and malachite), smooth obsidian, and wrinkly black rocks. When we shone a light through those small black rocks, the inside took on a transluent amber color.

Sometimes we were lucky and found geodes that, when broken open, revealed beautiful quartz crystals. The rocks we collected are now in my rock garden in my backyard. My grandkids love to look at them.

I thought back to my childhood going with my family on a Sunday afternoon drive to a large parkway not far from our house. We usually walked along a path through the woods to a river appropriately named Rocky River. We would carefully choose some flat stones to skip across the water.

My dad was good at skipping rocks. His rocks skimmed the surface, making concentric circles all the way across the river. However, many of my rocks immediately went splash and sunk.

Thinking back now to rock skipping reminds me of Pentecost and the way the early Christians spread the Good News of Jesus Christ. They made ripples traveling from one town to another just as a stone skips across a river.

My small stone has taken on three meanings. It reminds me to turn over my problems, concerns, and stress to Jesus. My pretty little stone reminds me that it is just one small part of God's wonderful creation. And finally, it reminds me of the way the gospel of Jesus Christ has spread throughout the world from person to person and town to town.

A FAITH ODYSSEY REVISITED
June 2017

Have you ever come away so thrilled and excited from visiting a place that you just had to see it again? I have visited the Musical Instruments Museum in Phoenix three times, but I could easily return because I learn something new during each visit. My third visit was with two of my grandchildren, and looking at the many instruments through their ears and eyes was an entirely different experience.

Perhaps you enjoy watching a movie more than once or reading a book the second time. Even when you know the plot of the movie or book, there can be some little nuance that perhaps you previously missed. That movie or book can still be just as exciting as the first time you experienced it.

Years ago my husband and I took our four children on a vacation trip to Carlsbad Caverns. We were astounded at the beauty and vastness of the caverns. We marveled at the long thin stalactites hanging from the ceiling and the stalagmites growing up from the floor. We all peered into a deep hole that supposedly had no bottom. The formations were incredible, each room more magnificent than the last.

We ate our lunch inside the cave. We rode the elevator to the top and then walked down again, repeating our morning trip through the caverns. That evening we sat in a large amphitheater and watched the bats coming out of the cave. The next morning my husband asked our children if they wanted to head for home or walk through the caverns again. Everyone said, "Again, let's go again before we go home." In a day and a half, our family walked completely through the cave three times. We could not get enough of the beauty and magnificence of Carlsbad Caverns.

Were you here at Gilbert Presbyterian Church on Sunday, October 9th? On that beautiful day, we held a Faith Odyssey in the courtyard. If I remember correctly, the temperature was perfect and a slight breeze was blowing. We were on an odyssey, a journey of walking around the patio enjoying the fellowship with one another and becoming reacquainted with the ministry and mission of the committees at GPC. We talked with the committee members and read their displays and handouts. We found out about their present activities and heard their dreams and wish list for the future. It was an exciting time to learn more about each committee and group at GPC.

Starting on Sunday, July 9th through July 30th, we will revisit our Faith Odyssey at GPC. This time our journey will be in the Education Building rather than outside. The committees will update us as to their goals. They will explain what they have accomplished since October and any challenges they may have had. As you walk around and explore, consider how you might respond to the dreams of GPC. Some ventures may require our time, others our talent, and almost all will require our treasure. Consider how you can best serve God and Jesus Christ through the work of the committees and other groups at Gilbert Presbyterian Church.

Remember all the gifts God has given you as you serve others.

THE STEWARDSHIP OF PRAYER
August 2017

One morning while eating breakfast, my friend, Sue Groves, called and wanted to know if she could stop by my house for a few minutes around 2:15 pm. "Yes, of course," I said. She said that she had a gift for both of us. What could it be?

That afternoon Sue came by with a small gift bag decorated with an angel. Inside was the gift wrapped in tissue paper. I carefully unwrapped it and discovered a card with two identical bracelets, each made of white and silver cord with a small silver cross. The card said, "PRAYER PARTNER BRACELETS." Two bracelets, one for you and one for your prayer partner. Commit now to hold each other in prayer, offering each other support on life's journey toward faith, healing, forgiveness, wisdom..." I felt tears in my eyes.

We helped each other put our bracelets on our wrists. At that moment we were committed to think and pray for one another. Every time I look at my bracelet, I think of my friend and her infectious smile and caring personality. I think of the way she encourages me to strive for the best in whatever I do, whether it be exercising or playing the piano. I pray that she will have a good day, she will have the knowledge and patience to help her clients, and she will be safe driving her car around the East Valley. While Sue was on vacation visiting friends and family

417

in her home state, I prayed that she would have a wonderful time and safe journey.

Sue likewise prays for me to have the courage to face my medical challenges and for the wisdom of my doctors. She prays for my family, my children and grandchildren. Sue has said to me that when she looks at the bracelet on her wrist she thinks of God, our faith, and all our blessings and joys. Furthermore, the cross on the bracelet reminds us of Jesus, His teachings, and why He died for us.

There are 92 individuals on the Prayer Chain at Gilbert Presbyterian Church. Of course most are members of our church, but others are winter visitors and friends of our GPC family. Our Prayer Chain connects people from all over the country in many different states. It is mind boggling to consider the extent of our prayers.

At times I have been the recipient of these prayers. It is very comforting to know, when we are hurting, others are praying for us. We receive prayers from people we might not even know, and likewise we may be praying for those unknown to us. That does not matter. We can feel the presence of God and of prayers all around us. We pray for those with medical problems, in surgery, we pray for babies being born, we pray for safe journeys, and we pray for those looking for work. We pray for our teachers and children in school and our young people in college.

We love to hear feedback that the surgery was a success, the person is healed, and someone found work in their chosen field. If the person cannot be healed, we pray that he or she will feel the calming presence of God. And should that person pass away, we pray for their family that they may find peace in their belief and knowing their loved one is in heaven.

Yes, there is power in our prayers. Are you on the Prayer Chain? Do you have a personal prayer partner like I do? Sue's friendship means so much to me, and now I feel ever closer to her since we are prayer partners.

There is stewardship in our prayers. We give of ourselves and our time when we pray for others. There is no better way to help others than by prayer.

"LOOK BOTH WAYS BEFORE CROSSING THE STREET"
September 2017

In June my son, Alan, was driving me home from my appointment with my oncologist. We were both in our own thoughts as to what my doctor had said. The liver biopsy that was done only a few days ago showed the melanoma from my eye had metastasized into the liver. That confirmed the scan of the previous week showing cancer in the lungs and liver. The doctor had explained that I would immediately begin immunotherapy on June 28 with treatments every three weeks. To both of us, this latest news of cancer was devastating.

Alan was driving south on Dobson, ready to turn left onto US 60. At the top of the on-ramp, both of us saw the freeway clogged with traffic. He then made a quick u-turn and headed up to Southern. That must have been quite an accident on the freeway to cause an almost complete standstill. Alan broke our silence as he was driving on Southern.

He asked me, "It is easy to learn a lesson when we have good news, but what lesson is there in the bad news you received today?" I really did not have to do much thinking for an answer to his question. A few months ago, if someone had asked me how long I expected to live, I would have perhaps said to age

90. After all, I exercise, eat right, am involved with my family, friends, and church, and I am in good health. Now, after what the doctor said, living to 90 may not be possible.

Then I thought of the people who were in the accident on US 60. I had no idea of their condition, but with the traffic like it was, I would guess someone was injured. I am sure they were not expecting to be involved in an accident. They might have been looking forward to their evening at home with their loved ones, but now their evening was probably going to be spent in a hospital.

What lesson did I learn from my bad news of cancer or the bad news for the accident victims on the freeway? That's easy. Life is tenuous, like a thin silver thread. At any moment that thread may be broken — we don't know when, where, or by what means but it will be broken. What does that mean to us?

Thank God and praise God for every moment you have. Live in the present. Appreciate and love your family and friends, listen to them and pray for them. Enjoy nature. Look at the magnificent rainbow in the sky, the moon, stars, sunrise and sunset, summer storms, and the mountains. Listen to the birds that sing. Look at that wild bunny hopping in the backyard of your home — I did and even got a picture of him posing on my pavers!

For the short time each of us has on earth, enjoy and celebrate life. Think of the legacy you are leaving your loved ones. That legacy can be your gift of giving a portion of your time, talents, and treasures to help others.

A few weeks after the appointment mentioned above, my oncologist wanted me to see a doctor at Mayo Clinic. The purpose of that visit was to see if I might qualify for one of their cancer research studies. If my treatment here is not working, then I will be going to Mayo Clinic. My daughter, Karen, flew in from Philadelphia to go with me.

At the end of our visit, Karen asked my Mayo doctor if he had any advice for me. With a smile on his face he said, "Yes, look both ways before crossing the street." We both laughed. I am sure Karen was thinking of the number of times she had said that to her sons, and likewise, I thought of all the times I had said it to Karen and her siblings. I also thought of all the times my mother had said it to me. The same age-old advice was passed from one generation to the next.

A few days later I thought again about what the doctor had said. Of course the literal meaning is excellent advice. But figuratively, it also is good advice. In any decision we make in life, we need to consider all options or possibilities before we decide to cross that street. Throughout life we make many decisions — some small and others big.

In our youth we decide what college to attend, and then we ask ourselves whether to accept that job or this. We decide whether to get married and have kids, and we ask ourselves whether to get a dog for the kids; and if so, what kind? Then finally, in our retirement years, we decide whether to stay in our homes or move.

As you meander along that path of life, consider all your options — are there any obstacles along the way? Is it clear to cross? Ask God for guidance, and make your decision without looking back. Yes, look both ways, in all directions, before crossing the street.

Life is tenuous, and it's filled with options. Choose wisely, enjoy each day, and live it to the fullest. Thank God and praise Him for all the gifts He has given you, especially for the gift of His son, Jesus Christ!

THE MELODIES OF LIFE
October 2017

Thirteen years ago, late November 4th Arizona time, the phone rang. I answered. My son-in-law said, "Listen." I then heard the first cry of my newborn grandson 2,000 miles away. That was music to my ears. I cried, too. A baby before he/she is born is surrounded by a melody of life — the mother's melody from the rhythm of her heartbeat.

We all are born with rhythm. Some children are quick and lively, jumping from one activity to another — presto with staccato. Other children are more quiet and pensive with a more moderate speed and tempo — definitely more legato. Every child seems to be born with a particular style and tempo that does not change significantly as he/she grows and develops.

A child's emotions seem to be right on the surface — happy one minute and crying out in anger and disappointment the next minute. At times, the child can be very carefree and happy, experiencing life in a major key. All at once, discord and dissonance may occur, and now life to the child is in a minor key.

All it takes on a piano to make a major key into a minor key is the slip of a finger. As we grow older and gain in maturity, we begin to realize that disappointments will happen — they are facts of life.

Further, at times there are lessons to be learned in our disappointments. As easily as it is to slip our finger from major to minor, we can just as easily slip our finger and our attitude from minor back to major.

My husband and I and our four children each had a unique melody. Many times our family was in beautiful harmony, working together. In contrast, there were times when the melody of one tried to overpower the melody of another. Add a collie named Lassie to the mix, and our family could sound discordant.

Somehow, though, at the end of the day, all that dissonance resolved itself into a beautiful harmony — sleep. There is nothing more beautiful than looking at four sleeping children and a dog at the end of day — the wonderful melody of sleep.

Nature is full of melodies. As a child in Ohio, I enjoyed listening to the crunching of the dry fall leaves under my shoes as I marched off to school. In the spring we listened for the chirping of the first robin. I remember my first visit to Niagara Falls. I could hear the water rolling over the rocks and the roar of the falls even before we saw the falls. As the roar became louder and louder, I felt more excited.

I remember listening to the crickets during the summer. Also, let's not forget the melody of thunder reverberating from one mountain to another during the summer monsoon storms. The thunder and the accompanying rain was music to our ears when we lived in the mountains of Eastern Arizona.

There are melodies that remind us of certain periods of our lives. I still get teary eyed when I hear the strains of "Pomp and Circumstance." I remember my high school and college graduations, my four children's graduations, and my granddaughter's graduations. Her brother will soon be the next grandchild in my family to graduate from high school. Mendelssohn's "Wedding March" is another melody we do not forget.

Then "Happy Birthday" is sung at every birthday party from a child's first to an elder's 100th.

I feel joyful melodies when I help others. When I was teaching, I felt glad when the students understood the lesson. It was a delight to watch the students work harmoniously on some math concept.

When we help others, we sing a song of joy whether we are packing lunches, helping with Feed My Starving Children, contributing to the hurricane and earthquake victims, lighting candles, or being a greeter, usher, worship leader, choir member, or bell ringer. There is a wonderful melody of joy created by helping others.

For some people, the last few stanzas of life are like a large symphonic orchestra. We sit back and listen intently to the orchestra and then, all at once, there is a loud crashing cymbal and complete silence. The orchestra members silently walk off the stage leaving the audience in awe and wonder. We also silently leave the auditorium, deep in our thoughts as to the music we just heard. We just experienced seeing and hearing a beautiful melody coming to a close much too soon.

For others, there is a gradual decline due to illness and/or old age. Their melody becomes slower and slower, with every measure more quiet than the one before until it is hardly heard at all. All the while the angels in heaven are singing ever more loudly, rejoicing that a believer will soon be home. Just as we do not choose our birth, we do not choose our final stanza of life —only God knows.

Acknowledgments

Have you ever had someone in your life who strongly suggested you do something such as lead a committee, perhaps make a speech, or write an article? At the time you thought what a wonderful idea, but certainly that was not for you. That person saw something in you that you did not see in yourself. I had such an experience back in May 2002 when Rocky Mackey suggested that I write articles for *The Crossroads,* our church newsletter. At the time I felt it was an impossible task for me to undertake. If it weren't for Rocky's insistence that I write articles for *The Crossroads* then these articles would never have been written. Then, of course, there would be no book. I'm not sure if she was completely aware of what she unleashed in me, but here it is. I thank you, Rocky, for insisting that I take up writing even though I argued with you right from the beginning that writing was not my major, math was my major.

I wish to thank all the editors of *The Crossroads* for being patient with me getting my articles in on time. Rocky was the editor when I began, then Ed Blake, and finally Tanja Bauerle. I wish to thank our Administrative Assistant, Carole Blake, and her staff of proofreaders who diligently read over my articles before publication in *The Crossroads*. And let us not forget Pastor Terry Palmer, ever encouraging me in my writing.

It is impossible to name everyone in the congregation at Gilbert Presbyterian Church who encouraged me and said that they enjoyed my monthly articles. Thanks go to all those who briefly made a comment and I immediately thought, that can be an article. I don't remember exactly what was said, but I thank you. And special thanks go to our winter visitors who took their time to e-mail me that they liked a particular article for that month.

Special thanks go to my children, David, Ann, Alan, and Karen for encouraging, commenting and asking if I wrote an article for that month. And for my grandchildren who would call up and say, "Grandma I read your article and I liked it." If it weren't for my family I might have quit long ago. And thanks to my family that this project is my legacy to the church. All money received from the book will go to up-grading the Gilbert Presbyterian Church sign out front.

Then very special thanks go to my book writing team. Thanks to my son, Alan, for heading it up, leading the way, and giving organization to the project. Throughout the years I had expressed a desire to put my articles into a book. The first time Alan and I discussed it I had about 20 articles, hardly enough for a book. My idea kept coming up but never anything was done. Finally, we said that this is it. Let's do it now in 2017. Thanks go to Anne Barton and Judy Walmsley without whose hours in proofreading, editing, and formulating the biblical index would have made this project impossible. And to my daughter Karen, for writing my beautiful biography.

I thank everyone, friends, church family, and my own family for giving me encouragement and being so involved in my project. With blessings to all, I thank you. Eloise R. Annis

Biography

Eloise M. Robinson was born on May 21, 1939, in Portsmouth, Ohio, the middle child and only daughter of Omar J. Robinson and Mildred DeMaris Robinson. Her brothers are Calvin and Gilbert Robinson. Her father was a civil engineer for Alcoa (Aluminum Company of America), and her mother taught Latin and French. Her father was quiet and stoic; mother was social and enjoyed music,

specifically playing hymns on the piano, and that love of music and piano was passed on. When Eloise was in the 3rd and 4th grades, her father built the family home in Lakewood. She remembered going to the construction site after school and on weekends and marveling at the complicated design process that went into the project. She decided she wanted to be become an engineer, like her father. But unfortunately in the

1950's, opportunities for women in engineering did not exist so she became a teacher, like her mother.

Eloise attended The Ohio State University and majored in mathematics and education. In her Junior year advanced physics lab, where she was the only girl in the room, she met her future husband. On the first day of class, the room was full and a kind gentleman, not intimidated by "the smart girl taking physics" gave up his seat for her. Many "watermelon dates" later, she married that kind man, Roy Annis, on June 10, 1961.

Roy and Eloise moved to Arizona in 1962 with a high school math teaching job waiting for her in Morenci. Coming from the flat lands and big city of Northern Ohio to the mountains and small copper mining town of Eastern Arizona was quite a shock. However, she and Roy adjusted quite quickly, taking up a hobby of rock hunting while hiking in the mountains. In 1964 they moved to Tempe, Arizona, where Eloise pursued a Master of Natural Sciences degree from Arizona State University. Upon earning the Master's degree, she worked as a statistician for the Arizona State Department of Health.

In 1969, Roy and Eloise moved back to Morenci where Roy obtained a position as chemist with Phelps Dodge Mining Corporation. At that time, life was focused on raising four children (David, Ann, Alan, and Karen), church, and teaching. When Eloise saw a need in the community, she took action to solve the need. Morenci had no early childhood education programs when she moved there. Even before academic studies proved the benefits of preschools, Eloise inherently knew their value and started Morenci's first preschool at the Presbyterian Church in town.

In 1982 Eloise returned to Arizona State University,

to obtain a Master's degree in Engineering. She was accepted into a special program for math teachers wanting to obtain an engineering degree. Upon graduating in 1983, she wanted very badly to become an engineer, but it was not to be. Ironically she returned to teaching in a special program helping unemployed and underemployed women obtain community college training and employment.

The possibility of returning to school while raising children was not lost on Eloise's own children as her two daughters did the same as they earned their doctoral degrees. The love of learning and education has been passed on!

In 1996 Roy retired and they moved to Gilbert, Arizona. Eloise quickly settled into a new church and school home. She started teaching mathematics at Chandler/Gilbert Community College and taught there for 12 years. She enthusiastically jumped into her church life at Gilbert Presbyterian Church. She served as an ordained Elder of Gilbert Presbyterian Church and a member of Session, responsible for church governance. She joined choir, bell choir and the church orchestra. Through the church pianist/organist, Eloise rekindled her love of music and took up piano lessons. She has enjoyed the process of learning and the beautiful music produced. In 2002, Eloise was recruited to write stewardship articles for the monthly church newsletter, The Crossroads. Incredibly, Eloise produced over 150 stories that have been compiled in this book.

Eloise also took up a new hobby, fitness. She had long wanted to "get into shape" but wasn't sure how to successfully achieve that goal. Prompted by a benign comment from her son, Eloise found a personal trainer who helped her lose 40 pounds and keep it off for years. Her health and success was motivating to many, proof of what could be achieved at any age.

Eloise also enjoys traveling. Because Roy had been many places when he was younger, and because his health was poor after retirement, they did not have the opportunity to travel much together. Their only post-retirement trip was to Yellowstone National Park. However, after Roy passed away in 2003, Eloise became an adventurous traveler. She traveled to Europe, the Arctic Circle, United Kingdom, Norway, Sweden, Denmark, France, Italy, and to over half the states in the Union, including Alaska and Hawaii. Her last big trip was to the Holy Land — she had always wanted to go, and she finally went in February 2014.

Despite a lifetime of experiences that others can only dream of, Eloise's main joy has been the experience of raising four children (including their many accomplishments) and being grandmother to eight wonderful grandchildren — Desiree, David, Matthew, Nathan, Lucas, Aaron, Aidan, and Alana.

Eloise has had a remarkable impact on those who have been privileged to know her. This includes, of course, her family. Her circle of influence is huge — she has inspired her students with her educational skills (including the encouragement she provided), her fellow churchgoers with her faith and trust in the Lord, her medical caregivers while she has gone through extraordinary challenges, and her friends and neighbors who have marveled at her willingness to accept change and turn it into positive outcomes for herself and others.

Biblical Index

Made in the USA
San Bernardino, CA
25 November 2017